Routledge Revivals

A Grammar of the Arabic Language

A Grammar of the Arabic Language

R. Sterling

Routledge
Taylor & Francis Group

First published in 1904 by Kegan Paul, Trench, Trübner & Co. Ltd

This edition first published in 2018 by Routledge
2 Park Square, Milton Park, Abingdon, Oxon, OX14 4RN
and by Routledge
711 Third Avenue, New York, NY 10017

Routledge is an imprint of the Taylor & Francis Group, an informa business

© 1904 Taylor & Francis

Publisher's Note
The publisher has gone to great lengths to ensure the quality of this reprint but points out that some imperfections in the original copies may be apparent.

Disclaimer
The publisher has made every effort to trace copyright holders and welcomes correspondence from those they have been unable to contact.

A Library of Congress record exists under ISBN: 38034208

ISBN 13: 978-1-138-60340-0 (hbk)
ISBN 13: 978-1-138-60342-4 (pbk)
ISBN 13: 978-0-429-46212-2 (ebk)

A GRAMMAR

OF THE

ARABIC LANGUAGE

A GRAMMAR

OF THE

ARABIC LANGUAGE

BY

The Rev. R. STERLING M. A., M. B., B. S.,

Missionary of the Church Missionary Society,

Gaza, Palestine.

LONDON

KEGAN PAUL, TRENCH, TRÜBNER & Co. LIMITED

Dryden House, Gerrard St. W.

1904

To the

Reverend D. S. MARGOLIOUTH, D. Litt., Laudian Professor
of Arabic in the University of Oxford,

The Author respectfully dedicates this work.

PREFACE.

The chief feature of this work is its suitability to the needs of the student whether at home or in the East under native teachers. The native methods of treatment have been largely followed in the belief that they conduce to a more thorough knowledge and appreciation of the genius of the language. The aim has been to produce a practical work: to emphasize the more important parts of the Grammar and to introduce only such matter as is essential to the acquirement of a practical knowledge of the language. Another feature of the work is the extensive Glossaries. These not only illustrate the peculiar structural character of the language but are of a nature to facilitate the progress of the student. They comprise I Triliteral Verbs (showing the vowel of the middle radical in both preterite and aorist) with their Nouns of Action, II Derived Verbs in common use, III Nouns of Action of Triliteral Verbs, IV Tables of (*a*) Adjectives, (*b*) Nouns of Excess, (*c*) Nouns of Instrument, (*d*) Irregular Plurals. These Verbs etc. are all arranged on their respective measures in alphabetical order, with their meanings in English. The native grammars have been freely consulted, especially the excellent little work فَصْلُ ٱلخِطَاب

I have to acknowledge my great indebtedness to Muallim Elias Halaby and Muallim Naṣri Farr of Gaza for their co-operation and valuable assistance. My best thanks are also due to Professor D. S. MARGOLIOUTH for suggestions and for the revision of the greater portion of the proofs.

Gosforth
Newcastle-upon-Tyne
January 1904.

CONTENTS

PART I

ORTHOGRAPHY

	Page
The Alphabet	1
The Vowels	6
Other Orthographical Signs.	7
The Pause.	10
The Accent	11
Anomalies in Writing	11

ETYMOLOGY

Parts of Speech.	13
Servile Letters	13
Measures of Words	14
The Verb.	16
The Annexed Pronouns.	19
Simple Form of the Triliteral.	20
The Six Measures of the Triliteral	21
Observations on the Derived Forms.	22
Rules for the Formation of the Verb	23
The Quadriliteral Verb	26
Table of Derived Forms.	27
Changes of the Weak Letters.	28
Assimilation	30
Forms of the Verb in respect to its Root Letter	32
Changes peculiar to each Form	33
The Corroborative نُون	38
The نُون of Precaution	40
Tables of Triliteral Verbs	41
Meanings of the Derived Forms.	47
The Derivative Nouns	61
The Primitive Noun.	85
The Gender of Nouns	85
Feminine Nouns	86
Number.	91

Page

The Dual 91
The Plural 92
The Regular Masculine Plural 92
The Regular Feminine Plural 94
The Irregular or broken Plural 96
The Noun of Relation 98
The Diminutive 102
The Numerals 107
The Pronouns 112
The Article 119
Collective Nouns 122
Classification of Nouns 123

PART II

SYNTAX

Declension 125
Indeclension 125
Regents 126
Cases 127
Division of the Signs of Declension 128
Implied Signs of Declension 131
The Nunation 132
States of the Noun in Declension and Indeclension 133
Imperfectly Declined Nouns 134
Indeclinable Nouns 137
Definite Nouns 138
The Sentence 140
The Nominative Case 140
The Verbal Sentence 141
The Subject of a Passive Verb 144
The Nominal Sentence 146
Words which affect the Subject and Predicate 158
The Accusative Case 180
The Genitive Case 197

THE PREPOSITION

NOUNS IN CONSTRUCTION

The Appositives 214
Moods of the Verbs 226
The Subjunctive Mood. Accusative Particles 226
The Conditional and Imperative Moods. Apocopative Particles . . . 229
The Conditional Particles أَمَّا, لَوْ, لَوْلَا, لَوْمَا, لَمَّا 233
Tenses of the Verb 235

Page

The Negative Particles 238

The Particles س , سَوْفَ , قَدْ 238

The Letter نُون 239

Verbs of Wonder 240

Verbs of Praise and Blame 241

Derived Nouns which govern as Verbs 243

Appendix 245

Tables of Derived Forms of the Verb 247

Triliteral Verbs arranged according to their medial radical 247

Derived Verbs 258

Nouns of Action Triliteral 281

Adjectives 298

Nouns of Excess 306

Nouns of Instrument 309

Irregular Plurals 314

   (a). Paucity 315

   (b). Multitude 320

   (c). of Plurals 337

PART FIRST.

ORTHOGRAPHY.

THE ALPHABET.

The alphabet أَلْحُرُوفُ ٱلْهِجَائِيَّةُ contains twenty-eight
letters which are all consonants.

They are written and read from right to left.
Their forms are modified in accordance with their
position in a word, whether at the beginning, middle,
or end, and whether single or joined to others.

Their names, forms, numerical value and approximate
pronunciation are given in the following table.

Numerical Value.	Numerical Order.	Final.	Medial.	Initial.	Detached.	Name.	
١	١	ﻝ	..	١	١	أَلِف	Aleph
٢	ب	ب	ـبـ	بـ	ب	بَآء	Bā
٣	ج	ت	ـتـ	تـ	ت	تَآء	Tā
٤	د	ث	ـثـ	ثـ	ث	ثَآء	Thā
٥	ه	ج	ـجـ	جـ	ج	جِيْم	Jɪm
٦	و	ح	ـحـ	حـ	ح	حَآء	Hā
٧	ز	خ	ـخـ	خـ	خ	خَآء	Khā

1

Numerical Value.	Numerical Order.	Final.	Medial.	Initial.	Detached.	Name.
٨	ح	ـد	..	د	د	دَال Dāl
٩	ط	ـذ	..	ذ	ذ	ذَال Dhāl
١٠	ي	ـر	..	ر	ر	رَآء Rā
٢٠	ك	ـز	..	ز	ز	زَاي Zain
٣٠	ل	ـس	ـسـ	سـ	س	سِيْن Sīn
٤٠	م	ـش	ـشـ	شـ	ش	شِيْن Shīn
٥٠	ن	ـص	ـصـ	صـ	ص	صَاد Ṣād
٩٠	س	ـض	ـضـ	ضـ	ض	ضَاد Ḍhād
٧٠	ع	ـط	ـطـ	طـ	ط	طَآء Ṭā
٨٠	ف	ـظ	ـظـ	ظـ	ظ	ظَآء Dhā
٩٠	ص	ـع	ـعـ	عـ	ع	عَيْن ‘Ain
١٠٠	ق	ـغ	ـغـ	غـ	غ	غَيْن Gh(r)ain
٢٠٠	س	ـف	ـفـ	فـ	ف	فَآء Fā
٣٠٠	ش	ـق	ـقـ	قـ	ق	قَاف Ḳāf
٤٠٠	ت	ـك	ـكـ	كـ	ك	كَاف Kāf
٥٠٠	ث	ـل	ـلـ	لـ	ل	لَام Lām
٩٠٠	خ	ـم	ـمـ	مـ	م	مِيْم Mīm
٧٠٠	ذ	ـن	ـنـ	نـ	ن	نُوْن Nūn
٨٠٠	ض	ـه	ـهـ	هـ	ه	هَآء Hā
٩٠٠	ظ	ـو	..	و	و	وَاو Wāw
١٠٠٠	غ	ـى	ـيـ	يـ	ى	يَآء Yā

ا preceded by ل has the form لا and is reckoned a letter of the alphabet by the native grammarians being called Lām-Aleph. It serves to distinguish the long vowel ا (ā) from ا; and follows the letter و.

These letters except Aleph, all end in a bold stroke when detached or terminating a word; when joined to the following letter this stroke is replaced by a small upward curve.

The letters ا د ذ ر ز و are not joined to the left.

The Numerical Order of the letters is represented by the mnemonic words اَبَجَدْ هَوَز حُطِى كَلَمَنْ سَعْفَضْ قِرشَتْ ثَخَذْ ضَظَعْ. Their employment as numerals is confined to mathematical works, and the record of historical events.

For ordinary use the decimal system of numeration is employed اَلرَّقْمُ الهِنْدِيّ in the same way as in all Indo-Aryan languages, viz.

• ١ ٢ ٣ ٤ ٥ ٦ ٧ ٨ ٩ ١٠ ١١ ١٢ ١٩٠٢.

0, 1, 2, 3, 4, 5, 6, 7, 8, 9, 10, 11, 12, 1902.

PRONUNCIATION. اَللَّفْظِ

ا is (I) a weak aspirate depending for its sound on the accompanying vowel, as for instance *almanack*, *illusion*, *ulterior*, (II) a sound resembling the glottal catch, (III) a sign of lengthening of the vowel.

ب is *b.*

ﺕ is a soft dental, softer than our *t*.

ﺙ as *th* in *theory, thin*. (Classical pronunciation).

ﺝ as *s* in *measure*. (In Egypt *g* in good).

ﺡ is a strong and smooth pectoral sound produced by the forcible expulsion of the breath through an almost closed glottis as in a deep sigh.

ﺥ is a vibratory guttural sound produced on expiration by the oscillation of the appendages of the throat as in the Scotch word *loch*, and the German *ch* as in *ich*.

ﺩ is a soft dental.

ﺫ is like *th* in *that, than, these*. (Classical pronunciation).

ﺭ is as *r* (English) distinctly articulated in all positions.

ﺯ is as *z* distinctly articulated.

ﺱ is as *s* but with more of a hissing sound as in *kiss*.

ﺵ is as *sh* in *sherbet*.

ﺹ is a 'lisping' *s* pronounced somewhat as in *sod*.

ﺽ is extremely difficult to pronounce correctly, the tongue is rolled against the cheek; it is an aspirated ﺩ strongly pronounced.

ﻁ has a broader and more open sound than *t*.

ﻅ has the same affinity to ﻁ as ﺙ has to ﺫ having a broad and open sound something like *th* in *this*.

ﻉ is a strong guttural produced by quick and forcible closure of the wind-pipe with the emission of the breath.

غ is a strong guttural produced as in the effort of gargling and sounds similar to "*ghr*" in English.

ف as *f*.

ق is a strong guttural *k* produced as in the cawing of a crow.

ك ل م ن ه و as our *k. l. m. n. h. w.*

ي as *y*.

The pronunciation of these letters as a whole, can only be adequately acquired from the lips of Arabic speaking people.

Special attention however should be given to the letters ق غ ظ ط ض ص ر خ اَلْأَحْرُفُ الْمُفَخَّمَةُ which have a broad sound when vowelled by ‑, also the name of God أَلله when preceded by ‑ or ‑.

The other letters are called اَلْحَرُوفُ الْمُرَقَّقَةُ.

It may be observed that the only letter having a nasal sound is the ن when preceding ي, مَن أَحَبَّ أَنْ يَأْخُذَ فَلْيَأْتِ.

This sound is called غُنَّة (having the nasal sound).

The letters are further regarded as:

I. Strong صَحِيْحَة (Sound).

II. Weak (مُعْتَلَّة).

The latter are ا و ي and resemble vowels in pronunciation and use, the rest are all strong.

The Aleph (Hemzeh) resembles the weak letters in admitting of change, اَلْإِعْلَال.

The Weak Letters when unvowelled are called أَحْرُفٌ لِيْنٍ (soft) but should they be preceded in this state by a homogeneous vowel they are called أَحْرُفُ مَدٍّ *letters of prolongation.*

The letters are sub-divided according to their place of utterance (مَخْرَج) into:

I. Gutturals ا.ح ع خ ع غ ه ق ك ي

II. Linguals .ر ز س ش ص ض

III. Dentals .ت ث ج د ذ ط ظ ل ن

IV. Labials .ب ف م و

The Linguals and Dentals except ج are also called Solar letters (أَلْحُرُوفُ ٱلشَّمْسِيَّةُ) because one of their number begins the word أَلشَّمْسُ The Sun.

When the article (أَلْ) precedes any of the Solar letters its ل is elided in pronunciation, and the symbol ّ is placed over the initial letter of the word to indicate that it is doubled.

The remaining letters are called Lunar letters for a similar reason أَلْقَمَرُ The Moon. (أَلْحُرُوفُ ٱلْقَمَرِيَّةُ).

THE VOWELS. أَلْحَرَكَاتُ

The vowels are three in number and are only diacritical signs and written above or below the consonants to which they belong, أَلْكَسْرَةُ ـِ . أَلْفَتْحَةُ ـَ . أَلضَّمَّةُ ـُ .

They are also used as terminations of inflection أَلْإِعْرَابُ in nouns and the moods of verbs.

With an Indefinite Noun the case endings are doubled

‑ ‑ ‑ and form the Nunation اَلتَّنْوِيْن which has

the force of the Indefinite Article.

‑ ‑ represents the Nominative Case اَلرَّفْع.

‑ ‑   „   „ Accusative Case اَلنَّصْب.

‑ ‑   „   „ Genitive Case اَلخَفْض.

The Nunation in the Accusative Case requires an Aleph

except when the noun ends in ة or ـا حَيَاةً. سَمَاءٌ.

OTHER ORTHOGRAPHICAL SIGNS. اَلضَّوَابِط

(1) ‑ سُكُون.

(2) ‑ مَدَّة.

(3) ‑ شَدَّة.

(4) ‑ هَمْزَةُ اْلقَطْع.

(5) ‑ هَمْزَةُ اْلوَصْلِ.

(1) ‑ اَلسُّكُوْن.

The symbol ‑ اَلسُّكُوْن is placed over an unvowelled

letter as مِنْ or قَدْ, the ن or د is called silent سَاكِنَة.

The م or ة is vowelled مُتَحَرِّكَة. It is not usual to

place ‑ over a letter of prolongation.

(2) ‑ اَلْمَدَّة.

Hemzeh أ followed by Aleph أا is written آ as أَأْمَنَ = آمَنَ.

The sign is called اَلْمَدَّة.

It is also used in اَلْأَسْمَاءُ اْلمَمْدُوْدَة to indicate that an

Aleph of prolongation is followed by a Hemzeh as صَحْرَاءٍ.

8

(3) ـّ اَلشَّدَّةُ.

The symbol ـّ signifies that the letter over which it is placed is doubled in pronunciation.

The first letter is silent, and the second has the vowel upon the ـّ.

(4) اَلْهَمْزَةُ (Compression).

It is of two kinds هَمْزَةُ ٱلْوَصْلِ and هَمْزَةُ ٱلْقَطْعِ.

(5) هَمْزَةُ ٱلْوَصْلِ (Conjunction).

The sign ـ is placed over the initial ا when not directly beginning a sentence, to indicate that the Aleph is elided, and the preceding vowel joined to the following consonant.

This Elision occurs in:

I. The Article, as أَخُو ٱلْمَلِكِ "The brother of the king".

II. In the Imperative of the Triliteral Verb أَسْرِعْ وَٱنْزِلْ.

III. The Preterite (both voices), Imperative, and the Nouns of Action of the Derived Forms, from the sixth onwards.

IV. In the Nouns:

Two	إِثْنَتَان	Son	إِبْنَم
Man	إِمْرُؤٌ	Name	إِسْم
Woman	إِمْرَأَة	Son	إِبْن
Oath	أَيْمُن	Daughter	إِبْنَة
Anus	إِسْت	Two	إِثْنَان

Its vowel at the beginning of a sentence is ِ‍ except in I the Article اَلْ;

II the Imperative of the Triliteral, the middle letter of which in the Imperfect tense has ‍ُ اُنْصُرْ.

To help نَصَرَ يَنْصُرُ

When the letter which precedes the ٱ is silent it takes ِ‍.

Exceptions are فِي, ي, مِنْ, and the Imperative of Doubled verbs which take ‍ُ when preceding اَلْ.

مُدُّ, كُمْ, هُمْ, اَنْتُمْ take ‍ُ.

The ٱ is omitted in the following instances:

I. The introductory formula بِسْمِ ٱللّٰهِ (بِاسْم). (In the name of God).

II. In the word اِبْن when used in a genealogical series between two proper nouns, the first of which is the name of the son, and the second the name of the father.

III. In the اَلْ when preceded by لِ and after ٱ the Particle of Interrogation لِلرَّجُلِ (اَلِٱلرَّجُلِ). To the man.

Is thy son .....?   اَٱبْنُكَ اَبْنُكَ.

Is the water .....?   اَٱلْمَآءُ اَلْمَآءُ.

THE POINT OF DISJUNCTION. (٦) ‍ُ هَمْزَةُ ٱلْقَطْعِ

هَمْزَةُ ٱلْقَطْعِ *is the hiatus* which is felt before the vowel which it introduces is uttered, and unlike هَمْزَةُ ٱلْوَصْلِ it occurs as a root letter not only in the beginning but in the middle and end of a word.

It takes any vowel and is always pronounced, as
أَكْرِمْ أَبَاكَ وَإِلَهَ إِبْرَاهِيمَ وَإِسْحَاقَ .

In the beginning of a word it is written with the chair
إِصْبَع . أَنْمُل . أَكَلَ   ١ (Aleph). (كُرْسِي)

In the middle of a word when followed by an ١ or
when silent it takes the chair homogeneous to the vowel
of the preceding letter, as رَأْس . بِئْمُر . سُؤَال .

If vowelled and not followed by ١ the hemzeh takes
the chair homogeneous to its own vowel, as لَوُّمَ . سُئِلَ . سَأَلَ .

In the end of a word if preceded by a vowel, it
takes the chair homogeneous to the preceding vowel as
قَرَأَ . ظَمِئَ . مَرْؤُ but when not preceded by a vowel it
is written without a chair, شَيْء . جُزْء . ضَوْء .

Many words are not written according to these rules,
as مَسْئَلَة .

The expression أَخُطُّ ٱلْهِجَاءَ "I write out the alphabet"
contains all the vowels and orthographical signs.

THE PAUSE. أَلْوَقْف

In reading, the following changes are to be observed
when a pause occurs.

I. The final short vowels and the Nunation are dropped
except in the case of ٍ the final نُون only is dropped
and is replaced in pronunciation by the Aleph.

II. ة with or without the Nunation is pronounced ه.

THE ACCENT. اَلنَّبْرَةُ

In all other respects Arabic is pronounced as it is written; long vowels as such, and short vowels as such.

The first syllable is accentuated in words whose vowel sounds are all long or all short; where a long vowel succeeds a short one, it receives the accent.

When a letter is doubled by ّ both letters must be distinctly pronounced.

ANOMALIES IN WRITING. إِقَامَةُ ٱلْهِجَاءِ

مَا "What" when used interrogatively and preceded by certain prepositions drops its ا as:

With what shall I come before the Lord? بِمَ أَتَقَدَّمُ
إِلَى ٱلرَّبِّ.

What do you desire? فِيمَ تَرْغَبُ.

How long will you pursue your evil course? حَتَّامَ
تَتَمَادَى فِي شَرِّكَ.

For what do you weep? عَلَامَ تَبْكِي.

The ا is represented by ٖ in the following instances and pronounced.

But	لَكِن	Ishmael	إِسْمٰعِيل
But	لَكِنَّ	Aaron	هٰرُون
This	هٰذَا	Isaac	إِسْحٰق
These two	هٰذَانِ	Abraham	إِبْرٰهِيْم

12

These	هٰؤُلَاءِ	God	أَللّٰه
This (fem.)	هٰذِهٖ	The God	أَلْاِلٰه
That	ذٰلِكَ	Here	هٰهُنَا
Those	أُولٰئِكَ	Most merciful	أَلرَّحْمٰنُ
Three	ثَلٰثَة	Angel	مَلٰئِكَة
Thirty	ثَلٰثُونَ		

In the masc. plural of the Preterite and Imperative and the apocopated form of the Aorist ا is written but not pronounced; as, لَمْ يَأْتُوا . اِعْلَمُوا . جَلَسُوا .

All nouns having وو side by side may drop one in writing but not in pronunciation دُوُد . كُوُوس . كُوُس . دُوُود .

مِن when followed by مَا (relative) becomes مِمَّا

عَن	,,	do.	,,	مَا	,,	عَمَّا
أَن	,,	do.	,,	لَا	,,	أَلَّا
إِن	,,	do.	,,	لَا	,,	إِلَّا
إِن	,,	do.	,,	ما	,,	إِمَّا

Note. The ت as a rule does not occur as the final letter of a noun except it is a root letter as بَيْت house, حُوت whale, تُوت mulberry, سُكُوت quietness. Exceptions بِنْت daughter, أُخْت sister. The ت is called أَلتَّآءُ ٱلْمَبْسُوطَةُ . The ة, أَلتَّآءُ ٱلْمَرْبُوطَةُ never occurs as the final letter of a verb.

PARTS OF SPEECH. اَقْسَامُ ٱلْكَلَامِ

There are three parts of Speech in Arabic:

I. The Verb ٱلْفِعْلُ.

II. The Noun ٱلْاِسْمُ.

III. The Particle ٱلْحَرْفُ.

The اِسْم *includes:*

(*a*). The Noun.

(*b*). The Pronoun.

(*c*). The Adjective.

(*d*). The Adverb.

(*e*). The Participles.

(*f*). Some Interjections.

The حَرْف *includes:*

(*a*). The Preposition حَرْفُ جَرٍّ.

(*b*). The Conjunction حَرْفُ عَطْفٍ.

(*c*). Some Interjections حُرُوفُ ٱلنِّدَاءِ.

(*d*). Some Interrogatives حُرُوفُ ٱلاِسْتِفْهَامِ.

(*e*). Other Particles حُرُوفُ ٱلتَّوْكِيدِ وَٱلنُّدْبَةِ.

SERVILE LETTERS. حُرُوفُ ٱلزِّيَادَةِ

These letters are used to inflect the noun and conjugate the verb.

They are ten in number and together form the word سَأَلْتُمُونِيْهَا. "You have asked me about them", i. e. the

Servile letters. All increase in verbs or nouns is effected
by these letters, the only exception being the doubling
of the middle or last radical of the root as اِحْمَرَّ .تَقَدَّمَ.
صَيَّاح . جَوَّال

Words are modified in meaning by prefixes, suffixes
and by the insertion of letters; most words in the
language may thus be referred to significant roots,
consisting of three or four letters. The various modi-
fications in form are spoken of as the "measures of
words". The typical root employed to represent such
changes is فَعَل.

These measures, which are peculiar to verbs and
nouns, are the following:

Verbs.

(I). Triliteral verbs have six measures:

(1) فَعَلَ يَفْعِلُ   (2) فَعَلَ يَفْعُلُ   (3) فَعِلَ يَفْعِلُ

(4) فَعُلَ يَفْعَلُ   (5) فَعُلَ يَفْعُلُ   (6) فَعِلَ يَفْعِلُ

(II). Derived verbs from the triliteral have ten measures:

(1) فَعَّلَ   (2) فَاعَلَ   (3) أَفْعَلَ   (4) تَفَعَّلَ   (5) تَفَاعَلَ

(6) إِنْفَعَلَ   (7) إِفْتَعَلَ   (8) إِفْعَلَّ   (9) إِسْتَفْعَلَ   (10) إِفْعَوْعَلَ

(III). The quadriliteral verb has the measure:

فَعْلَلَ   يُفَعْلِلُ

(IV). Derived verbs from the quadriliteral have three
measures:

(1) تَفَعْلَلَ يَتَفَعْلَلُ   (2) إِفْعَلَلَّ يَفْعَلِلُّ   (3) إِفْعَنْلَلَ يَفْعَنْلِلُ

Nouns.

(V). The measures of the derived nouns.

(VI). The triliteral primitive nouns have ten measures:

(1) فَعَل (2) فُعُل (3) فِعِل (4) فَعُل (5) فَعِل

(6) فِعَل (7) فُعَل (8) فُعْل (9) فَعْل (10) فِعْل

(VII). The quadriliteral primitive nouns have five measures:

(1) فَعْلَل (2) فُعْلُل (3) فِعْلِل (4) فِعْلَل (5) فِعَلّل

(VIII). The quinqueliteral nouns have four measures:

(1) فَعَلَّل (2) فُعَلِّل (3) فِعَلّل (4) فَعْلَلِل

(IX). The measures of the plurals.

THE VERB. اَلْفِعْلُ

The verb in its simplest form is of *two kinds.*

I. Triliteral مُجَرَّدٌ ثُلَاثِىٌّ as فَعَلَ To do.

II. Quadriliteral مُجَرَّدٌ رُبَاعِىٌّ as دَحْرَجَ To roll.

(The latter are comparatively few in number).

Both these root forms may be increased by one, two,
or three letters and thus produce Derived Forms.

The *root letters* are called حُرُوف أَصْلِيَّةٌ and may be
either Strong or Weak (the verb being named Strong
or Weak according to the absence or presence of these
letters).

The *letters of increase* are called حُرُوف زَائِدَةٌ .

Verbs may be either Transitive مُتَعَدٍّ or Intransitive
لَازِمٌ .

Intransitive Verbs may be made Transitive by:

(*a*) the use of a preposition;

(*b*) the prefixing of Hemzeh;

(*c*) doubling the medial radical; as,

To bring	جَاءَبِ	To come	جَاءَ
To cause to sleep	نَوَّمَ	To sleep	نَامَ
To raise	أَقَامَ	To rise	قَامَ

Some verbs are both Transitive and Intransitive as:

To build, to live long	عَمَّرَ	To come	جَاءَ
To do good	أَحْسَنَ	To fear	خَافَ
To make or be distant	أَبْعَدَ	To snatch	خَطَفَ
To raise, to stay	أَقَامَ	To separate	فَصَلَ
To learn	تَعَلَّمَ	To be poor	عَالَ
		To possess, to reign	مَلَكَ

The ordinary paradigm verb is فَعَلَ for the Triliteral and فَعْلَلَ for the Quadriliteral.

فَعَلَ is the third person sing. masc. of the Preterite. As the root form of the verb, it is the simplest and is consequently used as the standard of comparison or "measure" (وَزْن) for all verbs and Derivative Nouns.

It is usually rendered into English by the Infinitive. The first letter of any Triliteral verb is called its فَاء, the second its عَيْن, and the third its لَام; and in the Quadriliteral the second لَام is called أَللَّامُ ٱلثَّانِيَةُ.

Inflection. The verb is inflected to express Voice, Mood, Tense, Number, Person and Gender.

Voice. There are two Voices, the Active and the Passive. The Active is called صِيْغَةُ ٱلْمَعْلُومِ "the known" because the agent of the verb is known as,

Zaid beat the man ضَرَبَ زَيْدٌ ٱلرَّجُلَ.

The Passive Voice is called صِيْغَةُ ٱلْمَجْهُولِ "The unknown" because the agent is unknown; as,

The man was beaten ضُرِبَ ٱلرَّجُلُ.

The Active Verb is called أَلْفِعْلُ ٱلْمَعْلُومُ.

The Passive أَلْفِعْلُ ٱلْمَجْهُولُ.

Moods. The moods of the verb are three viz: — the Indicative, the Imperative and the Subjunctive. The Imperative is derived from the Imperfect Tense of the Indicative. The Subjunctive may be used in various senses i. e. Jussive, Hortative, Conditional etc.

Tenses. The Indicative Mood has both Perfect and Imperfect Tenses. The Subjunctive has only the Imperfect Tense. The verb strictly speaking has not Tenses but forms which express states.

Action not time is indicated; one a finished act, the Perfect; and the other an unfinished act, the Imperfect whose completion may be in the immediate present or in the near or far distant future. The Perfect Action includes all past tenses of other languages, the Imperfect includes all imperfect tenses.

By prefixing لَ to the Imperfect a present signification is imparted to the action of the verb, and by prefixing س or سَوْفَ a near or far distant future is respectively indicated.

Note. It is more accurate to speak of the Preterite and Aorist Tenses. The former to express a known finished act; the latter to express an indefinite and unfinished one.

Numbers. There are three numbers: the singular اَلْمُفْرَدُ, the dual اَلْمُثَنَّى, and the plural اَلْجَمْعُ.

Persons. There are three persons: the first اَلْمُتَكَلِّم "the speaker", the second اَلْمُخَاطَبُ "the person addressed", and the third اَلْغَائِبُ "the absent."

Genders. There are two genders: the masc. اَلْمُذَكَّرُ and the fem. اَلْمُؤَنَّثُ.

The numbers, persons, and genders are expressed by means of Personal Pronouns joined to the different forms of the verb.

THE ANNEXED PRONOUNS. اَلضَّمَائِرُ ٱلْمُتَّصِلَةُ

The Pronouns which are united to the verb in the Nom. Case in the process of its inflexion are six, نَا, ن, ت, ي, و, ا.

1st person sing. masc. or fem. Preterite	تُ
2nd ,, ,, masc. ,,	تَ
,, ,, ,, fem. ,,	تِ
Fem. plural for all Persons and Tenses	نَ
Masc. plural all forms	و
1st person plural Preterite	نَا
2nd person fem. sing. Aorist and Imperative	ي
For the dual	ا

Of these ت, ن, نَا are strong pronouns and the rest (اوي) weak.

When the strong pronouns are joined to a verb its

لَام is made silent ضَرَبْتُ, and when the weak pronouns
are joined to a verb the final letter of the verb takes
a vowel homogeneous to the annexed weak pronoun
إِضْرِبِي, تَضْرِبِيْنَ, ضَرَبُوا; but in the verbs ending in a weak
letter the homogeneous vowel is implied on the dropped
final letter as غَزَوْا for غَزَوُوا.

Note. The First Personal Pronoun in the Aorist Sing.
and Plural, the second person sing. of the Aorist, and
Imperative, and the third person sing. masc. and fem. of
the Aorist and Preterite are regarded as "hidden" مُسْتَتِرَة
in the verb, but when the noun follows the verb of
the third person the latter is regarded as not containing
a pronoun as ضَرَبَ زَيْدٌ ٱلرَّجُلَ.

Simple Form of the Triliteral Verb Sound.
Active Voice.

THE PRETERITE. ٱلْمَاضِى

Plural.		Dual.		Singular.		
Fem.	Masc.	Fem.	Masc.	Fem.	Masc.	
فَعَلْنَ	فَعَلُوا	فَعَلَتَا	فَعَلَا	فَعَلَتْ	فَعَلَ	3rd Per.
فَعَلْتُنَّ	فَعَلْتُم	فَعَلْتُمَا		فَعَلْتِ	فَعَلْتَ	2nd ,,
فَعَلْنَا					فَعَلْتُ	1st ,,

THE AORIST. ٱلْمُضَارِعُ

Plural.		Dual.		Singular.		
يَفْعَلْنَ	يَفْعَلُونَ	تَفْعَلَانِ	يَفْعَلَانِ	تَفْعَلُ	يَفْعَلُ	3rd Per.
تَفْعَلْنَ	تَفْعَلُونَ		تَفْعَلَانِ	تَفْعَلِينَ	تَفْعَلُ	2nd ,,
نَفْعَلُ					أَفْعَلُ	1st ,,

THE IMPERATIVE. اَلْاَمِرُ

Plural.		Dual.		Singular.		
Fem.	*Masc.*	*Fem.*	*Masc.*	*Fem.*	*Masc.*	
إِفْعَلْنَ	إِفْعَلُوا		إِفْعَلَا	إِفْعَلِي	إِفْعَلْ	2nd Per.

Passive Voice.

THE PRETERITE.

Plural.		Dual.		Singular.		
Fem.	*Masc.*	*Fem.*	*Masc.*	*Fem.*	*Masc.*	
فُعِلْنَ	فُعِلُوا	فُعِلَتَا	فُعِلَا	فُعِلَتْ	فُعِلَ	3rd Per.
فُعِلْتُنَّ	فُعِلْتُم	فُعِلْتُمَا		فُعِلْتِ	فُعِلْتَ	2nd „
فُعِلْنَا				فُعِلْتُ		1st „

THE AORIST.

Plural.		Dual.		Singular.		
يُفْعَلْنَ	يُفْعَلُونَ	تُفْعَلَانِ	يُفْعَلَانِ	تُفْعَلُ	يُفْعَلُ	3rd Per.
تُفْعَلْنَ	تُفْعَلُونَ		تُفْعَلَانِ	تُفْعَلِينَ	تُفْعَلُ	2nd „
نُفْعَلُ				أُفْعَلُ		1st „

There are six measures of the Triliteral Verb depending for their arrangement upon the vowels with which
the Medial Radical is pointed in the Preterite and Aorist.

I.	فَعَلَ يَفْعِلُ	ضَرَبَ يَضْرِبُ
II.	فَعَلَ يَفْعُلُ	نَصَرَ يَنْصُرُ
III.	فَعِلَ يَفْعَلُ	عَلِمَ يَعْلَمُ
IV.	فَعَلَ يَفْعَلُ	مَنَعَ يَمْنَعُ
V.	فَعُلَ يَفْعُلُ	فَضُلَ يَفْضُلُ
VI.	فَعِلَ يَفْعِلُ	حَسِبَ يَكْسِبُ

The first and second measures are generally transitive and of most frequent occurrence therefore are called دَعَائِمُ ٱلاْبْوابِ "principal forms".

In the first three measures the vowel of the ع of the Preterite differs from that of the Aorist, in the last three the vowel is the same.

In the fourth measure the ع or ل must be of the حُرُوف ٱلحَلْقِ but not every verb possessing these guttural letters is found in the measure.

The fourth measure is generally transitive.

The fifth measure is always intransitive and implies inherent qualities.

The sixth measure is rarely found, there being only about ten verbs and most of them begin with مِثَال وَاوِّي و .

DERIVED FORMATIONS OF THE VERB.

The increase of letters is invariably accompanied by an increase or modification of the meaning of the root form. There are twelve Derived Forms but eight only are of frequent occurrence. They are inflected precisely as the root form. It is of the utmost importance that the student should acquire a perfect familiarity with the Derived Forms.

There is no branch of Arabic study which is of such extreme importance, as the verb in Arabic is not simply the "Key-stone" of the "Arch of Speech" but the Arch itself.

The student should be able to recognize at a glance any verb of any formation and in whatever Tense and Mood it may be, together with its Derived Nouns.

In order to accomplish this, it is necessary to have a thorough knowledge of (*a*) the Rules for the formation of the verb اَلْفِعْلِ بِنَاءُ, (*b*) the changes which the weak letters undergo اَلْإِعْلَالُ, and (*c*) the subject of Insertion or Assimilation اَلْإِدْغَـامُ which are accordingly treated of before the Weak Verbs.

RULES FOR THE FORMATION OF THE VERB.

بِنَاءُ ٱلْفِعْلِ

The Preterite Active. The vowels of the Preterite in the Active Voice (اَلْمَاضِيُّ ٱلْمَعْلُومُ) are fethahs فَعَلَ except in the medial radical of the triliteral, which may take any vowel فَعِلَ and the Servile Hemzeh اِ in the five and six lettered verbs which is ِ. اِنْفَعَلَ اِفْتَعَلَ اِفْعَلَّ اِسْتَفْعَلَ اِفْعَالَّ اِفْعَوْعَلَ. (In certain verbs the vowels are implied رَمَى مَـدَّ قَامَ) رَمَيَ مَدَدَ قَوَمَ for

The Preterite Passive اَلْمَاضِيُّ ٱلْمَجْهُولُ is formed from the Preterite Active by giving ُ to the penultimate consonant and ِ to every vowelled letter preceding it.

V. تُفُوعِلَ   I. فُعِّلَ

VI. أُنْفُعِلَ   II. فُوعِلَ

VII. أُفْتُعِلَ   III. أُفْعِلَ

IX. أُسْتُفْعِلَ   IV. تُفُعِّلَ

The Aorist Active اَلْمُضَارِعُ ٱلْمَعْلُوم is formed from the Preterite Active by prefixing one of the four letters (أَنَيْتُ) ا, ت, ي, ن. Servile Hemzeh is suppressed wherever it occurs.

The vowel of the prefix is ــُ except in the four lettered verbs فَعَّلَ, فَاعَلَ, أَفْعَلَ, فَعْلَلَ where it is ــُ.

The penultimate consonant has ــَ except in the triliteral where it may be any of the three vowels, and in the fourth and fifth Derived Forms where it takes ــِ.

VI. يَنْفَعِلُ | IV. يَتَفَعَّلُ | يَفْعُلُ

VII. يَفْتَعِلُ | V. يَتَفَاعَلُ | I. يُفَعِّلُ

VIII. يَفْعَلُّ | | II. يُفَاعِلُ

IX. يَسْتَفْعِلُ | | III. يُفْعِلُ

X. يَفْعَوْعِلُ |

The Aorist Passive اَلْمُضَارِعُ ٱلْمَجْهُول has the same form as the Aorist Active. Its vowels are ــُ for the prefix and ــَ for the penultimate consonant.

III. يُفْعَلُ   يُفْعَلُ

IV. يُتَفَعَّلُ   I. يُفَعَّلُ

V. يُتَفَاعَلُ   II. يُفَاعَلُ

يُفْعَلّ VIII.	يُنْفَعَلُ VI.
يُسْتَفْعَلُ IX.	يُفْتَعَلُ VII.

The Imperative Active (أَلْأَمْرُ) is formed from the 2nd per. Aorist Active by suppressing the characteristic letter of the Aorist تَ, and if the following radical be silent Hemzeh is prefixed. The vowel of the Hemzeh is ـِ except in the triliteral which has ـُ on the ع (of the Aorist) where it takes ـُ and in the measure أَفْعَلَ where it retains ـَ.

إِنْفَعِلْ VI.	أَفْعِلْ III.	تَفْعَلُ	from	إِفْعَلْ
إِفْتَعِلْ VII.	تَفَعَّلْ IV.	تَفْعُلُ	from	أُفْعُلْ
إِفْعَلّ VIII.	تَفَاعَلْ V.			فَعِّلْ I.
إِسْتَفْعِلْ IX.				فَاعِلْ II.

The final vowel is apocopated.

This form of Imperative commands the 2nd person only of the Active Voice. To command the 1st and 3rd persons in the Active or Passive Voices لِ is prefixed to the Aorist and the final vowel is apocopated.

لِيُفْعَلْ	لِيَفْعَلْ
لِنُفْعَلْ	لِنَفْعَلْ

In verbs whose final radical is weak (نَاقِص), the weak letter is dropped in place of the vowel أَعْطِ, إِرْمِ, and in the following five measures the ن is dropped.

يَفْعَلَانِ   تَفْعَلَانِ   يَفْعَلُونَ   تَفْعَلُونَ   تَفْعَلِينَ

To express command in the Negative لَا with the Apocopated form of the Aorist is used.

لَا تَقْتُلْ.

THE QUADRILITERAL VERB. اَلْفِعْلُ ٱلرُّبَاعِىّ

The Quadriliteral Verb has three derived formations.

The first derived form expresses the consequence of the quadriliteral and corresponds with the fourth derived form of the triliteral.

The second derived form implies great intensity and corresponds with the eighth of the triliteral, and the third derived form corresponds with the sixth of the triliteral.

	Passive.			Active.	
Aorist.	Preterite.	Noun of Action.	Imperative.	Aorist.	Preterite.
يُفَعْلَلُ	فُعْلِلَ	فَعْلَلَةً	فَعْلِلْ	يُفَعْلِلُ	فَعْلَلَ
يُتَفَعْلَلُ	تُفُعْلِلَ	تَفَعْلُلٌ	تَفَعْلَلْ	يَتَفَعْلَلُ	تَفَعْلَلَ I.
يُفْعَلَلُّ	أُفْعِلِلَّ	إِفْعِلَالٌ	إِفْعَلْلِلْ	يَفْعَلِلُّ	إِفْعَلَلَّ II.
يُفْعَنْلَلُ	أُفْعُنْلِلَ	إِفْعِنْلَالٌ	إِفْعَنْلِلْ	يَفْعَنْلِلُ	إِفْعَنْلَلَ III.

There are some other quadriliterals which were originally triliterals, but a letter has been added to them in an irregular way (i. e. not in accordance with the recognized Derived Forms), and therefore they cannot be called مَزِيدَاتٌ ثُلَاثِيَّةٍ, nor are they pure quadriliterals because the letters are not all radicals. They are called مُلْحَقَاتٌ بِالرُّبَاعِىّ Supplements of the Quadriliteral.

Examples:

To give to wear	(جِلْباب) جَلْبَبَ
To stuff the crop	حَوْصَلَ
To practise veterinary surgery	بَيْطَرَ
To overthrow	دَهْوَرَ
To wear a cap	قَلْنَسَ
To make one cleave to dust	جَنْدَلَ

TABLE OF DERIVED FORMS.

Noun of Object.	Noun of Agent.	Noun of Action.	Imperative.	Aorist Passive.	Aorist Active.	Preterite Passive.	Preterite Active.	
مُفَعَّل	مُفَعِّل	تَفْعِيلًا و تَفْعِلَةً	فَعِّلْ	يُفَعَّلُ	يُفَعِّلُ	فُعِّلَ	فَعَّلَ ١	Triliteral.
مُفَاعَل	مُفَاعِل	مُفَاعَلَةً و فِعَالًا	فَاعِلْ	يُفَاعَلُ	يُفَاعِلُ	فُوعِلَ	فَاعَلَ ٢	
مُفْعَل	مُفْعِل	إِفْعَالًا	أَفْعِلْ	يُفْعَلُ	يُفْعِلُ	أُفْعِلَ	أَفْعَلَ ٣	
مُتَفَعَّل	مُتَفَعِّل	تَفَعُّلًا	تَفَعَّلْ	يُتَفَعَّلُ	يَتَفَعَّلُ	تُفُعِّلَ	تَفَعَّلَ ٤	
مُتَفَاعَل	مُتَفَاعِل	تَفَاعُلًا	تَفَاعَلْ	يُتَفَاعَلُ	يَتَفَاعَلُ	تُفُوعِلَ	تَفَاعَلَ ٥	
مُنْفَعَل	مُنْفَعِل	اِنْفِعَالًا	اِنْفَعِلْ	يُنْفَعَلُ	يَنْفَعِلُ	اُنْفُعِلَ	اِنْفَعَلَ ٦	
مُفْتَعَل	مُفْتَعِل	اِفْتِعَالًا	اِفْتَعِلْ	يُفْتَعَلُ	يَفْتَعِلُ	اُفْتُعِلَ	اِفْتَعَلَ ٧	
...	مُفْعَلّ	اِفْعِلَالًا	اِفْعَلَّ	...	يَفْعَلُّ	...	اِفْعَلَّ ٨	
مُسْتَفْعَل	مُسْتَفْعِل	اِسْتِفْعَالًا	اِسْتَفْعِلْ	يُسْتَفْعَلُ	يَسْتَفْعِلُ	اُسْتُفْعِلَ	اِسْتَفْعَلَ ١٩	
مُتَفَعْلَل	مُتَفَعْلِل	تَفَعْلُلًا	تَفَعْلَلْ		يَتَفَعْلَلُ	تُفُعْلِلَ	تَفَعْلَلَ	Quadriliteral.
مُفْعَنْلَل	مُفْعَنْلِل	اِفْعِنْلَالًا	اِفْعَنْلِلْ		يَفْعَنْلِلُ	اُفْعُنْلِلَ	اِفْعَنْلَلَ	
مُفْعَلَلّ	مُفْعَلِلّ	اِفْعِلْلَالًا	اِفْعَلِلَّ		يَفْعَلِلُّ	اُفْعُلِلَّ	اِفْعَلَلَّ	

PERMUTATION OR CHANGES OF THE WEAK LETTERS. اَلْاِعْلَالُ

The Weak Letters are ا, و, ى أَحْرُفُ ٱلْعِلَّةِ.

They may be:

(1) Changed for one Another.

(2) Made Silent.

(3) Dropped.

The Hemzeh اَلْهَمْزَة *may be represented by any of the Weak Letters.*

CHANGES OF THE HEMZEH. اِعْلَالُ ٱلْهَمْزَةِ

I. Hemzeh silent, preceded by Hemzeh vowelled is changed into the letter homogeneous to the vowel, ءَاَمَنَ آمَنَ, أُوْمِنُ أُوْمِنُ, إِئْمَان إِيْمَان.

II. Hemzeh silent, preceded by any other letter may be changed into the letter homogeneous to the vowel which precedes the Hemzeh, بِئْر بِيْر, بُؤْس بُوْس, رَأْس رَاس.

III. Hemzeh final, preceded by either و or ى silent is sometimes changed into the preceding letter and incorporated with it, وُضُوْء وُضُوّ مَجِيْء مَجِيّ.

Other common and recognized changes in the Hemzeh are:

The Aorist of رَأَى is يَرَى instead of يَرْأَى.

The Third Derivative of أَرْأَى is أَرَى instead of أَرْأَى.

The Imperatives of أَمَرَ, أَخَذَ, أَكَلَ are خُذْ, كُلْ, (أُوْمُرْ) مُرْ.

     „   „   of أَتَى is تِ or إِيْتِ.

The Imperatives of أَللَّفِيفُ ٱلمَفْرُوقُ as وَلِيَ وَقَى retain the sound letter only لِ, قِ.

سَأَلَ may be treated as the أَجْوَف.

سَأَلَ يَسْأَلُ اِسْأَلْ

سَالَ يَسَالُ سَلْ

CHANGES OF THE WEAK LETTERS.

إِعْلَالُ أَحْرُفِ ٱلعِلَّةِ

I. و silent, preceded by ◌َ is changed into ى, مِوْعَاد مِيعَاد.

ى silent, preceded by ◌ُ is changed into و, مُيْسِر مُوسِر.

ا preceded by ◌ُ or ◌ِ is changed into و or ى respectively,

شَاهَدَ becomes in the Passive شُوهِدَ.

مِفْتَاح , , , , Plural مَفَاتِيح.

II. A weak letter when silent, preceded by a homogeneous vowel and followed by a silent letter is dropped قُوّمْ قُمْ ,بِيّعْ بِعْ ,خَاْف خَفْ.

III. و and ى vowelled by ◌َ and preceded by ◌َ are changed into ا, قَوَمَ قَامَ ,رَمَىَ رَمَى.

(a) If the و of the نَاقِص occur after the third letter in a word it is always changed into ى, أَرْضَوْتُ أَرْضَيْتُ, يَرْضَوَانِ يَرْضَيَانِ.

(b) If the و be preceded by ◌ِ it is always changed into ى, رَضِوَ رَضِىَ, يَرْتَضِوُ يَرْتَضِىُ.

IV. و and ى when vowelled and preceded by a silent

letter, transfer their vowel to that letter يَبِيعِ يَبِيع
يَقْوُمُ يَقُوْمٌ; the weak letter is thereupon made homogeneous with the vowel يَهَابُ يَهْيَبُ ,يَخَافُ يَخْوَفُ.
But in certain nouns the change is not made أَدْوُر, اَعْيُن.

V. When و and ى come together and the first in
order is silent the و is changed into ى and incorporated سَيْوِد سَيِّد, طَوْىٰ طَىًّ.

VI. و and ي when vowelled by ـَ are dropped after
transferring their vowel to the preceding letter رَضِيُوا رَضُوا.

VII. When the ى is vowelled by ـِ and preceded by
ـِ it is always dropped, تَرْمِيِيْنَ تَرْمِيْنَ ,تَغْزِيِيْنَ تَغْزِينَ
مَاضِيِيْنَ مَاضِيْنَ but if the preceding vowel is ـَ the ى
is changed into و or the ـِ is transferred to the letter
before بِيعَ بُوْعَ بِيْعَ.

اَلْإِعْلَال is not permissable in Verbs of Wonder or in
Nouns of Comparison as their measure must be always
اَفْعَل.

ASSIMILATION. أُلْادِغَامُ

*Assimilation is the process by which one letter is attracted
to the sound of another.* The letter which has been assi-
milated is in certain cases incorporated into the other
which is in consequence doubled.

The following conditions must hold.

The two letters must be either I *Identical or Similar.*

II. *Side by side* in the same word but not in the
beginning.

I *Identical Letters*: Assimilation occurs in

(*a*) when the first is originally unvowelled as مَدَّ
from مَدَدَ;

(*b*) or is made silent by omitting the vowel مَدَّ
from مَدَدَ, or by transferring the vowel يَمُدُّ from يَمْدُدُ.

II. *In Similar Letters*:

This happens most frequently in verbs on the measure
اِفْتَعَلَ.

If the first radical is ط or ث or د the characteristic
ت of the measure is changed into the letter preceding it,
ثَارَ اِثَّارَ اِثْتَارَ, دَعَا اِدَّعَا اِدْتَعَى, طَرَدَ اِطَّرَدَ اِطْتَرَدَ.

If the first radical of the verb is ذ *or* ز the ت of
the measure is changed into ذ *or* د *or* ز,
ذَكَرَ اِذَّكَرَ اِذْتَكَرَ, زَادَ اِزْدَادَ اِزَّادَ اِزْتَادَ.

If the first radical of the verb is ص, ض *or* ظ the ت
is changed into ط, it may then be left or changed
again into ص, ض *or* ظ, ظَلَمَ اِظَّلَمَ, ضَجَعَ اِضْطَجَعَ
صَبَرَ اِصْطَبَرَ, ضَرَبَ اِضْطَرَبَ.

In the مِثَـال the و or ى is changed into ت,
وَحَدَ اِتَّحَدَ (اِوْتَحَدَ) يَسَرَ اِتَّسَرَ (اِيتَسَرَ).

In the measure اِنْفَعَلَ, if the first radical *is* م *the* ن
is changed into م. مَحَى اِنْمَحَى اِمَّحَى, مَحَقَ اِنْمَحَقَ اِمَّحَقَ.

When the annexed pronoun is ت preceded by د as
in تَعَدْتُ the د is omitted in pronunciation.

Assimilation in two words occurs when the first ends
with a silent letter and the second begins with the

same letter as قُلْ لَهُ but if the second letter is dis-similar, assimilation is optional مِنْ لَيِلٍ or مِلَّيلٍ.

FORMS OF THE VERB IN RESPECT TO ITS ROOT LETTERS.

تَقَاسِيمُ ٱلْفِعْلِ بِاعْتِبَارِ هَيْئَةِ حُرُوفِهِ ٱلْأَصْلِيَّةِ

The verb as we have seen is named in accordance with the nature of its root letters as Strong or Weak:

A: *Strong.*

When it is void of Weak Letters, Hemzeh and Doubling.

(Whole) اَلسَّالِمُ.

B: *Weak.*

I. When it is void of Weak Letters and contains Hemzeh or Doubling.

(Sound) اَلصَّحِيحُ.

II. When it contains Weak Letters.

(Weak) اَلْمُعْتَلُّ.

When two weak letters come together in the root the verb is called لَفِيف مَقْرُون (لَفَّ to fold) (قُرِنَ to be joined) but if a strong letter intervenes, the verb is called لَفِيف مَفْرُوق (فُرِقَ to be separate).

When the verb begins with و or ى it is called مِثَال as يَسُرَ, وَقَفَ.

When the medial radical is weak it is called أَجْوَف (Hollow) as قَالَ.

When the final radical is weak it is called نَاقِـص (Defective) as رَمَى.

The verb with ﺀ in its root is called مَهْمُوز (Hemzated).

The verb beginning with Hemzeh is called مَهْمُوزُ ٱلْفَاﺀ.

The verb whose medial radical is Hemzeh is called مَهْمُوزُ ٱلْعَيْن.

The verb which ends with Hemzeh is called مَهْمُوزُ ٱللَّام.

(a) سَالِم	{ ثُلَاثِيّ	قَتَلَ	
	رُبَاعِيّ }	دَحْرَج	
(b) صَحِيح	مُضَاعَف { ثُلَاثِيّ	مَدَّ	
	رُبَاعِيّ }	زَلْزَل	
	مَهْمُوز { ٱلْفَاﺀ	اَكَلَ	
	ٱلْعَيْن	سَاَلَ	
	ٱللَّام }	قَرَأَ	
(c) مُعْتَلّ	ٱلْفَاﺀ (ٱلْمِثَال)	وَعَدَ	يَسُرَ
	ٱلْعَيْن (ٱلْاَجْـوَف)	قَالَ	بَاعَ
	ٱللَّام (ٱلنَّاقِص)	غَزَا	رَمَى
	ٱلْعَيْن وَٱللَّام (لَفِيف مَقْرُون)	شَوَى	طَوَى
	ٱلْفَاﺀ وَٱللَّام (لَفِيف مَفْرُوق)	وَقَى	وَفَى

ٱلْمِثَالُ

Verbs beginning with و having ‑ on the ع of the Aorist drop the و in the Aorist, Imperative and Maṣdar.

34

وَعَدَ يَعِدُ عِدَةٌ عِدْ

وَرِثَ يَرِثُ رِثْ

In the Masdar a ة final is added to compensate for
the و which has been dropped.

Some verbs drop the و although they have ـَ on the ع
of the Aorist وَقَعَ يَقَعُ ،وَضَعَ يَضَعُ ،وَدَعَ يَدَعُ ،وَسِعَ يَسَعُ،
وَذَرَ يَذَرُ ،وَطِئَ يَطَأُ.

The Masdars of these exceptions also take the final ة.

THE HOLLOW VERB. أَلأَحْوَفُ

When تُ or نَ، نَا (Strong Pronouns in the Nom.
Case) are annexed to the أَجْوَف verb (i. e. when the ل
of the verb has to be silent) the weak letter is dropped.

قَامْتُ قُمْتُ ،خَافْنَا خِفْنَا، يَبِيْعْنَ يَبِعْنَ.

The same change occurs in the third, sixth, seventh
and ninth Derivative Formations.

اِنْقَادَ اِنْقَدْنَا ،اِسْتَقَامَ اِسْتَقَمْنَا، أَجَازَ أَجَزْنَا، اِجْتَازَ اِجْتَزْنَا

The third and ninth Derivative Formations of the
أَجْوَف add a final ة in the Masdar for the weak letter
which is dropped إِقَامَة، إِسْتِقَامَة.

If the ع in the Aorist of the Triliteral has ـُ the ف
in the Preterite after dropping the weak letter takes ـُ
قَامَ يَقُومُ قُمْتُ ،قَالَ يَقُولُ قُلْتُ; if the ع have ـَ or ـِ the
ف must have ـِ خَافَ يَخَافُ خِفْتُ، بَاعَ يَبِيْعُ بِعْتُ.

In the Derivative Formations the vowel of the ف
remains unchanged:

I. In the Preterite Passive of the Triliteral أَجْوَف the
و when present is changed into ى and the preceding
ـَ into ـِ, قَالَ قُولَ قِيْلَ, بَاعَ بُيِعَ بِيْعَ.

The vowel of the ف in the Triliteral of tne Passive
Voice should be ـِ but when the ف in the Active Voice
has ـُ then the former takes ـُ,

(Passive بُعْتُ)   بَاعَ يَبِيْعُ بِعْتُ (Active)

   ,,   (صِنْتُ)   صَانَ يَصُوْنُ صُنْتُ   ,,

II. In the sixth and seventh Derived Forms the Hemzeh
takes ـُ and the و when present is changed into ى,

إِنْقَادَ أُنْقُوِدَ إِنْقِيدَ, إِعْتَادَ إِعْتُوِدَ إِعْتِيْدَ.

THE DEFECTIVE VERB. أَلنَّاقِصُ

When the و plural pron. and the ى sing. fem. pron.
second pers. are annexed to a Defective verb in the Aorist
its weak letter is dropped.

If the ع have ـِ it remains and if ـَ or ـُ it has to
agree with the و or ى respectively:

3rd person plur. masc. يَخْشَوْنَ يَخْشَوْنَ

2nd   ,,   sing. fem. تَغْزُوِيْنَ تَغْزِيْنَ

2nd   ,,   sing. masc. تَرْمِيُوْنَ تَرْمُوْنَ

The ل of the Defective Triliteral (نَاقِصْ) reverts to
its original form when an annexed pronoun is joined
to it, غَزَا غَزَوْتُ, رَمَى رَمَيتُ; but in verbs of more than

three letters it is changed into ى irrespective of its
original form.

If the ع have ◌ِ in the Preterite the weak letter is
dropped in the third person fem. sing. and dual,

غَزَا غَزَتْ غَزَتَا .رَمَى رَمَتْ رَمَتَا

The weak letter is dropped in the Aorist when preceded by حَرْف جَزْم (particle of Apocopation), and it is
also dropped in the Imperative which retains the vowel of
the ع, اِرْمِ, يَرْمِ لَم.

VERBS WITH TWO WEAK LETTERS. اَللَّفِيْف

I. The first letter of the لَفِيْف مَفْرُوق behaves as the
مِثَال, وَلِيَ يَلِي.

II. The third letter of the لَفِيْف verbs behave as the
نَاقِص, وَقَى تَقِيْنَ تَوْقِيِيْنَ.

The Imperative of لَفِيْف مَفْرُوق verbs retain one letter
only, وَقِّى قِ, وَفِى فِ, وَلِيَ لِ.

THE NOUN OF ACTION. اَلْمَصْدَر

Verbs beginning with و having ◌ِ on the ع of the
Aorist drop the و and affix ة instead وِعْد عِدَة.

In the third and ninth Derivative Formations of the
Hollow Verb اجْوَف the weak letter is dropped and ة
affixed, أَقَامَ إِقْوَام إِقَامَة, إِسْتَقَامَ إِسْتِقْوَام إِسْتِقَامَة.

The Defective Verbs (نَاقِص) which insert ‌ا before the last radical, change the weak letter into Hemzeh, إِنْقَضَى إِنْقِضَاى إِنْقِضَاء, إِجْتَلَى إِجْتِلَاو إِجْتِلَاء.

In the fourth and fifth Derived Forms the ‌ء of the measure is changed into ‌ء and the ‌و when present into ‌ى, then the ‌ى is dropped because of two silent letters i. e. (‌ى and نُوْنُ ٱلتَّنْوِيْنِ) coming together,

تَرَجَّى تَرَجُّو تَرَجِّي تَرَج, تَسَامَى تَسَامُو تَسَامٍ.

These rules also apply to many nouns, as رِدَاء , كِسَاء, أَدِل.

ACTIVE PARTICIPLE OR NOUN OF AGENT.

إِسْمُ ٱلْفَاعِلِ

The Noun of Agent of the Triliteral Hollow Verb changes the weak letter into ‌ء (Hemzeh) قَـائِـل قَـاوِل, بَايِع بَائِع.

The Noun of Agent of the Triliteral نَاقِص drops the weak letter in the Nominative and Genitive Cases, and retains ‌ء, غَازٍ غَازُوْ, رَامٍ رَامِىْ.

PASSIVE PARTICIPLE OR NOUN OF OBJECT.

إِسْمُ ٱلْمَفْعُولِ

The Noun of Object of the Triliteral Hollow Verb:

I. drops the ‌و of the measure;

II. makes the weak letter silent by transferring its vowel to the preceding vowelless consonant;

III. and the preceding vowel homogeneous; as,

صَانَ مَصْوُوْن مَصُون ,بَاعَ مَبْيُوع مَبِيْع

Exceptions to this rule are the uncontracted forms:

مَقْوُوْل , مَقُوْوْد , مَدْيُوْن , مَدْوُوْف , مَخْيُوط.

The Noun of Object of the Defective Verbs (نَاقِص) which have not ـِ on the ع of the Aorist, change the و of the measure into ى and the preceding vowel is made ـِ then the two ى are incorporated;

رَمَى مَرْمُوى مَرْمِيّ ,حَشِيَ مَخْشُوى مَخْشِيّ.

The Derived Forms of the نَاقِص verbs drop their final letter in pronunciation when accompanied by the tanween مُصْطَفًى.

The same rule applies to nouns ending with ا

فَتًى originally فَتَىٌ
عَصًى ,, عَصَوٌ

ـَ نْ , نَّ نْ

THE CORROBORATIVE ن. نُوْنُ ٱلتَّوْكِيْدِ

The Energetic Mood is formed by annexing ـَ نَّ , نْ to the Aorist and Imperative after oaths, requests, prohibitions, questions.

The final vowel of the verb is changed into ـَ
لَا تَفْعَلَنَّ لا تَفْعَلَنْ.

When a weak letter has been dropped because of the concurrence of two silent letters it is restored on the final letter being vowelled ‏قُمْ قُومَنَّ, اِرْمِ اِرْمِيَنَّ‎.

The ‏نَّ, نْ‎ - are sometimes separated from the verb either by ‏ن‎ sign of fem. or ‏ا, و, ى‎ weak pronouns in Nominative Case.

In the first instance ‏ا‎ is placed between the ‏ن‎ fem. and ‏ن‎ of assurance ‏اِضْرِبْنَ اِضْرِبْنَانِّ‎.

In the second instance the weak pronoun is dropped except the ‏ا‎ and the ‏ل‎ of the verb retain their vowel ‏تَضْرِبُنَّ (تَضْرِبُونَنَّ)‎.

The Defective verbs having ‏ـ‎ on the ‏ع‎ retain these letters ‏إِرْضَيِنَّ, اِخْشَوُنَّ‎.

The ‏نْ‎ does not occur after the ‏ا‎.

THE AORIST WITH ‏نَ‎ ‏أَلتَّوْكِيدُ‎

يَفْعَلَنَّ يَفْعَلْنَانِّ	يَفْعَلانِّ تَفْعَلانِّ	يَفْعَلَنَّ تَـفْعَلَنَّ
تَفْعَلُنَّ تَفْعَلْنَانِّ	تَفْعَلانِّ	تَفْعَلَنَّ تَـفْعَلِنَّ
نَفْعَلَنَّ		أَفْعَلَنَّ

IMPERATIVE.

إِفْعَلُنَّ إِفْعَلْنَانِّ	إِفْعَلانِّ	إِفْعَلَنَّ إِفْعَلِنَّ

WITH ‏نْ‎

. . . . . يَفْعَلُنْ	. . . . .	يَفْعَلَنْ تَـفْعَلَنْ
تَفْعَلُنْ	. . . .	تَفْعَلَنْ تَـفْعَلِنْ
نَفْعَلَنْ		أَفْعَلَنْ

IMPERATIVE.

إِفْعَلُنْ	. . . . .	إِفْعَلَنْ إِفْعَلِنْ

نُوْنُ ٱلوِقَايَةِ ن OF PRECAUTION. ن

To prevent the last letter of the verb from taking
when followed by ی of the first person the ی becomes نی.

It is also used with the "Particles that Resemble
Verbs" (أَلْحُرُوفُ ٱلْمُشَبَّهَةُ بِٱلْأَفْعَالِ) لَعَلَّ, لٰكِنَّ, لَيْتَ, إِنَّ, أَنَّ,
and with the particles:

Near, With لَدُنْ   عَن From   مِن From, of.

PRETERITE ACTIVE.

	1st PERSON.		2nd PERSON.			3rd PERSON.		
	Plural.	Singular.	Plural.	Dual.	Singular.	Plural.	Dual.	Singular.
سالم	فَعَلْنَا	فَعَلْتُ	فَعَلْتُمْ	فَعَلْتُمَا	فَعَلْتَ	فَعَلُوا	فَعَلَا	فَعَلَ
			فَعَلْتُنَّ		فَعَلْتِ	فَعَلْنَ	فَعَلَتَا	فَعَلَتْ
مُضَاعَف	مَدَدْنَا	مَدَدْتُ	مَدَدْتُمْ	مَدَدْتُمَا	مَدَدْتَ	مَدُّوا	مَدَّا	مَدَّ
			مَدَدْتُنَّ		مَدَدْتِ	مَدَدْنَ	مَدَّتَا	مَدَّتْ
مهموز الفاء	أَكَلْنَا	أَكَلْتُ	أَكَلْتُمْ	أَكَلْتُمَا	أَكَلْتَ	أَكَلُوا	أَكَلَا	أَكَلَ
			أَكَلْتُنَّ		أَكَلْتِ	أَكَلْنَ	أَكَلَتَا	أَكَلَتْ
العين »	سَأَلْنَا	سَأَلْتُ	سَأَلْتُمْ	سَأَلْتُمَا	سَأَلْتَ	سَأَلُوا	سَأَلَا	سَأَلَ
			سَأَلْتُنَّ		سَأَلْتِ	سَأَلْنَ	سَأَلَتَا	سَأَلَتْ
اللام »	قَرَأْنَا	قَرَأْتُ	قَرَأْتُمْ	قَرَأْتُمَا	قَرَأْتَ	قَرَأُوا	قَرَآ	قَرَأَ
			قَرَأْتُنَّ		قَرَأْتِ	قَرَأْنَ	قَرَأَتَا	قَرَأَتْ
مثال واوي	وَعَدْنَا	وَعَدْتُ	وَعَدْتُمْ	وَعَدْتُمَا	وَعَدْتَ	وَعَدُوا	وَعَدَا	وَعَدَ
			وَعَدْتُنَّ		وَعَدْتِ	وَعَدْنَ	وَعَدَتَا	وَعَدَتْ
مثال يائي	يَسَرْنَا	يَسَرْتُ	يَسَرْتُمْ	يَسَرْتُمَا	يَسَرْتَ	يَسَرُوا	يَسَرَا	يَسَرَ
			يَسَرْتُنَّ		يَسَرْتِ	يَسَرْنَ	يَسَرَتَا	يَسَرَتْ
أجوف	خِفْنَا	خِفْتُ	خِفْتُمْ	خِفْتُمَا	خِفْتَ	خَافُوا	خَافَا	خَافَ
			خِفْتُنَّ		خِفْتِ	خِفْنَ	خَافَتَا	خَافَتْ
ناقص	رَمَيْنَا	رَمَيْتُ	رَمَيْتُمْ	رَمَيْتُمَا	رَمَيْتَ	رَمَوْا	رَمَيَا	رَمَى
			رَمَيْتُنَّ		رَمَيْتِ	رَمَيْنَ	رَمَتَا	رَمَتْ
»	حَشِينَا	حَشِيتُ	حَشِيتُمْ	حَشِيتُمَا	حَشِيتَ	حَشُوا	حَشِيَا	حَشِيَ
			حَشِيتُنَّ		حَشِيتِ	حَشِينَ	حَشِيَتَا	حَشِيَتْ
لفيف مفروق وَقَيْنَا	وَقَيْتُ	وَقَيْتُمْ	وَقَيْتُمَا	وَقَيْتَ	وَقَوْا	وَقَيَا	وَقَى
لفيف مقرون	طَوَيْنَا	طَوَيْتُ	طَوَيْتُمْ	طَوَيْتُمَا	طَوَيْتَ	طَوَوْا	طَوَيَا	طَوَى
			طَوَيْتُنَّ		طَوَيْتِ	طَوَيْنَ	طَوَتَا	طَوَتْ

	1st PERSON.		2nd PERSON.				3rd PERSON.				
	Plural	Singular.	Plural.	Dual.	Singular.		Plural.	Dual.	Singular.		
سَالِم	نَفْعَلُ	أَفْعَلُ	تَفْعَلُونَ تَفْعَلْنَ	تَفْعَلَانِ	تَفْعَلِينَ تَفْعَلُ	تَفْعَلْنَ	يَفْعَلُونَ يَفْعَلْنَ	تَفْعَلَانِ يَفْعَلَانِ	تَفْعَلُ يَفْعَلُ		
مُضَاعَف	نَمُدُّ	أَمُدُّ	تَمُدُّونَ تَمْدُدْنَ	تَمُدَّانِ	تَمُدِّينَ تَمُدُّ	يَمْدُدْنَ	يَمُدُّونَ	تَمُدَّانِ يَمُدَّانِ	تَمُدُّ يَمُدُّ		
مَهْمُوزُ ٱلْفَاء	نَأْكُلُ	آكُلُ	تَأْكُلُونَ تَأْكُلْنَ	تَأْكُلَانِ	تَأْكُلِينَ تَأْكُلُ	يَأْكُلْنَ	يَأْكُلُونَ	تَأْكُلَانِ يَأْكُلَانِ	تَأْكُلُ يَأْكُلُ		
« ٱلْعَيْن	نَسْأَلُ	أَسْأَلُ	تَسْأَلُونَ تَسْأَلْنَ	تَسْأَلَانِ	تَسْأَلِينَ تَسْأَلُ	يَسْأَلْنَ	يَسْأَلُونَ	تَسْأَلَانِ يَسْأَلَانِ	تَسْأَلُ يَسْأَلُ		
« ٱللَّام	نَقْرَأُ	اقْرَأُ	تَقْرَأُونَ تَقْرَأْنَ	تَقْرَأَانِ	تَقْرَإِينَ تَقْرَأُ	يَقْرَأْنَ	يَقْرَأُونَ	تَقْرَأَانِ يَقْرَأَانِ	تَقْرَأُ يَقْرَأُ		
مِثَال وَاوِيّ	نَعِدُ	أَعِدُ	تَعِدُونَ تَعِدْنَ	تَعِدَانِ	تَعِدِينَ تَعِدُ	يَعِدْنَ	يَعِدُونَ	تَعِدَانِ يَعِدَانِ	تَعِدُ يَعِدُ		
مِثَال يَائِيّ	نَيْسُرُ	أَيْسُرُ	تَيْسُرُونَ تَيْسُرْنَ	تَيْسُرَانِ	تَيْسُرِينَ تَيْسُرُ	يَيْسُرْنَ	يَيْسُرُونَ	تَيْسُرَانِ يَيْسُرَانِ	تَيْسُرُ يَيْسُرُ		
اجَوَف	نَخَافُ	أَخَافُ	تَخَافُونَ تَخَفْنَ	تَخَافَانِ	تَخَافِينَ تَخَافُ	يَخَفْنَ	يَخَافُونَ	تَخَافَانِ يَخَافَانِ	تَخَافُ يَخَافُ		
نَاقِص	نَرْمِي	أَرْمِي	تَرْمُونَ تَرْمِينَ	تَرْمِيَانِ	تَرْمِينَ تَرْمِي	يَرْمِينَ	يَرْمُونَ	تَرْمِيَانِ يَرْمِيَانِ	تَرْمِي يَرْمِي		
»	نَخْشَى	أَخْشَى	تَخْشَوْنَ تَخْشَيْنَ	تَخْشَيَانِ	تَخْشَيْنَ تَخْشَى	يَخْشَيْنَ	يَخْشَوْنَ	تَخْشَيَانِ يَخْشَيَانِ	تَخْشَى يَخْشَى		
لَفِيْف مَفْرُوق	نَفِي	أَفِي	تَفُونَ تَفِينَ	تَفِيَانِ	تَفِينَ تَفِي	يَفِينَ	يَفُونَ	تَفِيَانِ يَفِيَانِ	تَفِي يَفِي		
» مَقْرُون	نَطْوِي	أَطْوِي	تَطْوُونَ تَطْوِينَ	تَطْوِيَانِ	تَطْوِينَ تَطْوِي	يَطْوِينَ	يَطْوُونَ	تَطْوِيَانِ يَطْوِيَانِ	تَطْوِي يَطْوِي		

IMPERATIVE ACTIVE.

Plural.		Dual.	Singular.		
إِفْعَلْنَ	إِفْعَلُوا	إِفْعَلَا	إِفْعَلِي	إِفْعَلْ	سَالِم
أُمْدُدْنَ	مُدُّوا	مُدَّا	مُدِّي	مُدَّ	مُضَاعَف
كُلْنَ	كُلُوا	كُلَا	كُلِي	كُلْ	مَهْمُوْزُ ٱلْفَاء
سَلْنَ	سَلُوا	سَلَا	سَلِي	سَلْ	» الْعَيْنِ
إِسْأَلْنَ	إِسْأَلُوا	إِسْأَلَا	إِسْأَلِي	إِسْأَلْ	» اللَّام
إِقْرَأْنَ	إِقْرَأُوا	إِقْرَأَا	إِقْرَأِي	إِقْرَأْ	مِثَال وَاوِيّ
عِدْنَ	عِدُوا	عِدَا	عِدِي	عِدْ	مِثَال يَأْثِي
أُوسِرْنَ	أُوسِرُوا	أُوسِرَا	أُوسِرِي	أُوسِرْ	أَجْوَف
خَفْنَ	خَافُوا	خَافَا	خَافِي	خَفْ	نَاقِص
إِرْمِيْنَ	إِرْمُوا	إِرْمِيَا	إِرْمِي	إِرْمِ	»
إِخْشَيْنَ	إِخْشَوْا	إِخْشَيَا	إِخْشَي	إِخْشَ	لَفِيْف مَفْرُوْق
فِيْنَ	فُوا	فِيَا	فِي	فِ	»
إِطْوِيْنَ	إِطْوُوا	إِطْوِيَا	إِطْوِي	إِطْوِ	» مَقْرُوْنَ

PRETERITE PASSIVE.

1st PERSON.		2nd PERSON.			3rd PERSON.		
Plural Singular.		Plural.	Dual.	Singular.	Plural.	Dual.	Singular.
فُعِلْنَا فُعِلْتُ		فُعِلْتُمْ فُعِلْتُنَّ	فُعِلْتُمَا	فُعِلْتَ فُعِلْتِ	فُعِلُوا فُعِلْنَ	فُعِلَا فُعِلَتَا	فُعِلَ فُعِلَتْ
بِعْنَا بِعْتُ		بِعْتُمْ بِعْتُنَّ	بِعْتُمَا	بِعْتَ بِعْتِ	بِيعُوا بِعْنَ	بِيعَا بِيعَتَا	بِيعَ بِيعَتْ
صِنَّا صِنْتُ		صِنْتُمْ صِنْتُنَّ	صِنْتُمَا	صِنْتَ صِنْتِ	صِينُوا صِنَّ	صِينَا صِينَتَا	صِينَ صِينَتْ

AORIST PASSIVE.

1st PERSON.		2nd PERSON.			3rd PERSON.		
Plural Singular.		Plural.	Dual.	Singular.	Plural.	Dual.	Singular.
نُفْعَلُ أُفْعَلُ		تُفْعَلُونَ تُفْعَلْنَ	تُفْعَلَانِ	تُفْعَلُ تُفْعَلِينَ	يُفْعَلُونَ يُفْعَلْنَ	يُفْعَلَانِ تُفْعَلَانِ	يُفْعَلُ تُفْعَلُ
نُبَاعُ أُبَاعُ		تُبَاعُونَ تُبَعْنَ	تُبَاعَانِ	تُبَاعُ تُبَاعِينَ	يُبَاعُونَ يُبَعْنَ	يُبَاعَانِ تُبَاعَانِ	يُبَاعُ تُبَاعُ
نُصَانُ أُصَانُ		تُصَانُونَ تُصَنَّ	تُصَانَانِ	تُصَانُ تُصَانِينَ	يُصَانُونَ يُصَنَّ	يُصَانَانِ تُصَانَانِ	يُصَانُ تُصَانُ

PRETERITE ACTIVE.

1st PERSON.		2nd PERSON.				3rd PERSON.		
Plural.	Singular.	Plural.	Dual.	Singular.	Plural.	Plural.	Dual.	Singular.

AORIST ACTIVE.

1st PERSON		2nd PERSON			3rd PERSON		
Plural / Singular		Plural	Dual	Singular	Plural	Dual	Singular
نَأْمَنُ / آمَنُ		تَأْمَنُونَ / تَأْمَنُ	تَأْمَنَانِ	تَأْمَنِينَ / تَأْمَنُ	يَأْمَنُونَ / يَأْمَنَّ	تَأْمَنَانِ / يَأْمَنَانِ	تَأْمَنُ / يَأْمَنُ
نَلُومُ / أَلُومُ		تَلُومُونَ / تَلُومَنَ	تَلُومَانِ	تَلُومِينَ / تَلُومُ	يَلُومُونَ / يَلُومَنَ	تَلُومَانِ / يَلُومَانِ	تَلُومُ / يَلُومُ
نَرَى / أَرَى		تَرَوْنَ / تَرَيْنَ	تَرَيَانِ	تَرَيْنَ / تَرَى	يَرَوْنَ / يَرَيْنَ	تَرَيَانِ / يَرَيَانِ	تَرَى / يَرَى
نَنْبِرُ / أَنْبِرُ		تَنْبِرُونَ / تَنْبِرْنَ	تَنْبِرَانِ	تَنْبِرِينَ / تَنْبِرُ	يَنْبِرُونَ / يَنْبِرْنَ	تَنْبِرَانِ / يَنْبِرَانِ	تَنْبِرُ / يَنْبِرُ
نَبِيعُ / أَبِيعُ		تَبِيعُونَ / تَبِعْنَ	تَبِيعَانِ	تَبِيعِينَ / تَبِيعُ	يَبِيعُونَ / يَبِعْنَ	تَبِيعَانِ / يَبِيعَانِ	تَبِيعُ / يَبِيعُ
نَغُرُّ / أَغُرُّ		تَغُرُّونَ / تَغْرُرْنَ	تَغُرَّانِ	تَغُرِّينَ / تَغُرِّينَ	يَغُرُّونَ / يَغْرُرْنَ	تَغُرَّانِ / يَغُرَّانِ	تَغُرُّ / يَغُرُّ
نَحْتَكِي / أَحْتَكِي		تَحْتَكُونَ / تَحْتَكِينَ	تَحْتَكِيَانِ	تَحْتَكِينَ / تَحْتَكِي	يَحْتَكُونَ / يَحْتَكِينَ	تَحْتَكِيَانِ / يَحْتَكِيَانِ	تَحْتَكِي / يَحْتَكِي

IMPERATIVE ACTIVE.

Plural.	Dual.	Singular.
أُوْمُوا أُوْمْنَ	أُوْمَا	أُوْمِي أُوْمْ
رَوا رَيْنَ	رَيَا	رَيْ رَ
إبْرَأُوا إبْرَأْنَ	إبْرَأَا	إبْرَإِي إبْرَأْ
بِيْعُوا بِعْنَ	بِيْعَا	بِيْعِي بِعْ
أُغْزُوا أُغْزُوْنَ	أُغْزُوَا	أُغْزِي أُغْزُ
إحْيَوْا إحْيَيْنَ	إحْيَيَا	إحْيِي إحْيَ

MEANINGS OF THE DERIVED FORMS.

فَعَّلَ

I. *This measure makes Intransitive Verbs Transitive and Transitive Verbs Causative* (مُتَعَدِّيَة).

To deliver	نَجَّى	To escape	نَجَا
To make secure	سَلَّمَ	To be secure	سَلِمَ
To multiply	كَثَّرَ	To abound	كَثُرَ
To put to flight	هَرَّبَ	To flee	هَرَبَ

II. *Expresses Intensity* (لِلْكَثْرَةِ).

I cut the rope in pieces	قَطَّعْتُ ٱلْحَبْلَ
I shattered the glass	كَسَّرْتُ ٱلزُّجَاجَ
He wounded himself severely	جَرَّحَ جِسْمَهُ
Many camels died	مَوَّتَتِ ٱلْإِبْلُ
Many sheep lambed	وَلَّدَتِ ٱلْغَنَمُ

48

Many trees blossomed	فَرَّخَ ٱلشَّجَرُ
Many camels kneeled down	بَرَّكَتِ ٱلنَّعَمُ
I shut many doors	غَلَّقْتُ أَبْوَابًا
"We have made the earth bring forth many fountains"	فَجَّرْنَا ٱلْآرْضَ عُيُونًا

III. *Makes a Verb of a Noun* .لِاِتِّخَاذِ ٱلْفِعْلِ مِنَ ٱلْإِسْمِ

To pitch a tent	خَيَّمَ (خَيْمَة tent)
To paint	صَوَّرَ (صُورَة picture)
To petrify	حَجَّرَ (حَجَر stone)
To collect troops	جَيَّشَ (جَيْش army)
To cast a horoscope	نَجَّمَ (نَجْم star)
To gild	ذَهَّبَ (ذَهَب gold)
To make dusty	غَبَّرَ (غُبَار dust)
To plaster	كَلَّسَ (كلْس lime)
„ „	جَصَّصَ (جَصّ cement)
To specify	نَوَّعَ (نَوْع kind)
To assimilate	جَنَّسَ (جِنْس genus)
To soil	تَرَّبَ (تُرَاب dust)

فَاعَلَ

This measure is invariably *Transitive* and conveys the idea of:

I. *Reciprocal* Action between the *Agent and Object* of the Verb.

To fight with	ضَارَبَ	To accompany	رَافَقَ

To converse	حَادَثَ	To smite	لاطَمَ
To address	خَاطَبَ	To quarrel with	خَاصَمَ
To fight with	حَارَبَ	To summon	حَاكَمَ
To share „	شَارَكَ	To live peaceably with	سَالَمَ
To fight „	قَاتَلَ	To correspond „	كَاتَبَ
To accompany	صَاحَبَ		

II. *Competition* لِلْمُغَالَبَة.

To compete with in running   جَارَى

To compete with in (knowledge)   فَاخَرَ فِي (ٱلْعِلْم)

To compete with in wrestling   صَارَعَ

To compete with in writing   جَارَيْـتُـهُ فِي ٱلْكِـتَـابَة

I tried to overcome him in

argument   غَلَبْتُهُ فِي ٱلجِدَال

     To emulate (honour)   شَارَفَ

To circumvent	مَاكَرَ	To induce to err	غَالَطَ
To deceive	خَادَعَ	To ensnare	كَايَدَ

III. *Dealing. Some verbs* on this measure *express the action of the state implied in the Triliteral* ٱلْمُعَـٰامَلَة.

To deal kindly	لاطَفَ	To be kind	لَطُفَ
To deal gently	لَايَنَ	To be gentle	لَانَ
To deal roughly	خَاشَنَ	To be rough	خَشُنَ
To deal pleasantly	آنَس	To be affable	أَنِسَ

IV. *Simple Action of* فَعَلَ (بِـمَـعْنَى ٱلثُّلَاثِيّ).

To bless	بَارَكَ	To continue	دَاوَمَ

4

To be hypocritical in religion دَافَقَ   To travel سَافَرَ

V. *Repetition* اَلْمُرَاجَعَة.

To try to do a thing repeatedly حَاوَلَ

To return frequently عَاوَدَ

To demand repeatedly طَالَبَ

To put off repeatedly مَاطَلَ

To review رَاجَعَ

VI. *The meaning of* أَفْعَلَ (بِمَعْنَى أَفْعَلَ).

To resemble شَابَهَ = أَشْبَهَ

May God give you health عَافَاكَ ٱللّٰهُ = أَعْفَاكَ ٱللّٰهُ

To lend or borrow دَايَنَ = أَدَانَ

VII. *Some Triliteral Intransitive verbs which require a preposition to make them Transitive are expressed on this measure without the preposition.*

He sat with the prince جَالَسَ ٱلْأَمِيرَ , جَلَسَ مَعَ ٱلْأَمِيرِ

He wrote to him كَاتَبَهُ , كَتَبَ لَهُ

To converse كَالَمَ   He attacked him وَاقَعَهُ

To address خَاطَبَ   To fall (وَقَعَ)

VIII. فَاعَلَ *when formed from the Noun of Time means to transact business in that time.*

Day	يَوْم	To hire by the day	يَاوَمَ
Night	لَيْل	,, ,, ,, ,, night	لَايَلَ
Month	شَهْر	,, ,, ,, ,, month	شَاهَرَ
Year	عَام	,, ,, ,, ,, year	عَاوَمَ
Hour	سَاعَة	,, ,, ,, ,, hour	سَاوَعَ

| Summer | صَيْف | To hire for the summer | صَايَفَ |
| Winter | شِتَآء | „ „ „ „ winter | شَاتَى |

IX. فَـاعَـلَ *is sometimes formed from the names of the members of the body.*

Fore-arm	سَاعِد	to help	سَاعَدَ
Upper-arm	عَضُد	„ „	عَاضَدَ
Back	ظَهْر	to aid	ظَاهَرَ
Waist	أَزْر	to strengthen	آزَرَ
Shoulder	كَتِف	to walk by the side	كَاتَفَ
Waist	خَصْر	„ „ „ „ „	خَاصَرَ
Side	جَنْب	„ stand „ „ „	جَانَبَ
Neck	عُنْق	„ embrace	عَانَقَ
Face	وَجْه	„ meet face to face	وَاجَهَ
Lip	شَفَة	„ speak with	شَافَهَ

أَفْعَلَ

I. *Triliteral Intransitive Verbs generally become either Transitive or Causative on this measure.*

To cause to come down	أَنْزَلَ	To come down	نَزَلَ
To cause to enter	أَدْخَلَ	To enter	دَخَلَ
To bring in	أَحْضَرَ	To be present	حَضَرَ
To cause to be distant	أَبْعَدَ	To be distant	بَعُدَ
To fulfil	أَتَمَّ	To be fulfilled	تَمَّ

II. *If they are originally Transitive they may take two Objects instead of one and three if they had two.*

I put a ring upon him	اَلْبَسْتُهُ خَاتَمًا
I shewed him Zaid standing	أَرَيْتُهُ زَيْدًا وَاقِفًا
He saw Zaid standing	رَأَى زَيْدًا وَاقِفًا
I informed Zaid that Amr was standing	أَعْلَمْتُ زَيْدًا عَمْرًا وَاقِفًا

III. *Finding* لِلْوُجْدَانِ.

I found him or it good	أَحْسَنْتُهُ
I found him praiseworthy	أَحْمَدْتُهُ
He found the matter great	أَكْبَرَ ٱلْأَمْرَ
He found the matter important	أَعْظَمَ ٱلْأَمْرَ

IV. *Change* لِلتَّغَيُّرِ.

The land became sterile	أَجْدَبَتِ ٱلْأَرْضُ
The land became desolate	أَقْفَرَتِ ٱلْأَرْضُ
The water became putrid	أَنْتَنَ ٱلْمَآءُ
The man became humpbacked	أَحْدَبَ ٱلرَّجُلُ
The dog suffered from the mange	أَجْرَبَ ٱلْكَلْبُ

V. *Motion to* لِلْقَصْدِ.

To approach (face)	أَقْبَلَ	To go to Nejd	أَنْجَدَ
To retreat (turn back)	أَدْبَرَ	To go to Yemen	أَيْمَنَ

VI. *Abundance* لِلْكَثْرَةِ.

He inflicted severe wounds	أَثْخَنَ جِرَاحَهُ
He gave him much to do	أَشْغَلَهُ

53

VII. *To be in season, the proper time* لِلحَيْنُونَةِ.

The crops became ripe for harvesting أَحْصَدَ ٱلزَّرْعُ

The child attained the age for weaning أَفْطَمَ ٱلطِّفْلُ

The foal became fit for riding أَرْكَبَ ٱلمُهْرُ

To be in spring أَرْبَعَ To be in autumn أَخْرَفَ

To be in summer أَصَافَ To be in winter أَشْتَى

VIII. The following Verbs have the *same meaning in both forms* فَعَلَ and أَفْعَلَ.

To light ضَاءَ أَضَآءَ To commit crime جَرَمَ أَجْرَمَ

To shed blood هَرَقَ أَهْرَقَ To string سَلَكَ أَسْلَكَ

To ripen (fruit) يَنَعَ أَيْنَعَ

تَفَعَّلَ

I. *Consequence of the first Derivative* فَعَّلَ لِلْمُطَاوَعَةِ.

He taught عَلَّمَ He learned تَعَلَّمَ

He sent forward قَدَّمَ He advanced تَقَدَّمَ

He cut in pieces قَطَّمَ It was cut تَقَطَّعَ

He scattered فَرَّقَ It was scattered تَفَرَّقَ

He justified بَرَّرَ He was justified تَبَرَّرَ

He made innocent بَرَّأَ He was counted innocent تَبَرَّأَ

II. *Appropriation* لِلْإِتِّخَاذِ.

To take a wife تَزَوَّجَ To take a stone as a

To take a son تَبَنَّى pillow تَوَسَّدَ حَجَرًا

To take a garment تَرَدَّى To take a body تَجَسَّدَ

To take dinner تَغَدَّى To take possession of تَمَلَّكَ

54

To take nourishment تَغَذَّى
To take a name تَسَمَّى
To take under the arm تَأَبَّطَ (إِبْط)

To gird on a sword تَقَلَّدَ
To take arms تَسَلَّحَ
To enslave, serve تَعَبَّدَ
To entrust تَوَلَّى
To serve تَخَدَّمَ

III. *Gradation* لِلتَّدْرِيج.

To proceed by degrees تَدَرَّجَ

He learned science, branch after branch تَعَلَّمَ ٱلْعِلْمَ فَرْعًا فَرْعًا

He had a military training تَدَرَّبَ فِي ٱلْفُنُونِ ٱلْعَسْكَرِيَّةِ

To advance step by step تَقَدَّمَ (قَدَم)

To walk gradually تَمَشَّى

The well was filled by degrees تَمَلَّأَ ٱلْبِئْرُ

(To be filled) إِمْتَلَأَ

To be elevated تَرَقَّى To be trained تَخَرَّجَ

To watch continuously تَرَقَّبَ To pursue (heel عَقِب) تَعَقَّبَ

He attended to the matter continually تَدَبَّرَ ٱلْأَمْرَ

(As though we said) كَانَ يُدَبِّرُ ٱلْأَمْرَ

To fall behind gradually تَخَلَّفَ

To be strengthened by degrees تَقَوَّى

To act with deliberation تَثَبَّتَ

To continue expecting تَوَقَّعَ

To improve تَحَسَّنَ

To follow persistently تَتَبَّعَ

IV. *Change* لِلتَّحَوُّلِ.

The matter was changed	تَغَيَّرَ ٱلْأَمْرُ
The question was transferred	تَحَوَّلَتِ ٱلْمَسْأَلَةُ
The clay became stone	تَحَجَّرَ ٱلطِّينُ
The water became muddy	تَكَدَّرَ ٱلْمَآءُ
To become hard	تَصَلَّبَ
The water froze	تَجَلَّدَ ٱلْمَآءُ
The affairs improved	تَحَسَّنَتِ ٱلْأَحْوَالُ

V. *Affectation* لِلتَّكَلُّفِ.

The coward affected courage	تَشَجَّعَ ٱلْجَبَانُ
The sick one simulated patience and endurance	تَجَلَّدَ ٱلْمَرِيضُ
The sorrowful one affected patience	تَصَبَّرَ ٱلْحَزِينُ
To be manly	تَرَجَّلَ

Many verbs on this measure may have this meaning when used in certain senses, as

The boy affected politeness before the prince	تَأَدَّبَ ٱلْغُلَامُ أَمَامَ ٱلْأَمِيرِ

تَفَاعَلَ

I. *Expresses the consequence of* فَاعَلَ (ٱلْمُطَاوَعَةِ).

It conveys the idea of Reciprocal Action between the Agents of the Verb.

Zaid and Amr became partners	تَشَارَكَ زَيْدٌ وَعَمْرٌو

To help one another	تَعَاوَن
To love one another	تَحَابَّ
To greet one another (reconciliation)	تَصَافَحَ
To be neighbours	تَجَاوَرَ
To covenant together	تَعَاهَدَ
To accompany one another	تَصَاحَبَ
To exchange greetings	تَبَارَكَ
To consult together	تَآمَرَ

II. *Feigning* لِلتَّظَاهُرِ.

To feign death	تَمَاوَتَ	To feign blindness	تَعَامَى
„ „ occupation	تَشَاغَلَ	„ „ sickness	تَمَارَضَ
„ „ ignorance	تَجَاهَلَ		

III. *Increase* لِلتَّكَاثُرِ.

The evil increased	تَفَاقَمَ ٱلشَّرُّ
The clouds became dense	تَكَاثَفَ ٱلغَيْمُ
Afflictions pressed upon me	تَتَابَعَت عَلَيَّ ٱلمَصَائِبُ
Many people kept coming	تَوَارَدَ ٱلقَوْمُ
The enemy increased	تَكَاثَرَ ٱلعَدُوُّ
To be closely packed	تَرَاكَمَ

IV. *Repetition of the act* لِتِكْرَارِ وُقُوعِ ٱلفِعْلِ.

To fall one by one (leaves)	تَسَاقَطَ	To scoff	تَلَاعَبَ
		To divert oneself	تَلَاهَى
To sway	تَمَايَلَ	To be affectionate	تَعَاطَفَ
To waddle	تَهَادَى	To return by degrees	تَرَاجَعَ

To follow a pro-fession	To hold aloof	تَقَاعَدَ
		تَعَاطَى

إِنْفَعَلَ

Expresses the Consequence of فَعَلَ *and is always Passive.*

The ship was wrecked	إِنْكَسَرَتِ ٱلسَّفِينَةُ
The house fell down	إِنْهَدَمَ ٱلْبَيْتُ
The rope was cut	إِنْقَطَعَ ٱلْحَبْلُ
The writing was effaced	إِمَّحَتِ ٱلْكِتَابَةُ (إِنْمَحَتْ)
The water was poured out	إِنْصَبَّ ٱلْمَآءُ
The prophet was troubled	إِنْزَعَجَ ٱلنَّبِيُّ
The army was defeated	إِنْغَلَبَ ٱلْجَيْشُ
He was gathered to his fathers	إِنْضَمَّ إِلَى آبَائِهِ
The cloth was folded	إِنْطَوَى ٱلْقِمَاشُ
The light was extinguished	إِنْطَفَأَ ٱلنُّورُ
The disciples went to the house	إِنْصَرَفَ ٱلتَّلَامِيذُ إِلَى ٱلْبَيْتِ

إِفْتَعَلَ

This form is *generally Passive* or *Reflexive.*

I. It expresses the *consequence of* فَعَلَ (ٱلْمُطَاوَعَةِ).

To gather	جَمَعَ	To be gathered	إِجْتَمَعَ
To mix	مَزَجَ	To be mixed	إِمْتَزَجَ
To spread	نَشَرَ	To be spread (news)	إِنْتَشَرَ
To spread	مَدَّ	do.	إِمْتَدَّ

| To burn | حَرَقَ | To be burnt | اِحْتَرَقَ |
| To restore | رَدَّ | To be restored | اِرْتَدَّ |

II. *Reflexive* لِلْاِتِّخَاذِ.

To gather wood	اِحْتَطَبَ	To take an apprentice	اِصْطَنَعَ
To engage a cook	اِطَّبَخَ	To milk	اِحْتَلَبَ
To take hold of	اِسْتَلَمَ	To take a servant	اِخْتَدَمَ
To follow a craft	اِحْتَرَفَ	To gain	اِكْتَسَبَ
To buy	اِشْتَرَى, اِبْتَاعَ	To bake bread (for oneself)	اِخْتَبَزَ

III. *Meaning of* تَفَاعَلَ.

| To fight together | اِقْتَتَلَ | To divide between | اِقْتَسَمَ |
| To strive together | اِخْتَصَمَ | To meet together | اِلْتَقَى |

إِفْعَلَّ

Fixed Colours and Defects (لِلْاَلْوَانِ وَٱلْعُيُوبِ).

To be red	اِحْمَرَّ	To be brown	اِسْمَرَّ
To be black	اِسْوَدَّ	To be blue	اِزْرَقَّ
To be green	اِخْضَرَّ	To be one-eyed	اِعْوَرَّ
To be white	اِبْيَضَّ	To be crooked	اِعْوَجَّ

اِسْتَنْفَعَلَ

I. *Request* لِلطَّلَبِ.

| To ask forgiveness | اِسْتَغْفَرَ | To seek to copy | اِسْتَنْسَخَ |

59

To ask permission	اِسْتَأْذَنَ	To seek help	اِسْتَعَانَ
To borrow something	اِسْتَعَارَ	To seek protection	اِسْتَجَارَ
To borrow „	اِسْتَقْرَضَ	To seek reinforce-	
To borrow money	اِسْتَدَانَ	ments	اِسْتَنْجَدَ

II. *Finding and Believing* لِلْوِجْدَانِ وَٱلِٱعْتِقَادِ.

He found his answer good	اِسْتَحْسَنَ جَوَابَهُ
He found the house large	اِسْتَكْبَرَ ٱلدَّارَ
He believed the oath to be lawful	اِسْتَحَلَّ ٱلْقَسَمَ
He found the matter important	اِسْتَعْظَمَ ٱلْأَمْرَ
He found the boy lovable	اِسْتَحَبَّ ٱلْغُلَامَ
He found the army great	اِسْتَكْثَرَ ٱلْجَيْشَ
He found his intellect small	اِسْتَصْغَرَ عَقْلَهُ
I found thy disposition sweet	اِسْتَحْلَيْتُ طِبَاعَكَ
I found his speech vile	اِسْتَقْبَحْتُ كَلَامَهُ
He believed in his generosity	اِسْتَجَادَهُ
He despised him	اِسْتَخَفَّ بِهِ
I found study wearisome	اِسْتَثْقَلْتُ ٱلدَّرْسَ

III. *Submission* لِلتَّسْلِيمِ وَٱلِٱتِّخَاذِ.

To surrender	اِسْتَسْلَمَ	To take as captive	اِسْتَأْسَرَ
To take or become a slave	اِسْتَعْبَدَ		
To take or become a slave	اِسْتَرَقَّ		

IV. *Change* لِلتَّحَوُّلِ.

The crooked became straight	اِسْتَقَامَ ٱلْمُعْوَجُّ

| The clay became hard | إِسْتَحْجَرَ ٱلطِّيْن |
| To be transformed | إِسْتَحَالَ |

إِفْعَالّ

This form intensifies the meaning of اِفْعَلّ.

| To be intensely red | إِحْمَارّ | To be white | اِبْيَاضّ |

إِفْعَوْعَلَ

Intensity and Beginning لِلْمُبَالَغَةِ وَٱلِابْتِدَاء.

To be humpbacked	إِحْدَوْدَبَ
To become rough	إِخْشَوْشَنَ
It was about to rain	إِحْلَوْلَقَتِ ٱلسَّمَآءُ أَنْ تَمْطُر
The fruit became ripe	إِحْلَوْلَى ٱلتَّمَر
The man stooped	إِحْقَوْقَفَ ظَهْرُ ٱلرَّجُل
The earth became covered with verdure	إِعْشَوْشَبَتِ ٱلْاَرْض

إِفْعَوَّلَ

Expresses great Intensity.

| To be heavy | اِعْلَوَّدَ | To be long or last long | إِخْرَوَّط |

DERIVATIVE NOUNS. الأسماء التي تشتق من الفعل

THE FOLLOWING NOUNS ARE DERIVED FROM THE VERB: —

NAMES.		MEASURES.	
		TRILITERAL.	DERIVED.
			Special.
Noun of Action.	المَصْدَر	Various.	Special.
Noun of Unity.	مَصْدَر المَرَّة	فَعْلَة	ة to Masdar.
Noun of Species.	مَصْدَر النَّوْع	فِعْلَة	As Noun of Unity with qualifying expression.
Noun of Action with م.	المَصْدَر المِيمِيّ	مَفْعَل	فَعَال . . . ٌ
Noun of Agent.	اسم الفَاعِل	فَاعِل	فِعَال . . . ٌ
Adjective Resembling the Agent.	الصِّفَة المُشَبَّهَة باسم الفَاعِل	Various.	فُعَال . . . ٌ
Noun of Superiority.	اسم التَّفْضِيل	أَفْعَل	. . .
Noun of Excess.	اسم المُبَالَغَة	Various.	. . .
Noun of Object.	اسم المَفْعُول	مَفْعُول	فَعَال . . . ٌ
The Measures	فِعْلان نِفْعِل	. . .	. . .
Noun of Time and Place.	اسم المَكَان والزَّمَان	مَفْعَل	مَفْعَل مِفْعَال مَفْعَلة
Noun of Instrument.	اسم الآلَة	مِفْعَل مِفْعال مِفْعَلة	. . .

THE NOUN OF ACTION. اَلْمَصْدَر

The word مَصْدَر is the Noun of Place from صَدَرَ to arise.

It is so called because it is regarded as the source of the verb and the derivative nouns. It expresses mere action, state, or being of the verb, and is unlimited by subject, object, or time; as

beating ضَرْب   sleeping نَوْم   ease سُهُوْلَة

The Noun of Action is never made feminine; but if it should express number or kind, it is rendered into dual or plural; as

I struck him twice ضَرَبْتُهُ ضَرْبَتَيْنِ   I struck him blows ضَرَبْتُهُ ضَرَبَاتٍ

It is often used with its own verb to strengthen the meaning of the verb; as

I beat him severely ضَرَبْتُهُ ضَرْبًا   I killed him outright قَتَلْتُهُ قَتْلًا

I fled outright هَرَبْتُ هَرْبًا

It is sometimes used as an adjective, and as a common noun; as

a righteous man رَجُل عَدْل   a holy spirit رُوْح قُدْس

letter تَحْرِيْر   building بِنَاء

It is formed from both transitive and intransitive verbs.

From triliteral verbs it is irregular in its formation. Some twenty-three measures are in common use. A verb may have several Nouns of Action especially if it has dif-

ferent shades of meaning which may be indicated by
the different vowels employed on the ع of the preterite.

The following measures are the most common:

فَعْل is formed from transitive verbs on the measures فَعِلَ, فَعَلَ

فُعُوْل   „   „   „ intransitive   „   „   „   „   فَعَلَ

فَعَل   „   „   „   „   „   „   „   „   فَعِلَ

فَعَالَ
فُعُوْلَ   are   „   „   „   „   „   „   „   فَعُلَ

فِعَال ,فَعَال express sounds.

فِعَالَة expresses trades and
offices.

فِعَال expresses flight and
refusal.

فُعَال expresses ailments.

فَعَلَان expresses violent or
continuous motion.

فُعْلَة expresses colour in
the abstract.

فَعِيْل expresses change of
place.

In the derived forms of the verb and the quadriliteral special measures are employed:
(See glossary).

فَعَّل takes تَفْعِلَة or تَفْعِيْل | سَلَّمَ to make safe تَسْلِمَة or تَسْلِيْم

قَدَّم to offer „ تَقْدِمَة „ تَقْدِيْم | سَلَّح „ arm, equip تَسْلِيْح „ تَسْلِيْحَة

Verbs weak on the medial radical (اَلْأَجْوَف) take the
measure تَفْعِيْل only:

نَوَّم to make to sleep تَنْوِيْم | قَوَّم to straighten تَقْوِيم

بَيَّض „ whiten تَبْيِيْض | هَيَّج „ agitate تَهْيِيْج

سَوَّد „ blacken تَسْوِيْد | سَيَّج „ fence تَسْيِيْج

شَيَّدَ to establish	تَشْيِيْد	حَوَّلَ to change into	تَحْوِيْل
قَيَّدَ ,, bind	تَقْيِيْد		

Defective Verbs and those whose final radical is hemzeh take the measure تَفْعِلَة only; as

زَكَّى to justify	تَزْكِيَة	سَوَّى to equalize	تَسْوِيَة
سَلَّى ,, divert (mind)	تَسْلِيَة	هَيَّأ ,, prepare	تَهْيِئَة
سَمَّى ,, name	تَسْمِيَة	هَنَّأ ,, congratulate	تَهْنِئَة
قَوَّى ,, strengthen	تَقْوِيَة	جَزَّأ ,, apportion	تَجْزِئَة

فَاعِل takes the measure فِعَال or مُفَاعَلَة; as

قَاتَلَ to fight قِتَال or مُقَاتَلَة warfare.

حَارَبَ ,, ,, (حِراب) or مُحَارَبَة warfare.

ضَارَبَ ,, ,, (blows) ضِرَاب or مُضَارَبَة.

خَالَفَ ,, oppose خِلَاف or مُخَالَفَة opposition.

نَاقَضَ ,, contradict (نِقَاض) or مُنَاقَضَة contradiction.

سَالَمَ ,, make peace with (سِلَام) or مُسَالَمَة.

جَاهَدَ ,, wage war against infidels جِهَاد or مُجَاهَدَة.

جَادَلَ ,, dispute جِدَال or مُجَادَلَة disputation.

(Not every verb has both forms in use).

Verbs which begin with servile ة (تَفَاعَلَ. تَفَقَّلَ) have ـَ on the penultimate consonant; as

تَقَدَّمَ to advance	تَقَدُّم	progress.
تَعَجَّبَ ,, wonder	تَعَجُّب	wonder.
تَقَاتَلَ ,, fight together	تَقَاتُل	
تَظَاهَرَ ,, pretend	تَظَاهُر	pretence.

تَصَوَّرَ to imagine   تَصَوُّر imagination.

تَوَاضَعَ ,, be humble   تَوَاضُع humility.

تَدَاخَلَ ,, interfere   تَدَاخُل interference.

تَدَحْرَجَ ,, roll   تَدَحْرُج rolling.

Derived forms of the verb beginning with أ, إ, and the quadriliteral, insert an ١ before the final radical and give ِ to every vowelled letter preceding the ١.

The penultimate consonant takes َ ; as

أَحْسَنَ to do good   إِحْسَان charity.

أَكْرَمَ ,, honour   إِكْرَام honour.

أَسْرَفَ ,, squander   إِسْرَاف prodigality.

أَقْنَعَ ,, convince   إِقْنَاع convincing.

إِنْقَاد ,, be led   إِنْقِيَاد being led.

إِنْكَسَرَ ,, be defeated, broken   إِنْكِسَار defeat.

إِتَّحَدَ ,, be united   إِتِّحَاد unity.

إِتَّخَذَ ,, take possession   إِتِّخَاذ assumption.

إِسْوَدَّ ,, be black   إِسْوِدَاد blackness.

إِسْتَعَدَّ ,, make oneself ready   إِسْتِعْدَاد preparation.

إِسْتَقَامَ ,, be upright   إِسْتِقَامَة uprightness.

إِسْتَفْهَمَ ,, seek to understand   إِسْتِفْهَام

أَتَمَّ ,, fulfil   إِتْمَام fulfilment.

أَعْلَنَ ,, reveal   إِعْلَان revelation.

أَلْهَمَ ,, inspire   إِلْهَام inspiration.

آمَنَ ,, believe   إِيمَان faith.

إِنْطَلَقَ	to depart	إِنْطِلَاق	departure.
إِنْقَلَبَ	„ be overthrown	إِنْقِلَاب	overthrow
إِبْتَدَأَ	„ begin	إِبْتِدَاء	commencement.
إِجْتَهَدَ	„ be diligent	إِجْتِهَاد	diligence.
إِحْمَرَّ	„ be red	إِحْمِرَار	redness.
إِسْتَعْمَلَ	„ use	إِسْتِعْمَال	use.
إِسْتَفَادَ	„ profit	إِسْتِفَادَة	profit.
إِسْتَحَقَّ	„ be worthy	إِسْتِحْقَاق	merit.

It will be seen from the foregoing examples that the Noun of Action is very frequently used as a noun.

NOUN OF UNITY. مَصْدَرُ ٱلْمَرَّة

The Noun of Unity expresses the doing of an action once (مَرَّة).

If is formed from triliteral verbs on the measure فَعْلَة i. e. by affixing the ة of unity to the Noun of Action on the measure فَعْل; as

I struck him one blow ضَرَبْتُهُ ضَرْبَةً.

The act of

helping	نَصْرَة	killing	قَتْلَة	dying	مَوْتَة
sitting	قَعْدَة	rejoicing	فَرْحَة	fleeing	فَرَّة
drinking	شَرْبَة	once.			

In the derived forms of the verb the Noun of Unity is expressed on the measure of the ordinary Masdar with ة affixed; as

I honoured him once أَكْرَمْتُهُ إِكْرَامَةً.

When the ordinary Maṣdar ends with ة as in the
derived forms of the أَجْوَف a word to limit its meaning
is placed after it; as

I raised him once only أَقَمْتُهُ إِقَامَةً وَاحِدَةً

I pitied him once رَحِمْتُهُ رَحْمَةً لَا غَيْر

I invited him once only دَعَوْتُهُ دَعْوَةً فَقَطْ

The dual and plural are formed in the usual way
after suppressing the final ة; as

I struck him blows ضَرَبْتُهُ ضَرَبَاتٍ

I struck him two blows ضَرَبْتُهُ ضَرْبَتَيْنِ

NOUN OF SPECIES. مَصْدَرُ ٱلنَّوْعِ

The Noun of Species expresses the manner of doing
the action which is indicated by the verb.

Triliteral verbs have the measure فِعْلَة; as

I rode like the prince رَكِبْتُ رِكْبَةَ ٱلْأَمِيرِ

I took a quick walk مَشَيْتُ مِشْيَةً مُسْتَعْجَلَةً

He died miserably مَاتَ مِيتَةَ ٱلشَّقِيِّ

He walked righteously سَارَ سِيْرَةَ ٱلْبَارِّ

He shouted like a lion صَرَخَ صِرْخَةَ ٱلْأَسَدِ

The mode or style of

sitting	جِلْسَة	laughing	ضِحْكَة	standing	وِقْفَة
sitting	قِعْدَة	running	رِكْضَة	throwing	صِرْعَة

Derived forms of the verb have the same measure as
1) the Noun of Unity or 2) the Noun of Action followed by some qualifying expression.

1) I departed like the fearing one   اِنْطَلَقْتُ اِنْطِلَاقَةَ ٱلْخَائِفِ

   I looked about like a fawn   اِلْتَفَتُّ ٱلْتِفَاتَةَ ٱلظَّبْيِ

   I praised God piously   سَبَّحْتُ ٱللّٰهَ تَسْبِيْحَةَ ٱلتَّقِي

2) I loved him like a brother   أَحْبَبْتُهُ مَحَبَّةَ ٱلْأَخِ لِأَخِيْهِ

   I fought with him courageously   قَاتَلْتُهُ مُقَاتَلَةَ ٱلشُّجَاعِ

   He trembled as with fear   اِرْتَعَدَ ٱرْتِعَادَ ٱلْخَائِفِ

NOUN OF ACTION WITH م.   اَلْمَصْدَرُ ٱلْمِيْمِيّ

The Noun of Action with م has the same meaning
as the ordinary Maṣdar.

Triliteral Verbs have the measure مَفْعَل; as

Selling	مَبَاع	Speaking	مَنْطَق	Seeing	مَرْأًى
Growth	مَنْبَت	Taste	مَذَاق	Hearing	مَسْمَع
Result	مَآل	Clothing	مَلْبَس	Beating	مَضْرَب
		Falling	مَوْقَع	Return	مَعَاد

Verbs beginning with و and having = on the ع of
the Aorist take the measure مَفْعِل; as

وَعَدَ to promise	مَوْعِد يَعِدُ	وَرِثَ to inherit	مَوْرِث يَرِثُ	inheriting.	
وَقَفَ „ stand	مَوْقِف يَقِفُ	وَصَلَ „ join	مَوْصِل يَصِلُ	joining.	

The following words are exceptions to the preceding rule:

Walking	مَسِيْر	Coming	مَجِيْئ	Old age	مَشِيْب
Ending	مَصِيْر	Returning	مَرْجِع		

In all verbs of more than three letters the Noun of
Action with م takes the measure of the Noun of Object; as

Rending	مُمَزَّق	Trusting	مُتَّكَل	Spacious	مُتَّسَع
Praying	مُصَلَّى	Deducing	مُسْتَخْرَج	Recalling	مُسْتَرَدّ
Proceeding	مُنْبَثِق	Overthrow	مُنْقَلَب	Equalization	مُعَدَّل
Stooping	مُنْحَنَى	End	مُنْتَهَى	Opening	مُنْفَتَح
Taking	مُتَّخَذ	Deserving	مُسْتَحَقّ	Wavering	مُتَقَلَّب
Summary	مُجْمَل	Neglect	مُتَهَاوَن		

A ة is sometimes added; as

Exhortation	مَوْعِظَة	Hunger	مَجَاعَة	Fear	مَخَافَة
Consent	مَرْضَاة	Humiliation	مَذَلَّة	Excuse	مَعْذَرَة
Pardon	مَغْفَرَة				

THE NOUN OF AGENT OR ACTIVE PARTICIPLE.

$$إِسْمُ ٱلْفَاعِلِ$$

The Noun of Agent expresses intermittent action
only, and is formed from both transitive and intransitive verbs.

For triliterals its measure is فَاعِل; as

قَاتِل	one who kills.	قَائِل	one who says.
ضَارِب	,, ,, strikes.	آكِل	,, ,, eats.
رَامٍ	,, ,, throws.	مَادّ	,, ,, stretches.
جَالِس	,, ,, sits.	سَائِل	,, ,, asks.

بَائِع one who sells. | غَازٍ one who raids.

وَاعِد ,, ,, promises. | وَالٍ ,, ,, rules.

Verbs of more than three letters change the letter of the Aorist into مُ and vowel the penultimate consonant with =

مُقَدِّم قَدَّمَ offerer. | مُسَالِم سَالَمَ peaceful.

مُحْسِن أَحْسَنَ benefactor. | مُتَعَلِّم تَعَلَّمَ learner.

مُتَزَلْزِل تَزَلْزَلَ quaking. | مُتَحَارِب تَحَارَبَ mutual [warfare.

مُنْكَسِر إِنْكَسَرَ broken. | مُحْتَمِل إِحْتَمَل endurer.

مُدَحْرِج دَحْرَجَ roller. | مُحْرَنْجِم إِحْرَنْجَمَ pressing [(crowds).

مُحْمَرّ إِحْمَرَّ red. | مُسْتَحْسِن إِسْتَحْسَنَ approver.

مُحْدَوْدِب إِحْدَوْدَبَ hump- [backed. | مُقْشَعِرّ إِقْشَعَرَّ shudder- [ing with horror.

THE ADJECTIVE RESEMBLING THE AGENT.

ٱلصِّفَةُ ٱلْمُشَبَّهَةُ بِٱسْمِ ٱلْفَاعِلِ

The Adjective resembling the Agent is an Adjective of quality, and is generally formed from neuter verbs on the measures فَعِلَ يَفْعَلُ, فَعَلَ يَفْعَلُ. These verbs express inherent and permanent qualities in persons or things, and therefore the adjectives where derived from them possess similar qualities. They are formed from triliteral verbs on various measures as follows:

71

Measures.

فَعْل

عَذْب	sweet.	شَيْخ	aged.	رَطْب	tender.
سَهْل	easy.	صَعْب	difficult.	ثَبْت	firm.

فِعْل

جِلْف	uncouth.	دِقّ	thin.	خِصْب	fertile.

فُعْل

حُرّ	free.	دُوْن	mean.	حُلْو	sweet.
مُرّ	bitter.	صُلْب	hard.	سُخْن	hot.

فَعَل

حَدَث	youth.	عَزَب	unmarried.	حَسَن	handsome.
بَطَل	hero.	نَجَس	impure.		

فَعِل

دَنِس	soiled.	عَسِر	difficult.	خَشِن	rough.
فَرِح	joyous.	وَسِخ	dirty.	قَذِر	filthy.

أَفْعَل

أَصْفَر	yellow.	أَخْضَر	green.	أَزْرَق	blue.
أَحْمَر	red.	أَسْوَد	black.	أَبْيَض	white.
أَعْوَر	blue-eyed.	أَصَمّ	deaf.	أَعْقَد	tongue-tied.
أَعْرَج	lame.	أَعْمَى	blind.	أَخْرَس	dumb.

فَيْعِل

سَيِّد	lord.	ضَيِّق	narrow.	لَيِّن	soft.
طَيِّب	pleasant.	جَيِّد	good.	مَيِّت	dying.

Measures.

فَعِيْل

| نَظِيْف clean. | مَلِيْح good. | قَدِيْم old. |
| ظَرِيْف beautiful. | جَدِيْد new. | عَطِيْق „ |

فَعَال

| جَبَان coward. | حَصَان chaste. | شُجَاع brave. |
| | جَوَاد liberal. | عَيَآء incurable. |

فُعَال

| عُضَال distressing. | ضُخَام large. | ذُعَاف fatal. |
| عُقَام „ | شُجَاع brave. | زُعَاف „ |

فَعْلَان

| عَطْشَان thirsty. | عَرْقَان perspiring. | سَكْرَان drunken. |
| ظَمْآن „ | شَبْعَان satisfied. | غَضْبَان angry. |

فَاعِل

| حَارّ hot. | بَارِد cold. | فَاتِر lukewarm. |
| حَازِم resolute. | عَامّ general. | خَاصّ special. |

(See glossary).

فَعْلَان is commonly used to express hunger, thirst, and their opposites.

أَفْعَل expresses colour, defect, blemishes, and points of beauty.

From verbs of more than three letters the Adjective resembling the Agent is formed on the measure of the Noun of Agent.

Derived Forms.

I.   مُغَرِّد   singing bird.

II.   مُرَاءٍ   hypocrite.

III.   مُحْسِن   benefactor.   مُضِرّ   injurious.

    مُخْلِص   sincere.   مُنِيْر   shining.

    مُظْلِم   dark.   مُسِنّ   old (age).

    مُفْلِس   penniless.   مُشْرِق   shining.

    مُهْمِل   neglectful.   مُمْكِن   possible.

    مُؤْمِن   believer.   مُنْصِف   just.

    مُصِيْب   right.

IV.   مُتَجَبِّر   tyrant.   مُتَقَلِّب   fickle.

    مُتَجَعِّد   wrinkled.   مُتَوَسِّط   moderate.

    مُتَكَبِّر   proud.   مُتَأَدِّب   polite.

    مُتَمَدِّن   civilized.   مُتَرَدِّد   irresolute.

    مُتَجَمِّد   frozen.   مُتَوَحِّش   barbarian.

    مُتَعَبِّد   religious.

V.   مُتَكَاسِل   lazy.   مُتَظَاهِر   pretender.

    مُتَهَاوِن   neglectful.

VI.   مُنْحَرِف   deviating.   مُنْدَرِس   obliterated.

    مُنْخَفِض   lowered.   مُنْحَصِر   limited.

VII.   مُحْتَرِس   precautious.   مُخْتَلِف   different.

    مُكْتَفٍ   content.   مُكْتَئِب   vexatious.

    مُسْتَوٍ   straight.   مُعْتَدِل   temperate.

    مُتَّضِع   humble.

74

VIII. مُسْوَدّ black.   مُكْمَدّ opaque.

مُحْمَرّ red.

IX. مُسْتَحِيْل impossible.   مُسْتَدِيْر round.

مُسْتَعِدّ ready.   مُسْتَبِدّ arbitrary.

مُسْتَقِيْم upright.   مُسْتَهْزِئ scornful.

X. مُحْدَوْدِب hump-backed.

Note: Very few of these adjectives are formed from the first and second derived forms, because most of the latter are transitive.

Measures:

فَعْلَل

مُرَفْرِف fluttering.   مُتَمْتِم stammering.

مُوَسْوِس suggesting evil.

تَفَعْلَل I

مُتَفَلْسِف philosophizing. مُتَفَطْرِس self-admirer.

مُتَلَأْلِئ shining.

إِفْعَنْلَل II

مُكْفَهِرّ intensely dark. مُشْمَخِرّ very high.

The Comparison of Adjectives.

THE NOUN OF SUPERIORITY. اِسْمُ ٱلتَّفْضِيْل

Both the Comparative and Superlative degrees are formed from triliteral verbs on the measure أَفْعَل.

The Comparative degree is expressed by مِن following the measure; as

More accomplished than أَفْضَلُ مِن

The Superlative degree is expressed by prefixing the article to the measure, as اَلْأَفْعَلُ, or by putting the measure in construction with the noun qualified; as

He is the most accomplished man   هُوَ أَفْضَلُ رَجُلٍ

When the article is prefixed to the measure it agrees with the noun in gender and number; as

The most excellent men   اَلرِّجَالُ ٱلْأَفَاضِلُ

The most handsome women   اَلنِّسَاءُ ٱلْحُسْنَيَاتُ

The two richest men   اَلرَّجُلَانِ ٱلْأَغْنِيَانِ

The largest tree   اَلشَّجَرَةُ ٱلْكُبْرَى

When in construction with a definite noun, it may agree with the noun in gender and number or remain masculine singular.

Hind is the most accomplished of women

عِنْدٌ أَفْضَلُ ٱلنِّسَاءِ or هِنْدٌ فُضْلَى ٱلنِّسَاءِ

These are the two tallest men

هٰذَانِ أَطْوَلُ ٱلرِّجَالِ or هٰذَانِ أَطْوَلَا ٱلرِّجَالِ

These are the worst men

هٰؤُلَاءِ أَدْنِيَاءُ ٱلنَّاسِ or هٰؤُلَاءِ أَدْنَى ٱلنَّاسِ

(The fem. of أَفْعَلُ is فُعْلَى).

Comparatives formed from transitive verbs and verbs of loving, hating, etc. prefix the preposition لِ to the object; as

He seeks knowledge more than you   هُوَ أَطْلَبُ لِلْعِلْمِ مِنْكُمْ

When formed from verbs of knowing etc. they take the preposition ب with the object; as

He knows the truth better
than you هُوَ أَعْرَفُ بِالْحَقِّ مِنْكُمْ

Comparatives formed from intransitive verbs retain their preposition; as

هُوَ أَزْهَدُ فِي ٱلدُّنْيَا وَأَسْرَعُ إِلَى ٱلْخَيْرِ وَأَبْعَدُ عَنِ ٱلشَّرِّ وَأَقْرَبُ
مِنَ ٱلْحَقِّ وَأَصْبَرُ عَلَى ٱلنَّوَائِبِ.

He is more abstemious in worldly things, prompter to good, further from sin, nearer the truth, and more patient in afflictions.

Some adjectives from the very nature of the ideas they express do not admit of comparison, as those derived from the verbs.

To die مَاتَ   to pass away فَنِيَ   to live حَيِيَ.

Adjectives which express colour, defect, and points of beauty do not admit of comparison on this measure because they have already the form أَفْعَلُ without reference to degree.

Defective Verbs ٱلْأَفْعَالُ ٱلنَّاقِصَةُ as صَارَ, أَمْسَى, كَانَ and verbs which do not admit of conjugation as لَيْسَ, حَبَّذَا do not form adjectives of comparison.

The Noun of Superiority has invariably the meaning of the Noun of Agent.

Verbs of more than three letters and those which express colour, defect etc. take the Noun of Action in

the accusative case preceded by an adjective derived
from another verb to express comparison; as

He is speedier than they, هُوَ أَشَدُّ إِسْرَاعًا مِنْهُم

and less diligent than his brother. وَأَقَلُّ إِجْتِهَادًا مِنْ أَخِيهِ

He is a keener observer
than his companions. وَأَدَقُّ مُلَاحَظَةً مِنْ رُفَقَائِهِ

He is more famous than his
parents. هُوَ أَوْسَعُ شُهْرَةً مِنْ وَالِدَيْهِ

He is nearer to God, of quicker perception than others
and of more refined manners.

هُوَ أَكْثَرُ ٱقْتِرَابًا إِلَى ٱللّٰهِ, وَأَسْرَعُ إِدْرَاكًا مِنْ سِوَاهِ وَأَدْنَى ٱقْتِرَابًا
مِنَ ٱلْأَدبِ.

He is redder (or blacker) and lamer.

هُوَ أَشَدُّ حُمْرَةً (أَوْ سَوَادًا) وَأَكْثَرُ عَرَجًا.

THE NOUN OF EXCESS. إِسْمُ ٱلْمُبَالَغَةِ

This derived noun has the meaning of the Noun of
Agent to which is added the idea of intensity.

It has various measures, the most important of which
are the following:

فُعَلَة	فَعِيل	فَعُوْل	فِعِّيْل	فَعَّالَة	فَعَّال
فَاعِلَة	فُعُل	مِفْعِيْل	مِفْعَال	فَعِل	فَاعُوْل
					فُعُوْلَة

غَفَّار the Pardoner. تَوَّاب the Forgiving.

قَهَّار ,, Subduer. بَسَّام smiling.

فَيَّاض the Bountiful. بَرَّاق bright.

جَوَّال ,, traveller. عَلَّام learned.

خَوَّان ,, treacherous. مَنَّان benefactor.

غَدَّار ,, صَوَّام fasting person.

(See glossary).

THE MEASURES فَعِيْل and فَعُوْل

These two forms are common to the Noun of Agent
and Noun of Object; so that at one time they would
denote activity; as

patient صَبُوْر   sick مَرِيْض

and at another passivity; as

an apostle رَسُوْل   wounded جَرِيْح

When فَعُوْل indicates the Noun of Agent and فَعِيْل
the Noun of Object and are accompanied by their substantives they have the same form for masculine and
feminine; as

a wounded man رَجُل جَرِيْح   a patient man رَجُل صَبُوْر

,, ,, woman اِمْرَأَة جَرِيْح   ,, ,, woman اِمْرَأَة صَبُوْر

but if فَعُوْل indicates the Noun of Object and فَعِيْل the
Noun of Agent, or if their nouns are not mentioned
they add ة for the feminine; as

a woman intrusted with an important mission اِمْرَأَة رَسُوْلَة

a sick woman اِمْرَأَة مَرِيْضَة

Adjectives which are peculiar to the feminine fall under this rule, and some adjectives on the measure فَاعِل; as

pregnant	حَامِل	barren	عَاقِر	thin	ضَامِر
wet nurse	مُرْضِع	mother with infant	مُطْفِل		

THE NOUN OF OBJECT OR PASSIVE PARTICIPLE.

إِسْمُ ٱلْمَفْعُولِ

Triliterals have the measure مَفْعُول; as

مَضْرُوب	beaten	مَحْبُوب	loved	مَرْوِيّ	reported
مَقْتُول	killed	مَنْظُور	seen	مَبْلُول	wet
مَرْكُوب	ridden	مَدْفُون	buried	مَمْدُود	stretched
مَسْؤُول	responsible, asked	مَوْعُود	promised	مَأْثُور	tracked
مَوْقِيّ	protected	مَرْمِيّ	thrown	مَرْضِيّ	pleased
مَطْوِيّ	folded	مَبِيع	sold	مَقُول	spoken
مَصُون	guarded	مَغْزُوّ	raided		

In all other forms of the verb the Noun of Object follows the measure of the Noun of Agent, substituting ـَ for the ـِ of the penultimate consonant; as

educated	مُهَذَّب هَذَّبَ	reconciled	مُصَالَح صَالَحَ
hoped	مُتَرَجَّى تَرَجَّى	demanded	مُتَقَاضَى تَقَاضَى
employed	مُسْتَخْدَم إِسْتَخْدَمَ	rectified	مُصْلَح أَصْلَحَ
		gained	مُكْتَسَب إِكْتَسَبَ

The measure فَعَل has sometimes the meaning of the Noun of Object:

وَلَد	child.	مَوْلُوْد	born.
عَدَد	number.	مَعْدُوْد	counted.
سَلَب	booty.	مَسْلُوْب	spoiled.
جَلَب	imported goods	مَجْلُوْب	brought.
قَدَر	fate	مَقْدُوْر	determined.
نَسَق	order	مَنْسُوْق	arranged.

When the Noun of Object is formed from the names of the members of the body, it means to be diseased in that member; as

colic بَطْن مَبْطُوْن   heart disease مَفْوُوْد فُوَاد
chest complaint مَصْدُوْر صَدَر

THE NOUN OF PLACE AND TIME.

إِسْمُ ٱلْمَكَانِ وَٱلزَّمَانِ

The Noun of Place and Time is formed from both transitive and intransitive verbs.

Triliterals have the measure مَفْعَل the same as the Noun of Action with م : —

مَنْجَى	escape	مَدْخَن	chimney
مَأْوَى	settlement	مَزَار	place of pilgrimage
مَجَاز	bridge	مَصَبّ	mouth of a river
مَطْبَخ	kitchen	مَغْطَس	wash-basin
مَذْبَح	altar	مَحْفَل	meeting-place

مَقْعَد	seat	مَلْجَأ	refuge.
مَثْنَى	fold	مَرْعَى	pasture
مَنَام	sleep	مَنْبَع	source
مَكْتَب	study	مَخْرَج	exit
مَقْتَل	slaughter-house	مَحَطّ	platform
مَرْصَد	observatory	مَقَام	standing
مَجْمَع	gathering-place	مَرْسَح	hall, theatre
مَقَرّ	abode	مَشْرَب	watering trough
مَنْظَر	sight	مَنْهَل	„ for camels
		مَصْدَر	source

The ع of the measure is vowelled with ـِ in verbs whose first radical is weak أَلْمُعْتَلَّةُ ٱلْفَاء and in verbs whose ع in the Aorist is sound and vowelled with ـِ as;

a place	مَوْضِع	a place of mire	مَوْحِل
„ „ of standing	مَوْقِف	„ „ aimed at	مَقْصِد
„ „ „ putting	مَوْضِع	„ „ of fracture	مَكْسِر
„ „ „ lying cattle	مَرْبِض	„ „ „ falling	مَوْقِع
„ „ „ exhibition	مَعْرِض	„ „ „ gaming	
„ „ „ sitting		by lots	مَيْسِر
(assembly)	مَجْلِس	„ „ „ smiling	مَبْسِم

Some nouns take ـِ although the ع of the Aorist has ـُ ; as

Time or place of

Ascent	مَطْلِع	sunset	مَغْرِب
Place of Pilgrimage	مَنْسِك	sunrise	مَشْرِق

6

prostration in prayer,		residence	مَسْكَن
mosque	مَسْجِد	growing place	
slaughter	مَسْجَز	(plant)	مَنْبِت
falling (anything)	مَسْقَط	separation	مَفْرِق

The plural is formed by inserting ١ after the second radical and vowelling the following letter with ِ; as

refuges	مَآوٍ	pastures	مَرَاعٍ
goings forth	مَخَارِج	altars	مَذَابِح

The affix ة is dropped.

A ة is sometimes added to the measure to express abundance of the thing implied; as

A place abounding in

مَكْتَبَة	books	مَأْسَدَة	lions	مَفْعَاة	snakes
مَضْبَعَة	hyenas	مَقْبَرَة	graves	مَذْأَبَة	wolves

At other times the ة has no special signification; as

Halting place (residence)	مَنْزِلَة	cave	مَغَارَة
on the right hand	مَيْمَنَة	destruction (desert)	مَهْلَكَة
on the left hand	مَيْسِرَة	light-house	مَنَارَة
court of judgment	مَحْكَمَة	station	مَحَطَّة
school	مَدْرَسَة		

The following are exceptional: —

Time of birth	مِيْلاد (وَلَد)
for performance of an action	مِيْقَات
appointed time or place for fulfillment of promise }	مِيْعَاد

From verbs of more than three letters it is formed
as the Noun of Action with م : —

place (abode)	مُقَام	departure	مُنْصَرَف
hospital	مُسْتَشْفَى	gathered together, room	مُجْتَمَع
prayer (Church)	مُصَلَّى	meeting-place	مُلْتَقَى
abode	مُسْتَقَرّ	slope	مُنْحَدَر

NOUN OF INSTRUMENT. اِسْمُ ٱلْآلَةِ

The Noun of Instrument is applied to anything which
is used in performing the action of the verb; as

| bellows | مِنْفَاخ | from | نَفَخَ | to blow |
| curtain | سِتَار | ,, | سَتَرَ | ,, cover |

It is formed from derived and primitive nouns.

The derived nouns are taken from triliteral transitive
verbs only and have three regular measures: —

I مِفْعَل   II مِفْعَال   III مِفْعَلَة

The plural is formed in the same manner as the
Noun of Place and Time, i. e. by inserting ا after the
second radical and vowelling the third with ـِ

The plural of مِفْعَل and مِفْعَلَة is مَفَاعِل

The plural ,, مِفْعَال is مَفَاعِيل

مِفْعَل

مِسْعَر	fire-brand.	مِكْبَس	hand-press.
مِقْبَض	handle.	مِقْلَى	frying-pan.
مِقَصّ	scissors.	مِزْوَد	provision-bag.

مِلْقَط	tongs.	مِنْخَس	goad, spur.
مِحْقَن	syringe.	مِسَنّ	grind-stone.

مِفْعَال

مِزْمَار	flute.	مِقْذَاف	oar.
مِسْمَار	nail.	مِسْبَار	probe.
مِحْرَاث	plough.	مِقْرَاض	scissors.
مِنْفَاخ	bellows.	مِفْتَاح	key.
مِشْرَاط	lancet, scalpel.		

مِفْعَلَة

مِقْلَمَة	pen-case.	مِغْرَفَة	ladle.
مِسْطَرَة	ruler.	مِحْرَطَة	lathe.
مِظَلَّة	umbrella.	مِصْيَدَة	trap.
مِنْطَقَة	girdle, belt.	مِرْماة	small arrows.
مِصْفَاة	filter.	مِرْمَلَة	sand-sifter.
مِشْنَقَة	gallows.	مِحْبَرَة	inkstand.
مِخَدَّة	pillow.	مِرْآة	looking-glass.

The following are primitive nouns:

حَرْبَة	spear.	شَبَكَة	net.
مُخْل	lever, crow-bar.	نِيْر	yoke.
حَدَأَة	doubleheaded axe.	سَهم	arrow.
دَلْو	bucket.	فَحّ	trap.
قُفْل	lock	قِرْبَة	water-skin.
طَبْل	drum	كَلْبَتَان	pincers.
مَنْجَنِيق	catapult.		

THE PRIMITIVE NOUN. اَلْإِسْمُ ٱلْجَامِدِ

The Primitive Noun is one which cannot be referred
to any verbal root; it may have three, four, or five
letters.

There are ten measures of primitive triliteral nouns:

Camel	فِعِل إِبِل	6	Heart	فَعْل قَلْب	1
Shoulder	فَعِل كَتِف	7	Lock	فُعْل قُفْل	2
Grapes	فَعَل عِنَب	8	Load	فِعْل حِمْل	3
Arm	فَعُل عَضُد	9	Horse	فَعَل فَرَس	4
Sparrow-hawk	فُعَل صُرَد	10	Neck	فُعُل عُنُق	5

A letter may be dropped from the primitive triliteral
noun, as أَب for أَبُو; the dropped letter is generally و,
as in غَد, إِسْم, دَم, حَم, إِبْن, أَب, أَخ; it may, however,
he ة or ى, as يَدَى يَد, إِسْت سَنَة, فَم فَوَه; the dropped
letter is replaced by إ (آ) or ة, as سَنَة, صِلَة, إِبْن, إِسْم.

THE GENDER OF NOUNS. اَلْجِنْس

Nouns are of two genders:

I Masculine مُذَكَّر,   II Feminine مُؤَنَّث.

Feminine Nouns are of two kinds:

(a) Animate مُؤَنَّث حَقِيقِّي, as إِمْرَأَة woman.

(b) Inanimate غَيْر حَقِيقِّي or مَجَازِّي as ٱلشَّمْس the Sun.

Feminine Nouns are further subdivided into:

I Feminine by form مُؤَنَّث لَفْظِيّ, having as their suffixes ة, ◌َٰٓ, or ى (signs of feminine); as

| Mercy | رَحْمَة | Claim | دَعْوَى | Desert | صَحْرَآء |
| Virtuous | فَاضِلَة | Drunken | سَكْرَى | Red | حَمْرَآء |

II Feminine by meaning مُؤَنَّث مَعْنَوِيّ; as

| Earth | أَرْض | Soul | نَفْس | Mary | مَرْيَم |

FEMININE NOUNS. اَلْأَسْمَآء اَلْمُؤَنَّثَة

Feminine Nouns comprise:

I All nouns ending with any of the three signs of the feminine (1) ة, (2) ◌َٰٓ, and (3) ◌َى, except they be masculine proper nouns.

(1) Nouns and Adjectives made feminine by ة are:

(*a*) The Noun of Agent, as جَاهِلَة جَاهِل ignorant.

(*b*) All measures of the Noun of Attribute except فَعْلَان and أَفْعَل, as فَرِحَة فَرِح joyful سَيِّدَة سَيِّد lord, (but سَكْرَى سَكْرَان drunken حَمْرَآء أَحْمَر red).

(*c*) Nouns on the measure فَعِيل indicating the Noun of Agent, as سَرِيْعَة سَرِيْع hasty كَرِيْمَة كَرِيْم generous.

(*d*) The Noun of Object, as مَكْسُوْرَة مَكْسُوْر broken مَبِيْعَة مَبِيْع sold.

(*e*) Nouns on the measure فَعُوْل indicating the Noun of Object, as رَسُوْلَة رَسُوْل apostle رَكُوْبَة رَكُوْب beast for riding.

(*f*) Some common Nouns, as كَلْبَة كَلْب dog
غَزَالَة غَزَال gazelle مَلِكَة مَلِك king.

Note. Irregular Plurals of irrational objects are treated
as feminine singular; as

Hard hearts	قُلُوْب قَاسِيَة
Stern judges	قُضَاة قُسَاة
Capable teachers	مُعَلِّمُوْن مُسْتَعِدُّوْنَ
Beautiful books	كُتُب جَمِيْلَة
Capable intellects	عُقُوْل مُسْتَعِدَّة
Strong men	رِجَال أَقْوِيَآء

(2) Nouns on the measure أَفْعَل signifying colour or
defect are made feminine by ـآ, i. e. they take the
measure فَعْلَآء; as

Yellow	أَصْفَر صَفْرَآء	Red	أَحْمَر حَمْرَآء
Hump-backed	أَحْدَب حَدْبَآء		

(3) Nouns on the measure أَفْعَل, having the signification of the superlative degree, are made feminine by
ـى, i. e. they take the measure فُعْلَى, as

Most excellent	ٱلْأَفْضَل ٱلْفُضْلَى	Most handsome	ٱلْأَحْسَن ٱلْحُسْنَى
Greatest	ٱلْأَعْظَم ٱلْعُظْمَى	Greatest	ٱلْأَكْبَر ٱلْكُبْرَى
First	ٱلْأَوَّل ٱلْأُوْلَى	Smallest	ٱلْأَصْغَر ٱلصُّغْرَى
*Worse	ٱلْأَدْنَى ٱلدُّنْيَا		

*When the ى is preceded by ـِ it is written ١, as

88

دُنْيَا , عُلْيَا. Exceptions are اَلْحُلْوَى for اَلْحُلَيَا the sweetest اَلْقُصْوَى for اَلْقُصْيَا the farthest.

II Names of females; as

Mary مَرْيَم   Hind هِنْد   Zaynab زَيْنَب

III Common nouns and adjectives which denote females, as

Wet-nurse	مُرْضِع	Divorced	طَالِق
Pregnant	حُبْلَى	Giving birth	وَلُود
Mother	أُمّ	Sister	أُخْت

IV Names of countries, towns and tribes; as

Jerusalem	اَلْقُدْس	Jaffa	يَافَا
Syria	اَلشَّام	Egypt	مِصْر
Koreish	قُرَيْش		

V Names of fire and winds; as

Wind	رِيح	North wind	شَمَال
Hot South-westerly wind	هَيْف	South wind	جَنُوب
Pestilential hot wind	سَمُوم	East wind	صَبَا
Hot night wind	حَرُور	West wind	دَبُور
Blazing fire	سَعِير , لَظَى , صلآء	Fire	نَار
		Hell-fire سَقَر جَحِيم	

VI Double members of the body; as

Heel	عَقِب	Foot	رِجْل	Hand	يَد
Palm (hand)	كَفّ	Ear	أُذُن	Arm	ذِرَاع
Shoulder	كَتِف	Eye	عَيْن	Hip	وَرِك

also

Tooth	سِنّ	Womb	رَحِم
Liver	كَبِد	Rib	ضِلَع

Exceptions are:

Cheek	خَدّ	Elbow	مَرْفِق	Side	جَنْب
Finger	إِصْبَع	Maw	كَرْش		

The following nouns are of the feminine gender although they have a masculine termination:

Wine	خَمْر	Scorpion	عَقْرَب
Well	بِئْر	Hare	أَرْنَب
Cup	كَأْس	Eye	عَيْن
House	دَار	Water-wheel	مَنْجَنُون
Bucket	دَلْو	Catapult	مَنْجَنِيق
Leopard	فَهْد	Sun	اَلشَّمْس
Viper	أَفْعَى	Staff	عَصَا
Destination (traveller's)	نِوًى	Shoe	نَعْل
Bow	قَوْس	Razor	مُوسَى
Ship	فُلْك	Hyena	ضَبُع
Earth	أَرْض	Metre (Poetry)	عَرُوض
Soul	نَفْس	Coat of mail	دِرْع
Right hand, oath	يَمِين	Mill	رَحَى
Market	سُوق	Eagle	عُقَاب
Axe	فَأْس	War	حَرْب
		Paradise	اَلْفِرْدَوْس

The following nouns may be used either in the masculine or feminine gender:

Corn measure	صَاع	Arm	عَضُد
Hinder-part	عَجُز	Booth, shop	حَانُوت
Horse, mare	فَرَس	Lance	رُمْح
Nape of Neck	قَفَا	Knife	سِكِّين
Mirage	آل	Peace	سِلْم
Musk	مِسْك	Heaven, sky	سَمَآء
Salt	مِلْح	Iron pestle	فِهْر
Letters of the alphabet		White honey	ضَرَب
Article of dress	إِزَار	Honey	عَسَل
State, Condition	حَال	Spider	عَنْكَبُوت
Natural disposition	طِبَاع	Cooking-pot	قِدْر
Night-journey	سُرَى	Shin-bone	كُرَاع
Power	سُلْطَان	Night	لَيْل
Thumb or great toe	إِبْهَام	Intestine	مِعَى ، مَعًى
Peace, reconciliation	صُلْح	Large bucket	ذَنُوب
Forenoon	ضُحَّى	Breast	ثَدْى
Wedding	عُرْس	Wing	جِنَاح
Neck	عُنُق	Way	سَبِيْل
Tongue	لِسَان	Weapon	سِلَاح
Fox	ثَعْلَب	Barley	شَعِير
Well	قَلِيْب	Way	صِرَاط
Road	طَرِيْق	Gold	ذَهَب

NUMBER. اَلْعَدَدُ

There are three Numbers:

I. Singular مُفْرَد

II. Dual مُثَنَّى

III. Plural جَمْع

THE DUAL.

The dual adds اَنِ to the singular for the nominative,
and يَنِ for the genitive, as two men رَجُلَانِ, رَجُلَيْنِ.

Nouns of three letters, ending with ا or ى, restore
the ا or ى to its original form; as

Staff عَصَا عَصَوَانِ	Mill رَحَى رَحَيَانِ
Youth فَتَى فَتَيَانِ	

If the ا or ى occurs after the third letter it is
changed to ي; as

Bustard حُبَارَى حُبَارَيَانِ	Butt for shooting مَرْمَى مَرْمَيَانِ
Pregnant حُبْلَى حُبْلَيَانِ	

Nouns ending with آء (sign of fem.) change the Hemzeh
into و; as

Red حَمْرَآء حَمْرَاوَانِ	Desert صَحْرَآء صَحْرَاوَانِ

but if the آء is a root letter it must be left; as

Good reader قَرَّآء قَرَّاءَانِ

If the آء is not the sign of fem. it may be changed
into و or left; as

Dress كِسَاء كِسَاءَانِ كِسَاوَانِ   Heaven سَمَاء سَمَاءَانِ سَمَاوَانِ

Mantle رِدَاء رِدَاءَانِ رِدَاوَانِ

Triliteral nouns which have dropped a weak letter restore it in the dual if it is restored when joined to a pronoun; as

Brother أَخْ أَخُوكَ أَخَوَانِ   Hand يَدْ يَدُكَ يَدَانِ

Father أَبْ أَبُوكَ أَبَوَانِ   Blood دَمْ دَمُكَ دَمَانِ

Father-in-law حَمْ حَمُوكَ حَمَوَانِ

THE PLURAL. ٱلْجَمْعُ

The Plural is of two kinds:

I. Regular جَمْعٌ سَالِمٌ.

II. Irregular or Broken جَمْعٌ مُكَسَّرٌ.

The Regular Plural is again divided into:

I. The Regular Masculine Plural جَمْعُ ٱلْمُذَكَّرِ ٱلسَّالِمُ

II. The Regular Feminine Plural جَمْعُ ٱلْمُؤَنَّثِ ٱلسَّالِمُ

The Regular Plural is thus called because the singular form remains unchanged; the omission of ة (sign of fem.) is not considered as breaking the form.

THE REGULAR MASCULINE PLURAL.

The Regular Masculine Plural is formed by adding وْنَ' to the singular for the nominative case, and يْنِ for the accusative and genitive cases; as

Believers مُؤْمِنٌ مُؤْمِنُونَ مُؤْمِنِينَ

Nouns and adjectives which may take the regular masculine plural are:

I. The Proper Noun اَلْعَلَمُ when

(*a*) rational (*b*) void of ة (fem) (*c*) not a compound noun (as عَبْدُ ٱللّٰه).

II. The Common Noun إِسْمُ ٱلْجِنْسِ when

(*a*) rational (*b*) void of ة (fem) (*c*) in the diminutive form, as رَجُل رُجَيْل رُجَيْلُوْنَ.

III. Adjectives derived from verbs when

(*a*) rational (*b*) void of ة (fem) (*c*) not on the measures فَعْلَى feminine أَفْعَل and فَعْلَاء feminine فَعْلَان nor on the measures فَعِيْل and فَعُوْل when the sing. form of masculine and feminine is the same.

The following nouns are exceptions:

The Earth	أَرْض أَرْضُوْنَ	Children	إِبْن بَنُوْنَ
Worlds	عَالَم عَالَمُوْنَ	Years	سَنَة سِنُوْنَ
Relations	أَهْل أَهْلُوْنَ	Hundreds	مِئَة مِئُوْنَ

and عِشْرُوْنَ, twenty, thirty to ninety. تِسْعُوْنَ to ثَلَاثُوْنَ.

Derived Adjectives whose final letter is ى or ي drop the weak letter; and if the preceding vowel is ﹻ this ﹻ remains, but, if not, it agrees with the following letter; as

Proper Name	مُصْطَفَى مُصْطَفَوْنَ
One who exacts to the full	مُتَوَفِّي مُتَوَفُّوْنَ
Archer	رَامِي رَامُوْنَ

THE REGULAR FEMININE PLURAL.

The Regular Feminine Plural is formed by adding
اتٌ to the singular; the ة sign of feminine when present, is dropped.

Nouns which take the regular feminine plural are:

I. Proper names of women; as فَاطِمَة فَاطِمَات.

II. Every noun or adjective ending with ة whether masculine or feminine; as

Proper Name	طَلْحَة طَلْحَات
A very learned man	عَلَّامَة عَلَّامَات
An ignorant woman	جَاهِلَة جَاهِلَات
A wise woman	حَكِيمَة حَكِيمَات

III. Nouns ending with ى or اء signs of feminine except those on the measures أَفْعَل fem. فَعْلَى fem. فَعْلَان fem. فَعْلَاء; as

The best	اَلْفُضْلَى اَلْفُضْلَيَات
Inner part of hoof	خَلْقَاء خَلْقَاوَات
Deserts بَيْدَاء بَيْدَاوَات	Deserts صَحْرَاء صَحْرَاوَات

IV. Such common nouns as refer to irrational beings and inanimate objects when in the diminutive form; as

Small camels جَمَل جُمَيْلَات   Small coins دِرْهَم دُرَيْهِمَات

V. Adjectives referring to irrational beings of the male sex, as

Wild beasts (وُحُوش) مُفْتَرِسَات   Neighing horses (خَيْل) صَاهِلَات

Departing ones مُنْطَلِقَات

When the common noun is mentioned with the adjective the ة is added to the singular form of the adjective; as

Neighing horses خَيْل صَاهِلَة   Departing camels جِمَال مُنْطَلِقَة

Wild beasts وُحُوش مُفْتَرِسَة   Open eyes عُيُون مَفْتُوْحَة

Listening ears آذَان مُصْغِيَة

VI. The Noun of Action consisting of more than three letters; as

Offerings تَقْدِيْمَات   Supplications تَوَسُّلَات

Confessions إِعْتَرَافَات

VII. Every foreign noun of which no other form of plural is known; as

Pasha بَاشَا بَاشَوَات   Telegrams تَلِغْرَافَات

Primitive nouns which have not their middle radical weak and are on the measure فَعْلَة take ـَ on the ع in the plural; as

Page, face of   Rose وَرْدَة وَرَدَات

anything صَفْحَة صَفَحَات

but if the ع is weak it is left unvowelled; as

Meadow رَوْضَة رَوْضَات   Egg بَيْضَة بَيْضَات

Nut جَوْزَة جَوْزَات

If the noun is on the measure فِعْلَة, it may be left unvowelled; as

Darkness ظُلْمَة ظُلْمَات   Piece قِطْعَة قِطْعَات

or, it may have a vowel homogeneous to the vowel preceding, as ظُلُمَات قِطعَات.

The following take the regular feminine plural although not coming under the rules previously stated.

I. The words:

Heaven	سَمَآء	Bath	حَمَّام
Judicial roll	سِجِلّ	Tent	سُرَادِق

II. إِبْن آوَى, إِبْن عِرْس make their plurals:

Weasels	بَنَات عِرْس	Jackals	بَنَات آوَى

III. أُمّ mother, if rational, takes أُمَّهَات for plural; if irrational, it takes أُمَّات.

IV. Words preceded by ذَات take ذَوَات for plural; as

Hornets	ذَوَاتُ ٱلْأَذْنَابِ,	Quadrupeds	ذَوَاتُ أَرْبَع,
	ذَاتُ ٱلذَّنَبِ		ذَاتُ أَرْبَع

THE IRREGULAR OR BROKEN PLURAL.

جَمْعُ ٱلتَّكْسِيرِ

The Irregular Plural is formed by:

(*a*) changing the vowels, as أُسُد أَسَد (plur.) lions.

(*b*) rejecting letters, as رُسُل رَسُول (plur.) apostles.

(*c*) adding letters, as رِجَال رَجُل (plur.) men.

There are twenty-nine measures of the irregular plural of substantives and adjectives derived from tri-literal roots, and some nine measures of substantives and adjectives possessing four or more letters. A list

---

is given in the glossary with their singulars and meanings.

There are two other forms of the Irregular Plural namely:

(a). The Plural of Paucity جَمْعُ ٱلْقِلَّةِ. (b). Plural of Multitude جَمْعُ ٱلْكَثْرَةِ.

The Plural of Paucity indicates the numbers three to ten inclusive. It comprises:

(a). The Regular Plurals. (b). The following four measures of the Irregular Plurals.

Ribs	1 أَفْعُل أَضْلُع	Lads	3 فِعْلَة فِتْيَة
Loaves	2 أَفْعِلَة أَرْغِفَة	Nails	4 أَفْعَال أَظْفَار

The last measure is commonly found among the triliterals. The first and last measures may be made plural again, then they come under the plural of multitude.

Ribs	أَضْلُع أَضَالِع	Nails	أَظْفَار أَظَافِير

These two measures and their equivalents are called صِيْغَة مُنْتَهَى ٱلْجُمُوع.

When a noun has only one form of plural it necessarily indicates paucity and multitude; as

Men	رِجَال	Necks	أَعْنَاق
Hearts Affections	أَفْئِدَة		

The Plural of Multitude indicates any number from ten to infinity.

THE RELATIVE ADJECTIVE. اَلتِّسْبَةُ

I. The Relative Adjective is formed by affixing يّ to
the noun, after stripping it of the ة sign of fem. and
the signs of dual and plural when present; as

Manly	رَجُل رَجُلِيّ	Belonging to the Kibla	اَلْقِبلَةُ قِبْلِيّ
Earthly	أَرْض أَرْضِيّ	Nazarene	نَاصِرَة نَاصِرِيّ
Solar	شَمْس شَمْسِيّ	Belonging to the two sacred citi (Mecca and Medina)	رَمَانِ حَرَمِيّ
Mental	عَقْل عَقْلِيّ	Belonging to al-Irakaïn (Basrah and Koofah)	عِرَاقَانِ عِرَاقِيّ
Egyptian	مِصْر مِصْرِيّ	Belonging to Moslems	سْلِمُوْنَ مُسْلِمِيّ
Domestic (house)	بَيْت بَيْتِى	Relating to dates	ـمَر تَمْرِيّ
From Mecca	مَكَّة مَكِّيّ	Ecclesiastical	كَنِيسَةُ كَنَسِيّ

II. Singular Nouns with dual or plural forms (but
not dual or plural significations) retain them; as

Hamdūn	حَمْدُوْن حَمْدُوْنِيّ	Zeidān	زَيْدَان زَيْدَانِيّ
Hamdān	حَمْدَان حَمْدَانِيّ	Zeidūn	زَيْدُوْن زَيْدُوْنِيّ
		Anmar	أَنْمَار أَنْمَارِيّ

III. The Hemzeh of the feminine termination ءآ is
changed into و but if the Hemzeh represents an original weak letter such change is optional; as

Virgin	عَذْرَآء عَذْرَاوِيّ	Green	خَضْرَآء خَضْرَاوِيّ
Black beetle	خُنْفَسَآء خُنْفَسَاوِيّ	Red	حَمْرَآء حَمْرَاوِيّ

Robe	كِسَآءٌ كِسَاوِيّ كِسَائِيّ
Heaven	سَمَآءٌ سَمَاوِيّ سَمَائِيّ
Garment	رِدَآءٌ رِدَاوِيّ رِدَائِيّ

IV. ١, ى (Aleph) or ي final, in a three or four lettered noun, is generally changed into و, and sometimes an ١ is inserted before the و; the letter which precedes the و is thereupon vowelled with َ; as

Youth	فَتًى فَتَوِيّ	Pregnant	حُبْلَى حُبْلَوِيّ حُبْلَاوِيّ
Millstone	رَحًى رَحَوِيّ	Sorrowful	شَجِيّ or شَجٍ شَجَوِيّ
Mote	قَذًى قَذَوِيّ	Judge	قَاضِي or قَاضٍ قَاضَوِيّ
Staff	عَصًى عَصَوِيّ	High	عَلِيّ عَلَوِيّ
Meaning	مَعْنًى مَعْنَوِيّ	Earth	دُنْيَا دُنْيَوِيّ دُنْيَاوِيّ

but if the ي be preceded by a sound letter silent no change occurs; as

Gazelle   ظَبْيٌ ظَبْيِيّ

V. ي when preceded by a silent weak letter is changed into و; as

Living	حَيّ حَيَوِيّ	Fold	طَيّ طَوَوِيّ

VI. ١, ى (Aleph), and ي are dropped when they occur after the fourth letter, and when the second letter of a four lettered noun is vowelled; as

Frenchman	فَرَنْسَا فَرَنْسِيّ	High	مُسْتَعْلِي مُسْتَعْلِيّ
Bustard	حُبَارَى حُبَارِيّ	River in Damascus	بَرَدَى بَرَدِيّ

VII. َ on the middle radical of a triliteral noun becomes ِ; as

King	مَلِك مَلَكِيّ	Liver	كَبِد كَبَدِيّ

VIII. When the ل is a weak letter, words on the measure فَعِيْل drop the first ي and change the second into و; whereupon the ع is vowelled with ◌َ; as

High   عَلِيّ عَلَوِيّ

IX. Words on the measure فَعِيْلَة drop the ي and change the vowel of the ع to ◌َ; as

Church	كَنِيْسَة كَنَسِيّ	Enactment	فَرِيْضَة فَرَضِيّ

Exceptions: —

Nature	طَبِيْعَة طَبِيْعِيّ	Truth	حَقِيْقَة حَقِيْقِيّ
		Disposition	سَلِيْقَة سَلِيْقِيّ

X. Nouns which have dropped a weak letter generally restore it, and any letter which has been substituted for the dropped letter is omitted; as

Language	لُغَة لُغَوِيّ	Father	أَب أَبَوِيّ
Gum	لِثَة لِثَوِيّ	Blood	دَم دَمَوِيّ
Hundred	مِئَة مِئَوِيّ	Son	إِبْن بَنَوِيّ
Hand-maiden	أَمَة أَمَوِيّ	Brother	أَخ أَخَوِيّ
Year	سَنَة سَنَوِيّ	Hand	يَد يَدَوِيّ
To-morrow	غَد غَدَوِيّ	Father-in-law	حَم حَمَوِيّ
		Lip	شَفَة شَفَوِيّ شَفَهِيّ

Exceptions: —

Sister	أُخْت أُخْتِيّ	Daughter	بِنْت بِنْتِيّ
		Name	إِسْم إِسْمِي

XI. ُيّ and يّة final in nouns of more than three letters are dropped; as

Chair   كُرْسِيّ كُرْسِيّ

Native of Alexandria   أَلْإِسْكَنْدَرِيَّة إِسْكَنْدَرِيّ

XII. In compound proper nouns the يّ of relation is generally affixed to the second word أَلْـعَـجُـزُ, leaving the first أَلصَّدْرُ unchanged; as

Native of Bethlehem   بَيْتُ لَحْم بَيْتَ لَحْمِيّ

   „   of Bethel   بَيْتُ إِيْل بَيْتَ إِيْلِيّ

XIII. Sometimes it is formed from the first word; as

A native of Ramallah   رَامُ ٱللّٰهِ رَامِيّ

Name of a poet   أَمْرُوُ ٱلْقَيْس إِمْرِئِيّ

Proper names of men   مَعْدِي كَرِب مَعْدَوِيّ تَأَبَّطَ شَرًّا تَأَبَّطِيّ

and at other times a process called أَلـنَّحْـت (cutting) is employed, as in the proper names

عَبْدُ ٱلشَّمْس	عَبْشَمِيّ	عَبْدُ ٱلدَّار	عَبْدَرِيّ
آرِيُوس بَاغُوس	آرِيُوبَاغِيّ	عَبْدُ ٱلْقَيْس	عَبْقَسِيّ
عَبْدُ ٱللّٰه	عَبْدَلِيّ	حَضْرَمَوْت	حَضْرَمِيّ
تَيْمُ ٱللّٰه	تَيْمَلِيّ	إِمْرُوُ ٱلْقَيْس	مَرْقِسِيّ

XIV. The following words are formed irregularly:

Spiritual	رُوح رُوحَانِيّ	Names	صَنْعَاء صَنْعَانِيّ	
Divine	رَبّ رَبَّانِيّ	of towns	أَلرَّيّ أَلرَّازِيّ	
Nazarene (Christian)	نَاصِرَة نَصْرَانِيّ	tribes and	طَىّ طَائِيّ	
From Yemen	يَمَن يَمَانٍ	Countries.	أُمَيَّة أُمَوِيّ	

Materialist	دَهْر دُهْرِيّ	Names of towns tribes and Countries.	اَلْبَحْرَيْن بَحْرَانِيّ
From Tihamah	تِهَامَة تِهَام		سُلَيْم سُلَمِيّ
Bedouin	بَادِيَة بَدَوِيّ		اَلْأَنْبَاط نُبَاطِيّ

ABSTRACT NOUNS OF QUALITY. أَسْمَآءُ ٱلْكَيْفِيَّة

God-head	اَلْإِلـهِـيَّة	Manhood	رُجُولِيَّة
Humanity	إِنْسَانِيَّة	Substance	مَاهِيَّة
Lordship	اَلرُّبُوبِيَّة	Totality	جَمْعِيَّة
Capability of being understood	مَفْهُومِيَّة	Christendom	اَلنَّصْرَانِيَّة
		Judaism	اَلْيَهُودِيَّة

The termination وُت has a similar signification:

| Divinity | لَاهُوت | Humanity | نَاسُوت |
| Kingdom | مَلَكُوت | Pride | جَبَرُوت |

THE DIMINUTIVE. أَلتَّصْغِيرُ

I. For triliteral nouns the measure of the diminutive is فُعَيْل. It is formed by inserting يْ after the second radical, vowelling the first with ُ and the second with َ ; as

| Mountain | جَبَل جُبَيْل | Man | رَجُل رُجَيْل |
| | | Dog | كَلْب كُلَيْب |

II. In nouns of more than three letters, the letter which follows the ي of the measure takes َ except it be one of the three signs of the feminine, or ا of the plural, or آن servile in a proper noun or adjective; as

Dirham	دِرْهَم دُرَيْهِم	Black (fem.)	سَوْدَآء سُوَيْدَاء
Bird	عُصْفُور عُصَيْفِيْر	Companions	أَصْحَاب أُصَيْحَاب
Castle	قَلْعَة قُلَيْعَة	Man's name	سَلْمَان سُلَيْمَان
Proper fem. name	سَلْمَى سُلَيْمَى	Drunken	سَكْرَان سُكَيْرَان

III. The regular masc. and fem. plurals, and the plural of paucity form their diminutives regularly; as

Believers	مُؤْمِنُوْنَ مُوَيْمِنُوْنَ	Ribs	أَضْلُع أُضَيْلِع
Zaids	زَيْدُوْنَ زُيَيْدُوْنَ	Nails	أَظْفَار أُظَيْفَار
Hinds (proper name)	هِنْدَات هُنَيْدَات	Loaves	أَرْغِفَة أُرَيْغِفَة
Roses	وَرَدَات وُرَيْدَات	Youths	فِتْيَة فُتَيَّة

IV. The plural of multitude reverts to the singular of its form and takes the regular masc. plural in the case of nouns denoting rational masc. beings and the regular fem. plural in the case of irrational beings; as

Poets	شُعَرَاء شَاعِر شُوَيْعِرُوْنَ	
She camels	ذِيَاق نُوَيْقَات	Camels جِمَال جُمَيْلَات

V. Any letter which has been dropped from the original form of the noun is restored; as

Father	أَبّ أُبَيّ	Blood	دَم (دَمُو) دُمَيّ
Brother	أَخ أُخَيّ	Water	مَآء مُوَيْه
Sheep or goat	شَاة شُوَيْهَة		

and any letter which has been substituted for the dropped letter is omitted, except it be ة fem.; as

Hand-maiden	أَمَة أُمَيَّة	Name	إِسْم سَمُو سُمَيّ
Lip	شَفَة شُفَيْهَة	Mouth	فَم فُوه فُوَيْه
Daughter	بِنْت بُنَيَّة	Promise	عِدَة وُعَيْدَة
Son	إِبْن بَنُو بُنَيّ	Effort	جِدَة وُجَيْدَة

VI. A noun with servile ا for its second letter is changed into و; as

Horseman	فَارِس فُوَيْرِس	Scribe	كَاتِب كُوَيْتِب
Poet	شَاعِر شُوَيْعِر	Beater	ضَارِب ضُوَيْرِب
Seal	خَاتَم خُوَيْتِم		

VII. If the third or fourth letter is و, or ا not plural, this letter is changed into ي; as

Satan	شَيْطَان شُيَيْطِيْن	Glutton	أَكُوْل أُكَيِّل
Sultan	سُلْطَان سُلَيْطِيْن	Mill-stone	رَحَى رُحَيَّة
Bird	عُصْفُوْر عُصَيْفِيْر	Food	طَعَام طُعَيِّم
Handle	عُرْوَة عُرَيَّة	Boy	غُلَام غُلَيِّم
Book	كِتَاب كُتَيِّب	Wolf	سِرْحَان سُرَيْحِيْن
Old-woman	عَجُوْز عُجَيِّز	Brook	جَدْوَل جُدَيِّل
Youth	فَتَى فُتَيّ	Staff	عَصَا عُصَيّ

VIII. When the second letter is servile ا changed from ا, or its origin is unknown, it is changed into و; as

Ivory	عَاج عُوَيْج	Another	آخَر (أَأْخَر) أُوَيْخِر

IX. A noun with a weak letter which has undergone change reverts to its original form; as

Tusk	نَاب (نَيَب) نُيَيْب	Door	بَاب (بَوَب) بُوَيْب

Exceptions:

Feast   عِيْد (عَوَد) عُيَيْد   Night   لَيْلَة (لَيْل) لُوَيْلَة

X. Nouns feminine by meaning (without signs of fem.) if of three letters only, restore the ة of fem.; as

Eye   عَيْن عُيَيْنَة   Sun   شَمْس شُمَيْسَة

Hind (proper name) هِنْد هُنَيْدَة   House   دَار دُوَيْرَة

Tooth   سِنّ سُنَيْنَة   Sheep   غَنَم غُنَيْمَة

but, Scorpion   عَقْرَب عُقَيْرِب

Exceptions:

Sandal   نَعْل نُعَيْل   War   حَرْب حُرَيْب

Bow   قَوْس قُوَيْس   Arabs   عَرَب عُرَيْب

Herd of she camels ذَوْد ذُوَيْد   Cuirass   دِرْع دُرَيْع

XI. In cases where ambiguity would arise between the masculine and feminine the ة is not affixed, as in the fem. cardinal numbers three to ten inclusive, and in nouns which have a singular ending in ة; thus

Five   خَمْس خُمَيْس   Tree   شَجَر شُجَيْر

XII. Nouns with more than four radical letters in their root reject all after the fourth; as

Quince   سَفَرْجَل سُفَيْرِج   Spider   عَنْكَبُوت عُنَيْكِب

In compound nouns the first noun is made diminutive; as عَبْدُ ٱللّٰه عُبَيْدُ ٱللّٰه.

XIII. The diminutive cannot be applied to the names of God, or of high personages, to indeclinable nouns and names of such objects as do not admit of diminution; as

Glass زُجَاج   Sunday أَلْأَحَد   March آذَار

XIV. The diminutive is applied to the following verbs and indeclinable nouns contrary to rule:

I. Verbs of wonder أَفْعَالُ ٱلتَّعَجُّب; as

How beautiful is the sky   مَا أُحَيْسِنَ ٱلسَّمَآء

How sweet are the views of our

countries   مَا أُحَيْلَى مَنَاظِرَ بِلَادِنَا

II. Relative Pronouns أَسْمَآء ٱلْمَوْصُول; as

Plur.	Dual.	Sing.	
أَللَّذَيُّونَ (أَللَّذِينَ)	أَللَّذَيَّا (أَللَّذَانِ)	أَللَّذَيَّا (أَلَّذِى)	Masc.
أَللَّتَيَّاتِ (أَللَّوَاتِي)	أَلتَّيَّانِ (أَللَّتَانِ)	أَللَّتَيَّا (أَلَّتِى)	Fem.

III. Demonstrative Pronouns أَسْمَآء ٱلْإِشَارَة; as

Far object.	Middle Object.	Near Object.	
ذَيَّالِكَ (ذٰلِكَ)	ذَيَّاكَ (ذَاكَ)	ذَيَّا (ذَا)	Masc.
	تَيَّاكَ (تِيْكَ)	تَيَّا (تِي)	Fem.

XV. The following nouns are formed irregularly:

Sea	بَحْر أُبَيْحِر	Boys	صِبْيَة أُصَيْبِيَة
Man	رَجُل رُوَيْجِل	Lads	غِلْمَة أُغَيْلِمَة
Man	إِنْسَان أُنَيْسِيَان		

The diminutive is also used as a term of endearment and to express enhancement or contempt; as حُبَيِّب, كُلَيْب, بُنَيّ, أُبَىّ, أُخَىّ.

The very best	خُيَيْر	A great misfortune	دُوَيْهِيَة
A special friend	صُدَيِّق	An enemy	عُدَىّ

THE NUMERALS. اَلْعَدَدُ

THE CARDINAL NUMBERS. (أَصْلِيّ)

The cardinal numbers from 1 to 10 are:

Fem.	Masc.		Fem.	Masc.	
خَمْسَة	خَمْس	5	إِحْدَى	أَحَدٌ وَاحِدٌ	1
سِتّة	سِتّ	6	وَاحِدَة		
سَبْعَة	سَبْع	7	إِثْنَتَانِ	إِثْنَانِ	2
ثَمَانِيَة	ثَمَانٍ	8	ثَلَاثَة	ثَلَاثٌ	3
تِسْعَة	تِسْع	9	أَرْبَعَة	أَرْبَع	4
عَشَرَة	عَشْر	10			

1 and 2 stand for the noun and agree with it in gender and number. They can only be used with the noun for emphasis, in which case they follow it; as

رَجُلٌ وَاحِدٌ ,رَجُلَانِ إِثْنَانِ.

3 to 10 take the fem. form when the objects numbered are masc., and the masc. form when the objects numbered are fem. They govern a broken plural of the objects numbered in the genitive, and when possible take the plural of paucity.

Three women	ثَلَاثُ نِسَآءٍ	Three men	ثَلَاثَة رِجَالٍ	
Five loaves	خَمْسَةُ أَرْغِفَةٍ	Seven fishes	سَبْع سَمَكَاتٍ	

The cardinal numbers from 11 to 19 are:

Fem.	Masc.		Fem.	Masc.	
ثَلَاثَ عَشْرَةَ	ثَلَاثَةَ عَشَرَ	13	إِحْدَى عَشْرَةَ	أَحَدَ عَشَرَ	11
أَرْبَعَ عَشْرَةَ	أَرْبَعَةَ عَشَرَ	14	إِثْنَتَا عَشْرَةَ	إِثْنَا عَشَرَ	12

Fem.	Masc.		Fem.	Masc.
خَمْسَةَ عَشَرَ	خَمْسَ عَشْرَةَ	18 ثَمَانِيَةَ عَشَرَ ثَمَانِىَ عَشْرَةَ		
سِتَّةَ عَشَرَ	سِتَّ عَشْرَةَ	19 تِسْعَةَ عَشَرَ تِسْعَ عَشْرَةَ		
سَبْعَةَ عَشَرَ	سَبْعَ عَشْرَةَ			

15 ... 16 ... 17 (numbers at start of each line)

11 and 12. The gender of both numerals in 11 and 12 agrees with that of the objects numbered; as

Eleven women إِحْدَى عَشْرَةَ ٱمْرَأَةً   Eleven men أَحَدَ عَشَرَ رَجُلًا

Twelve women إِثْنَتَا عَشْرَةَ ٱمْرَأَةً   Twelve men إِثْنَا عَشَرَ رَجُلًا

Note 1 and 2 wherever they occur agree in gender with the objects numbered; as

Forty-one ewes إِحْدَى وَأَرْبَعُوْنَ نَعْجَةً

2 wherever it occurs is declined in the same manner as the dual; as

The twelve Apostles came جَاءَ ٱلْاِثْنَا عَشَرَ رَسُوْلًا

I saw twelve does رَأَيْتُ إِثْنَتَي عَشْرَةَ ظَبْيَةً

13 to 19. The numeral 10 agrees in gender with the object numbered whilst the units take the reverse gender. Both numerals are indeclinable and have َ in all cases; as

Thirteen men ثَلَاثَةَ عَشَرَ رَجُلًا   Thirteen women ثَلَاثَ عَشْرَةَ ٱمْرَأَةً

11 to 99 take the object numbered in the accus. sing.

The cardinal numbers 20 to 90 are:

70 سَبْعُوْنَ	40 أَرْبَعُوْنَ	20 عِشْرُوْنَ
80 ثَمَانُوْنَ	50 خَمْسُوْنَ	21 أَحَد وَعِشْرُوْنَ
90 تِسْعُوْنَ	60 سِتُّوْنَ	22 إِثْنَانِ وَعِشْرُوْنَ
		30 ثَلَاثُوْنَ

20 to 90 are common to both genders and have وْنَ in the nom. and يْنِ in the genitive and accus. cases.

The numerals from 100 to 900 are:

600 سِتُّ مِائَةٍ		100 مِائَةٌ	
700 سَبْعُ مِائَةٍ		200 مِائَتَانِ	
800 ثَمَانِى مِائَةٍ		300 ثَلَاثُ مِائَةٍ	
900 تِسْعُ مِائَةٍ		400 أَرْبَعُ مِائَةٍ	
		500 خَمْسُ مِائَةٍ	

100 is common to both genders and takes the object numbered after it in the genitive sing.

100 to 1000 take the noun after them in the genitive singular.

The numerals from 1000 upwards:

100.000 مِائَةُ أَلْفٍ		1000 أَلْفٌ	
200.000 مِائَتَا أَلْفٍ		2000 أَلْفَانِ	
300.000 ثَلْثُمِائَةِ أَلْفٍ		3000 ثَلَاثَةُ آلَافٍ	
400.000 أَرْبَعُمِائَةِ أَلْفٍ		4000 أَرْبَعَةُ آلَافٍ	
500.000 خَمْسُمِائَةِ أَلْفٍ		5000 خَمْسَةُ آلَافٍ	
1.000.000 أَلْفُ أَلْفٍ		11.000 أَحَدَ عَشَرَ أَلْفًا	
2.000.000 أَلْفَا أَلْفٍ		12.000 إِثْنَا عَشَرَ أَلْفًا	
3.000.000 ثَلَاثَةُ آلَافِ أَلْفٍ		13.000 ثَلَاثَةَ عَشَرَ أَلْفًا	

The thousands are put in the genitive plural after their units and the noun follows in the genitive sing.

Three thousand men	ثَلَاثَةُ آلَافِ رَجُلٍ
Ten thousand men	عَشَرَةُ آلَافِ رَجُلٍ

Numerals made up of thousands, hundreds, tens and units, may be compounded in two ways. (*a*) The thousands may be put first, followed by hundreds, units and tens or (*b*) this order may be reversed; as

أَرْبَعَةُ آلَافٍ وَسِتُّ مِائَةٍ وَأَحَدٌ وَثَلَاثُوْنَ

أَحَدٌ وَثَلَاثُوْنَ وَسِتُّ مِائَةٍ وَأَرْبَعَةُ آلَافٍ

THE ORDINAL NUMBERS. (تَرْتِيْبِيّ)

The Ordinal Adjectives from first to tenth are:

Fem.	Masc.		Fem.	Masc.	
سَادِسَة	سَادِس	sixth.	أَلْأُوْلَى	أَلْأَوَّلُ	the first.
سَابِعَة	سَابِع	seventh.	ثَانِيَة	ثَانِي	second.
ثَامِنَة	ثَامِن	eighth.	ثَالِثَة	ثَالِث	third.
تَاسِعة	تَاسِع	ninth.	رَابِعَة	رَابِع	fourth.
عَاشِرَة	عَاشِر	tenth.	خَامِسَة	خَامِس	fifth.

Fem.	Masc.	
حَادِيَة عَشْرَةَ	حَادِيَ عَشَرَ	eleventh.
ثَانِيَة عَشْرَةَ	ثَانِيَ عَشَرَ	twelfth.
ثَالِثَة عَشْرَةَ	ثَالِثَ عَشَرَ	thirteenth.
رَابِعَة عَشْرَةَ	رَابِعَ عَشَرَ	fourteenth.
خَامِسَة عَشْرَةَ	خَامِسَ عَشَرَ	fifteenth.

The ordinal numbers are formed on the measure of the noun of agent (except the first) and agree in gender with the noun.

The tens, hundreds, and thousands do not differ in form from the cardinal numbers.

11 to 19; the units of these take the article; as

The fifteenth ‏أَلْخَامِسَ عَشَرَ‎.

20 and upwards, both the decades and the units take the article and are united by ‏وَ‎; as

The thirty-fifth ‏أَلْخَامِسُ وَٱلثَّلَاثُوْنَ‎.

THE NUMERAL ADVERBS.

Once, twice, thrice etc are expressed by the words ‏مَرَّة, دَفْعَة, نَوْبَة‎ once in the accusative:

Twice	‏نَوْبَتَيْنِ دَفْعَتَيْنِ مَرَّتَيْنِ‎
Thrice	‏ثَلَاثَ دَفَعَاتٍ‎ or ‏ثَلَاثَ مَرَّاتٍ‎
Seventy times	‏سَبْعِيْنَ نَوْبَةً‎ or ‏مَرَّةً‎
Once and again	‏تَارَةً وَأُخْرَى‎

The Distributive Numerals are:

One by one	‏وَاحِدًا وَاحِدًا‎ or ‏مَوْحَدُ‎ or ‏أُحَادُ‎
Two by two	‏إِثْنَيْنِ إِثْنَيْنِ‎ or ‏مَثْنَى‎ or ‏ثُنَاء‎
Three by three	‏ثَلَاثَةَ ثَلَاثَةَ‎ or ‏ثُلَاثُ‎ or ‏مَثْلَثُ‎
Four by four, and soon	‏أَرْبَعَةَ أَرْبَعَةَ‎ or ‏مَرْبَعُ‎ or ‏رُبَاعُ‎

The Multiplicative Numerals:

Single	‏مُفْرَد‎	Pentagon, fivefold	‏مُخَمَّس‎
Double, twofold	‏مُثَنَّى‎	Hexagon, sixfold	‏مُسَدَّس‎
Triangle, triple, threefold	‏مُثَلَّث‎	Peptagon, sevenfold	‏مُسَبَّع‎
Square, quadruple, fourfold	‏مُرَبَّع‎	Octagon	‏مُثَمَّن‎

The Adjectival Numerals are:

Treble, consisting of three ثُلَاثِيّ   Dual, consisting of two ثَنَائِي

Quadruple   ,,   ,, four رُبَاعِيّ

Fractions are:

A half   نِصْف   A fourth رُبْع or رُبُع

A third ثُلْث or ثُلُث   A tenth عُشْر or عُشُر

Above a tenth the fractions are expressed by the
use of the words أَجْزَآء مِنْ ,جُزْء "parts of"; as

. ثَلَاثَةٌ مِنْ سَبْعَةَ عَشَرَ or only ثَلَاثَةُ أَجْزَآءٍ مِنْ سَبْعَةَ عَشَرَ جُزْأً ۱۷.

. وَاحِدٌ مِنْ أَحَدَ عَشَرَ or only جُزْء مِنْ أَحَدَ عَشَرَ جُزْأً ۱۱.

Approximate numbers are expressed by بِضْع "a few"
used with the units from three to nine, and نَيِّف "a
few more" used with the tens, hundreds and thousands.

PERSONAL PRONOUNS. (اَلضَّمَائِرُ اَلشَّخْصِيَّةُ)

These are of two kinds:

I. Annexed to the verb, noun, or particle.

II. Separate.

The Annexed Pronouns are of three kinds:

I. Those special to the nominative case, viz. ن ,ت ,ى ,ا ,و.

II. Those common to the accusative and genitive,
viz. ك ,ه ,ى.

III. That common to the nominative, accusative and
genitive, viz. نَا.

ANNEXED PERSONAL PRONOUNS. ٱلضَّمَائِرُ ٱلْمُتَّصِلَةُ

NOMINATIVE CASE.

Fem. Plural.	Masc.	Fem. Dual. Masc.	Fem. Singular. Masc.	
نَا	نَا	نَا	تُ	1st Person „
تُنَّ	تُمْ	تُمَا	تِ تَ	2nd „
نَ	(1)وُ	ا	...	3rd „

ACCUSATIVE AND GENITIVE CASES.

Plural.		Dual.	Singular.	
نَا	نَا	نَا	ي (نِ)	1st Person
كُنَّ	كُمْ	كُمَا	كِ كَ	2nd „
هُنَّ	هُمْ	هُمَا	هَا	هُ 3rd „

When these are annexed to a verb they are in the accus. case; to a noun or preposition in the genitive.

Our friend passed by and visited us صَدِيْقُنَا مَرَّ بِنَا فَزَارَنَا

هُ and هُمْ become هِ and هِمْ after ـِ or ي; as

According to their saying عَلَى قَوْلِهِمْ He is wrong ٱلْحَقُّ عَلَيْهِ

When the affixed pronouns are united to the regular masc. plural and dual or when the latter nouns are in construction, the نَ and نِ are omitted; as

The strikers of Amr ضَارِبُو عَمْرٍ His strikers ضَارِبُوهُ
The two books of Zaid كِتَابَا زَيْدٍ His two books كِتَابَاهُ

In the third person masc. pl. of the preterite and aorist, and the imperative plural, the ا is dropped when a pronoun is affixed; as

They did not love him لَمْ يُحِبُّوهُ   They did it فَعَلُوْهُ (فَعَلُوا)

Hear ye him إِسْمَعُوهُ

إِيَّا is a separate accusative particle and is used as a prefix for the affixed pronoun:

I. When a verb governs two accusatives; as

Give it to me أَعْطِنِي إِيَّاهُ   Give it to him أَعْطِهِ إِيَّاهُ

It is not necessary to put إِيَّا before the second accus. pronoun when the two are not of the same person; thus we can say

You asked me about it سَأَلْتُمُونِيْهَا   Give it to me أَعْطِنِيْهِ

I gave it to you أَعْطَيْتُكَهُ   Ask me about it سَلْنِيْهِ

but we cannot say,

I gave it to him أَعْطَيْتُهُهُ

II. When the accusative pronoun is separated from the verb; as

They will honour you يُكْرِمُونَكَ

They will honour both Zaid and you يُكْرِمُونَ زَيْدًا وَإِيَّاكَ

III. Where the accusative precedes the verb; as

Thee we worship إِيَّاكَ نَعْبُدُ

IV. When preceded by إِلَّا; as

I love none else but thee لَا أُحِبُّ إِلَّا إِيَّاكَ

Note. The second person plural preterite when followed by an affixed pronoun introduces a و; as

Ye did strike ضَرَبْتُمْ   Ye did strike me ضَرَبْتُمُونِى

SEPARATE PERSONAL PRONOUNS.

اَلضَّمَائِرُ ٱلْمُنْفَصِلَةُ

NOMINATIVE CASE.

Plural.		Dual.	Singular.		
Fem.	*Masc.*	*Common.*	*Fem.*	*Masc.*	
نَحْنُ		نَحْنُ		أَنَا	1st Person
أَنْتُنَّ	أَنْتُمْ	أَنْتُمَا	أَنْتِ	أَنْتَ	2nd ,,
هُنَّ	هُمْ	هُمَا	هِيَ	هُوَ	3rd ,,

Note: In أَنَا نَحْنُ 1st Person, and هُوَ هِيَ 3rd Person, the whole word is regarded as the pronoun; but in أَنْتَ أَنْتِ أَنْتُمَا أَنْتُمْ أَنْتُنَّ 2nd Person, and هُمَا هُمْ هُنَّ 3rd Person, أَنْ and هـ only are the pronouns:

					2nd Person.
Particle of address =	حَرْف خِطَاب = تَ,	pronoun أَنْ	أَنْتَ	
Sign of dual =	مَا,	» = تُ,	» أَنْ	أَنْتُمَا
Sign of masc. plur. =	م,	» = تُ,	» أَنْ	أَنْتُمْ
Sign of fem. plur. =	نَّ,	» = تُ,	» أَنْ	أَنْتُنَّ

				3rd Person.
Sign of dual =	مَا.........	»	هـ	هُمَا
Sign of masc. plur. =	م,.........	»	هـ	هُمْ
Sign of fem. plur. =	نَّ,.........	»	هـ	هُنَّ

The conjunctions وَ and فَ when joined to هُوَ and هِيَ may deprive them of their first vowels; as

فَهْيَ ،وَهْيَ ،فَهْوَ ،وَهْوَ

ACCUSATIVE CASE.

Plural.		Dual.	Singular.		
Fem.	*Masc.*	*Common.*	*Fem.*	*Masc.*	
إِيَّانَا	إِيَّانَا	إِيَّانَا		إِيَّايَ	1st Pers.
إِيَّاكُنَّ	إِيَّاكُم	إِيَّاكُمَا	إِيَّاكِ	إِيَّاكَ	2nd ,,
إِيَّاهُنَّ	إِيَّاهُمْ	إِيَّاهُمَا	إِيَّاهَا	إِيَّاهُ	3rd ,,

Note: إِيَّا is only the prefix of the accusative case.

Sign of the 1st person ي pronoun إِيَّا — إِيَّايَ
Sign of the 1st person plur. نَا ,, إِيَّا — إِيَّانَا

Particle of address = حَرْف خِطَاب = كَ pronoun إِيَّا — إِيَّاكَ
Sign of dual = مَا, ,, = كَ ,, إِيَّا — إِيَّاكُمَا
Sign of masc. plur. = م, ,, = كَ ,, إِيَّا — إِيَّاكُم
Sign of fem. plur. = نَّ, ,, = كَ ,, إِيَّا — إِيَّاكُنَّ

Particle of 3rd person = حَرْف غَيْبَة = هُ ,, إِيَّا — إِيَّاهُ
Sign of distinction between
  masc. and fem. = ١, ,, = ه ,, إِيَّا — إِيَّاهَا
Sign of dual = مَا. ,, = هُ ,, إِيَّا — إِيَّاهُمَا
Sign of masc. plur. = م, ,, = هُ ,, إِيَّا — إِيَّاهُمْ
Sign of fem. plur. = نَّ. ,, = هُ ,, إِيَّا — إِيَّاهُنَّ

THE RELATIVE PRONOUNS. أَسْمَاء ٱلْمَوْصُول

		Who.	Which.		That.	
Plural.		Dual.			Singular.	
Fem.	*Masc.*	*Fem.*	*Masc.*		*Fem.*	*Masc.*
ٱللَّوَاتِي	ٱلَّذِينَ	ٱللَّتَانِ	ٱلَّذَانِ		ٱلَّتِي	ٱلَّذِي	Nom.
ٱللَّاتِي ٱللَّاتِي	ٱلْأُولَى	ٱللَّتَيْنِ	ٱللَّذَيْنِ		,,	,,	Obj. Genitive.

مَا what, which, مَن who, أَي whoever, whatever, are
both relative and interrogative pronouns.

أَلْ who, which, is used with the nouns of agent and
object as a relative pronoun.

THE DEMONSTRATIVE PRONOUN. أَسْمَآءُ ٱلْإِشَارَةِ

Near Object (This).

Plural.	Dual.		Singular.		
Common.	Fem.	Masc.	Fem.	Masc.	
أُوْلَآءِ or أُوْلَى	تَانِ	ذَانِ	ذِي (ذِهِ تِهِ تَا)	ذَا	Nom.
,, ,,	تَيْنِ	ذَيْنِ	,,	,,	Gen. and Accus.

Middle Object (That).

أُوْلَائِكَ or أُوْلَاكَ	تَانِكَ	ذَانِكَ	تِيْكَ	ذَاكَ
,, ,,	تَيْنِكَ	ذَيْنِكَ	,,	,,

Distant Object (That).

أُوْلَالِكَ or أُوْلَالِكَ	تَانِّكَ	ذَانِّكَ	تِلْكَ	ذٰلِكَ
,, ,,	تَيْنِّكَ	ذَيتِّكَ	,,	,,

هُنَا here, هُنَاكَ there, and ثَمَّ there, are also demonstrative pronouns.

The demonstrative for near objects may have the
particle هَا (ٱلتَّنْبِيْهُ) prefixed to it; as

هٰذا هٰذِه   هٰذَانِ هٰاتَانِ   هٰؤُلَآءِ
هٰذَيْنِ هَاتَيْنِ

The هَا (ٱلتَّنْبِيْهُ) may also be prefixed to some of the

118

demonstrative pronouns for middle objects: (*a*). When addressing a female person the ـِ of the كَ in the dem. pron. for middle objects is generally changed into ـِ; as

ذلِكِ ٱلرَّجُلُ يَا ٱمْرَأَةٌ   أُوْلْئِكِ ٱلرِّجَالُ يَا ٱمْرَأَةٌ

(*b*). لَمَـا is annexed for the dual, (*c*) مُ is annexed for the plural masc., (*d*) نَّ is annexed for the plur. fem.; as

This is the opportunity, brethren	<div dir="rtl">تِلْكُمُ ٱلْفُرْصَةُ يَا إِخْوَتِي</div>
This is the book, men	<div dir="rtl">ذلِكُمَا ٱلْكِتَابُ يَا رَجُلَانِ</div>
Those are the men, O women	<div dir="rtl">أُوْلْئِكُنَّ ٱلرِّجَالُ يَا نِسَاءُ</div>

The relative pronoun always needs a صِلَة and عَائِد The صِلَة is the sentence or phrase following the relative and completing its meaning. The عَائِد is the pronoun contained in the صِلَة which connects it with the antecedent relative. It is better that this pronoun should be in the third person; as

Thou art the one who loves me   أَنْتَ ٱلَّذِي يُحِبُّنِي

If the عَائِد is in the accusative case it may be omitted; as

Thou art he whom I love   أَنْتَ ٱلَّذِي أُحِبُّ

The صِلَة of the article (when used with relative force) is always a noun of agent or noun of object.

The demonstrative pronoun is indeclinable but the dual form takes ١ for the nom., and ي for the accus. and genitive.

The interrogative pronouns are all indeclinable except أَيُّ.

The latter is declined like an ordinary noun; but in such a sentence as

I love whoever of them is wise أُحِبُّ أَيُّهُم حَكِيْمٌ it is indeclinable.

THE ARTICLE. أَلْ

أَدَاةُ ٱلتَّعْرِيْف Instrument of Definition.

The definite article is an inseparable particle prefixed to words and suffers no change for gender or number. It is used:

I. As the definite article.

(a). أَلْعَهْدِيّة for familiarity; as

Is this the book i. e. The book mentioned previously أَهٰذَا هُوَ ٱلْكِتَابُ

(b) أَلْجِنْسِيّة for distinguishing the genus; as

The lion is more daring than the wolf أَلْأَسَدُ أَجْرَأُ مِنَ ٱلذِّئْبِ

II. As the relative pronoun.

Zaid, the beater of Amr زَيْدٌ ٱلضَّارِبُ عَمْرًا

It may be زَائِدَة (redundant) as in the relative pronoun ٱلَّذِي and in some proper nouns, which have only become such through usage; as

أَلْمَدِيْنَةُ, ٱلْفَضْلُ, ٱلْحَرَمُ

There is no indefinite article in Arabic.

Nouns are classified; as

I. اِسْم جَامِد Primitive, opposed to اِسْم مُشْتَق Derived.

جَمَد to become solid.   اِشْتَقَ to derive.

II. اِسْم مُجَرَّد Containing root letters only, opposed

[to اِسْم مَزِيد فِيهِ Augmented.

جَرَّد to strip.   زَادَ to increase.

III. اِسْم عَلَم Proper Noun opposed to اِسْم جِنْس

[Common Noun.

IV. اِسْم جِنْس is either اِسْم عَيْنٍ denoting a concrete

object

or اِسْم مَعْنًى denoting an abstract

idea.

V. اِسْم عَلَم may be   مُفْرَد A single word

or مُرَكَّب compound.

مُرَكَّب may be (a)   إِسْنَادِيّ predicative or a pro-

position; as

تَأَبَّطَ شَرًّا "He carried mischief

under his arm".

(b) مُرَكَّب مَزْجِيّ Mixed Compound

which is not a pro-

position.

بَعْلَبَكَّ Baalbec.

(c) إِضَافِيّ Correlative, as

عَبْدُ ٱللّٰهِ]

VI. اِسْمٌ عَلَمٌ is aigain either

(a). مَنْقُوْلٌ transferred from some other use, being originally an adjective, noun of action, com. noun, verb, sentence, or name of sound.

Masc. = Nejeeb Excellent نَجِيْب
  Towfeek Divine aid تَوْفِيْق   = مَنْقُوْلٌ
  Khaleel Friend خَلِيْل

Fem. = Jameeleh Handsome جَمِيْلَة
  Wadād Love وَدَاد   = مَنْقُوْلٌ
  Nadah Dew نَدَى

(b). مُرْتَجَلٌ existing only as a proper name.

Masc. = Abraham إِبْرٰهِيْم
  David دَاوُود   = مُرْتَجَلٌ
  John حَنَّا

Fem. = Mary مَرْيَم
  Helena هِيْلَانَة   = مُرْتَجَلٌ
  Sarah سَارَة

Finally the اِسْمٌ عَلَمٌ may be:

(a). اِسْمٌ name, as Zaid.

(b). كُنْيَة sobriquet, name with prefix, as أَبُو, أُمُّ.

(c). لَقَبٌ title, as the Conqueror.

Masc. = Abu-Alatahia أَبُو ٱلْعَتَاهِيَّة
  Abu-Bakr أَبُوبَكْرٍ   = كُنْيَة

Fem. = Mother of believers أُمُّ ٱلْمُؤْمِنِينَ   ) = كُنْيَة

      Mother of Goodness أُمُّ ٱلْخَيْرِ)

A proper name may contain all three.

The كُنْيَة comes first, the إِسْم second, and the لَقَب third.

The إِسْم follows the declension of the كُنْيَة and the لَقَب may follow the declension of the noun or it may be مَقْطُوع or مُضَاف إِلَيْهِ.

Masc. = Sword of the state سَيْفُ ٱلدَّوْلَةِ)

      John the beloved يُوحَنَّا ٱلْحَبِيبُ) = لَقَب

Fem. = The little Jane حَنَّةُ ٱلصَّغِيْرَةُ)

      Mary the prophetess مَرْيَمُ ٱلنَّبِيَّةُ) = لَقَب

The proper noun is شَخْصِيّ if it refers to only one individual of a kind, and جِنْسِيّ if it be applied alike to every individual of a kind:

Proper name of the lion   أُسَامَة.

  ,,   ,,   of the hyena أُمُّ عَامِر.

COLLECTIVE NOUNS.

Collective Nouns are of two kinds:

I. إِسْمُ ٱلْجَمْع which implies multitude but has no singular of its form.

II. شِبْهُ ٱلْجَمْع which implies multitude and forms a singular by affixing ة (ٱلْوَحْدَة unity).

I. ‫اِسْمُ ٱلْجَمْع‬.

Swarm of bees	خَشْرَم	Army	خَمِيس
Women	نِسَآء	Tribe, People	قَوْم
A Company	مَعْشَر	People	أَهْل
Descendants	ذُرِّيَّة	People, Nation	شَعْب
Flock	قَطِيع	Horses	خَيْل
Herd of Gazelles	سِرْب	Multitude	مَلَأ
Tribe	قَبِيلَة	Company of Men up to ten	رَهْط
Family	أُسْرَة	Associates	بِطَانَة
Family	عَائِلَة	Individuals	نَفَر
Sect	طَائِفَة	Company	جَمَاعَة
Troop	عُصْبَة	Birds	طَيْر
Troop	عِصَابَة	Courtiers	حَاشِيَة

II. ‫شِبْهُ ٱلْجَمْع‬.

Bees	نَحْل	Pebbles	حَصَى
Figs	تِين	Hair	شَعْر
Words	كَلِم	Datestone	نَوَى
Seeds	حَبّ	Fish	سَمَك
Verses (Koran, Bible)	آى	Steps	دَرَج
Eggs	بَيْض	Net	شَبَك
Leaves	وَرَق	Brick	آجُرّ
Palm trees	نَخْل	Spear	قَنَا, قَنًى
Ducks	بَطّ	Ostrich	نَعَام

Trees	شَجَر	Reeds Spears	أَسَل
Doves	حَمَام	Stomachs	مَعِد
Flowers	زَهْر	Heads	هَام
Roses	وَرْد	Reed-pens	يَرَاع
Apples	تُفَّاح	Reeds	قَصَب
Geese	إِوَزّ	Pomegranates	رُمَّان
Hens	دَجَاج	Cows	بَقَر
Needs	حَاج	Wild Pigeons	يَمَام
Brushwood	أَجَم	Owls	بُوم

PART SECOND.

SYNTAX. أَلنَّحْوُ

from نَحَا to *purpose*.

Nahu is the branch of Arabic grammar which treats
of the state of the final letters of words as arranged
in sentences, in respect to the Declension or Indeclension
of such words.

Sentences may be composed of nouns only or of
nouns and verbs together; the particle merely intensifies the meaning of the sentence.

DECLENSION. أَلْإِعْرَابُ

from أَعْرَبَ to *speak plainly*.

Declension is the change in the final vowels of words
to shew the function of the words in a sentence. This
change is caused by governing words or regents, which
may be either expressed لَفْظِيَّة or understood مَعْنَوِيَّة.

INDECLENSION. أَلْبِنَآءُ

from بَنَى to *build*, and therefore what is immovable.
Indeclension is the retention of a particular vowel or

سُكُوْن on the end of a word for some assignable reason.

Note. Some words retain their سُكُوْن or vowels not because they are indeclinable but because they end in Aleph (ى ، ا) which does not admit of any vowel being placed over it; as

Youth   أَلْفَتَى   Stick   أَلْعَصَا

Or, because they have always the same function in a sentence, as سُبْحَـان which is always the absolute object.

The signs of Indeclension أَوْجُهُ ٱلْبِنَـآءِ are ٟ , ٍ , ً , ٠.
The ٍ and ٠ are common to the three parts of speech, as particles هَلْ, رُبَّ, verbs قُمْ, قَـامَ, nouns لَـدُنْ, أَيْـنَ
the ٟ and ً to the (a) noun and (b) particle.

(b) مُنْذُ , جَيْرِ   (a) حَيْثُ , أَمْسِ

REGENTS. أَلْعَوَامِلُ

Words which stand alone are never declined; to be declined they must be arranged in a sentence and stand in some relation to other words. The words which govern others are called regents. The regents which are expressed are:

(a) the verb, (b) the preposition, (c) the particles of apocopation جَوَازِمُ ٱلْفِعْـل, (d) the subjunctive particles نَـوَاصـبُ ٱلـفِـعْـلِ, (e) words which affect the form and meaning of the subject and predicate أَلنَّوَاسِـخُ, (f) words derived from the verb, viz. the nouns of agent, object, attribute, superiority, and action.

(g). Adverbs which have the function of verbs اَسْمَآء الْفِعْل. The regents which are understood are اَلْاَبْتِدَآء and اَلتَّجَرُّد. The governing word should always preceede the word governed.

CASES.

There are four cases in Arabic:

رَفْع Nominative   نَصْب Accusative

جَرّ or خَفْض Genitive and جَزْم Apocopative i. e., the dropping of the last vowel or weak letter. The nominative and accusative cases are common to nouns and verbs, the genitive is peculiar to nouns, and the apocopative to verbs.

The Signs of Declension are of two kinds:

I. Letters viz. و, ا, ى, ن.

II. Vowels viz. ِ , َ , ُ , ْ .

The latter are the original signs.

The signs of declension are either ظَاهِرَة expressed, or مُقَدَّرَة implied.

I. Words which take letters for their signs of declension, مَوَاطِنُ الْاِعْرَابِ بِالْحُرُوْف are:

(a). The five nouns — viz.

اَب father   اَخ brother   حَم father-in-law   فَم mouth and ذُو possessing, when in construction with nouns

and pronouns other than the suffix of the first person
singular يَآءُ ٱلْمُتَكَلِّمِ.

(*b*). The dual, ٱلْمُثَنَّى.

(*c*). The regular masculine plural and the like, viz.
the decades.

(*d*). The five forms which occur in the conjugation
of the aorist:

$$ يَفْعَلَانِ , تَفْعَلَانِ , يَفْعَلُوْنَ , تَفْعَلِيْنَ , تَفْعَلُوْنَ $$

11. Words which take vowels, مَوَاطِنُ ٱلْإِعْرَابِ بِٱلْحَرَكَاتِ;
are:

(*a*). The singular noun (*b*) the irregular plural (*c*) the
regular feminine plural (*d*) the aorist when without the
ن feminine and ن of assurance, and the expressed pronoun in the nominative case, ٱلضَّمِيْرُ ٱلْبَارِزُ وَٱلْمَرْفُوْعُ.

DIVISION OF THE SIGNS OF DECLENSION.

$$ أَوْجُهُ ٱلْإِعْرَابِ $$

This is as follows for the

Nominative ـُ , و , ا , ن.

Accusative ـَ , ـً , ا , ي , suppression of ن.

Genitive ـِ , ـٍ , ي.

Apocopative ـْ , suppression of ن , ٱلْإِعْرَابُ and weak
letters.

THE NOMINATIVE.

٢ is the sign of the nominative in every word which takes a vowel as a sign of declension; as

Zaid went ذَهَبَ رَيْدٌ

و in the five nouns and in the regular masculine plural; as

Thy father and the believers came جَاءَ أَبُوكَ وَٱلْمُؤْمِنُوْنَ

ا in the dual; as

The two men strove together ٱلرَّجُلَانِ تَخَاصَمَا

نُ ,ٱلْإِعْرَابُ, is retained in the five verbs as a sign of their being in the nominative (indicative); as

The men know ٱلرِّجَالُ يَعْلَمُوْنَ

THE ACCUSATIVE.

ِ is the sign of the accusative in every word which admits of a vowel as the sign of declension except the regular feminine plural; as

I saw Zaid رَأَيْتُ زَيْدًا

ٍ in the regular feminine plural; as

The women came riding جَاءَتِ ٱلنِّسَاءُ رَاكِبَاتٍ

ا in the five nouns; as

He loved thy brother أَحَبَّ أَخَاكَ

ي in the regular masculine plural and dual; as

I saw the two infidels and

the believers رَأَيْتُ ٱلْكَافِرَيْنِ وَٱلْمُؤْمِنِيْنَ

Suppression of ن، اَلْإِعْرَابُ, in the five verbs, as

They will never return لَنْ يَرْجِعُوا

THE GENITIVE.

ـِ is the sign of the genitive in every word where a vowel is used as a sign of declension except in words imperfectly declined; as

This is the son of Zaid هٰذَا ٱبْنَ زَيْدٍ

ـَ in nouns imperfectly declined; as

I saw the son of Ahmad رَأَيْتُ ٱبْنَ أَحْمَدَ

ي in the five nouns, the dual, and regular masculine plural; as مَرَرْتُ بِأَبِيكَ وَٱلْكَافِرَيْنِ وَٱلْمُؤْمِنِينَ.

I passed thy father, the two unbelievers and the believers.

THE APOCOPATIVE.

ـْ is the sign of the apocopative in verbs ending with strong letters not joined to expressed pronouns in the nominative case; as

I did not know لَمْ أَعْرِفْ

Suppression of ن occurs in the five verbs; as

Do not (ye two) strive with one another لَا تَتَخَاصَمَا

Suppression of the weak letters occurs in verbs ending with such letters when not joined to a manifest pronoun in the nominative case; as

Did you not know أَلَمْ تَدْرِ

IMPLIED SIGNS OF DECLENSION. تَقْدِيرُ ٱلإِعْرَابِ

I. All the vowels are implied on ا, ى because of
ٱلتَّعَذُّرُ *impossibility*; as

The youth came جَاءَ ٱلْفَتَى I saw the youth رَأَيْتُ ٱلْفَتَى
I beat him with the stick ضَرَبْتُهُ بِٱلعَصَا

II. ـُ and ـِ are implied on the و and ى when not
preceded by ـِ, لِلِٱسْتِثْقَالِ *for heaviness*; as

Behold the judge prays هُوَذَا ٱلقَاضِي يَدْعُو

III. Vowels are implied in nouns when in construction
with the ي, ٱلْمُتَكَلِّمُ, as this must be preceded by ـِ,
لِلْمُجَانَسَة *for agreement*; as

My friend went ذَهَبَ صَدِيْقِي

I saw my friend رَأَيْتُ صَدِيْقِي

I wrote with my pen كَتَبْتُ بِقَلَمِي

The و of the regular masculine plural is changed into
ي according to the rules of ٱلْإِعْلَال and is incorporated
with the ي; as

These are my lovers (Nominative) هَؤُلَاءِ مُحِبِّيَّ

The ـُ is implied when it is followed by هَمْزَةُ ٱلْوصْلِ; as
Serve God أَعْبُد ٱللّٰه

The vowels are implied in the pause and in rhyme; as
Fear God and you will be safe
from others خَفِ ٱللّٰهَ تَأْمَنِ ٱلغَيْرَ

Only he who fears God is
the hero إِنَّمَا مَنْ يَتَّقِيْ ٱللّٰهَ ٱلْبَطَلُ

The ن of declension which follows the five verbs in the nominative case may be implied when followed by the ن of protection اَلْوِقَـايَةُ and always when followed by the ن of assurance اَلتَّوْكِيْدُ; as

Do you love me? أَتُحِبُّوْنَنِي or أَتُحِبُّوْنِي

Will not ye two serve God? أَلَا تَعْبُدَانِّ ٱللّٰهَ

ى, ا, و are implied in pronunciation when followed by هَمْزَةُ ٱلْوَصْلِ; as

This is the judge's father هٰذَا أَبُوْ ٱلْقَاضِي

When the last letter in a word is dropped the sign of declension is implied upon it; as

This is a just judge هٰذَا قَاضٍ عَادِلٌ

The ِ is implied upon the ى and not on the ض.

The ن is omitted for تَـخْـفِـيْـف, *lightening*, and the ى, ا, و are dropped because of two silent letters coming together.

THE NUNATION. اَلتَّنْوِيْنُ

The Tanween or Nunation is a quiescent ن annexed to a declinable word, the ن being suppressed and the final vowel doubled; as رَجُلٌ, رَجُلٍ.

The tanween is of various kinds, the chief of these are:

I. تَنْوِيْنُ ٱلتَّمْكِيْنِ which is annexed to wholly declinable nouns; as رَجُلٌ, رِجَالٌ

II. تَـنْوِيْـنُ ٱلْعِـوَضِ which is annexed to the forms of certain forms of Plurals, when they end in weak letters in the nominative and genitive cases, the weak letter being dropped; and to the words كُــلّ, بَــعْــض instead of placing them in construction, ٱلْـمُـضَـاف إِلَيْـهِ ; and to إِذ when in construction with a noun of time; as

Maidens جَوَارٍ for جَوَارِي, كُلٌّ يَمُوْتُ for كُلُّ أَحَدٍ يَمُوْتُ,
وَحِيْنَ إِذْ for سَأَذْهَبُ إِلَى غَزَّةَ وَحِيْنَئِذٍ أَرَاكَ.

III. تَنْوِيْنُ ٱلْمُقَابَلَةِ which is annexed to the regular feminine plural so that it may resemble the ن of the regular masculine plural; as (مُؤْمِنِيْنَ), مُؤْمِنَاتٍ.

IV. تَنْوِيْنُ ٱلتَّنْكِيْرِ which is annexed to certain proper nouns that become indeclinable when used as common nouns; as

I passed Sibewaih and
another Sibewaih مَرَرْتُ بِسِيْبَوَيْهِ وَ سِيْبَوَيْهِ آخَرَ

V. تَنْوِيْنُ ٱلتَّرَنُّمِ which is used in poetry.

STATES OF THE NOUN IN DECLENSION AND INDECLENSION.

أَحْوَالُ ٱلْآسْمِ فِي ٱلْإِعْرَابِ وَٱلْبِنَآءِ

Nouns originally admit of declension.

Verbs originally do not admit of declension.

Particles are always indeclinable.

The Noun may be:

134

I. Wholly Declined مُعْرَبَة تَمَامًا admitting of the ـً
and تَنْوِيْنُ ٱلتَّمْكِيْنِ.

II. Imperfectly Declined مَمْنُوْع مِنَ ٱلصَّرْف not admitting of the ـً or تَنْوِيْنُ ٱلتَّمْكِيْنِ.

III. Indeclinable مَبْنِيٌّ.

Nouns which resemble verbs resemble them also in being imperfectly declined, that is, they do not take the تَنْوِيْن or ـً, and those nouns which resemble particles, resemble them also in being indeclinable.

ٱلْمَمْنُوْعُ مِنَ ٱلصَّرْف

The word صَرْف in this connexion signifies the tanween or according to some grammarians the tanween and ـً; therefore the expression مَمْنُوْعٌ مِنَ ٱلصَّرْف is the inability of a word to take the tanween and ـً. All words which are مَمْنُوْعَةٌ مِنَ ٱلصَّرْف take ـَ in the genitive and accusative cases.

IMPERFECTLY DECLINED NOUNS.

ٱلْأَسْمَاءُ ٱلْمَمْنُوْعَةُ مِنَ ٱلصَّرْف

These are the following:

I. Nouns.

(a). Proper Nouns which have undergone change in form but not in meaning, they are:

مُضَر	جُمَح	دُلَف	جُشَم	عُمَر
هُبَل	جُدَى	عُصَم	قُثَم	زُحَل
هُدَل	بُلَع	ثُعَل	قُزَح	زُفَر

(*b*). Proper Nouns which are on measures peculiar to the verb, as فَعَّلَ, فُعِلَ, and those measures which have as their prefix a servile letter which is also peculiar to the verb; as

شَمَّرُ, أَحْمَدُ, تَدْمُرُ, يَزِيْدُ, يَشْكُرُ

(*c*). Proper Nouns which have ان affixed to them; as

عُثْمَان, حَمْدَان, سَرْحَان

(*d*). Compound Proper Nouns when the second part only is declined مُرَكَّبٌ مَزْجِيّ; as

بَعْلَبَكَّ, حَضْرَمَوْتُ, مَعْدِى كَرِبُ

(*e*). Foreign Proper Nouns which have (1) more than three letters or (2) three letters with the second one vowelled; as

إِبْرَهِيْمُ, يُوْسُفُ

(*f*). Proper Nouns ending with ة whether masculine or feminine; as

طَلْحَة (Masc.)   فَاطِمَة (Fem.)

(*g*). Feminine Proper Nouns (1) not ending with ة and of more than three letters, or (2) of three letters, or (2) of three letters with the second vowelled; as

زَيْنَب, عَدَن.

II. Adjectives (1) which have undergone change in form but not in meaning; as

I saw other women   رَأَيْتُ نِسَآءَ أُخَرَ for أُخَرَ

(Nouns of Superiority are not made plural, dual, or feminine, unless they have the article or are in construction).

(2). Adjectives on the measure of verbs as أَحْمَر red. (These are the nouns of attribute and the nouns of superiority).

(3). Adjectives ending with ان having ـَ on the ف; as

Fem. سَكْرَى   drunken سَكْرَان

Adjectives come under these rules when they do not form their fem. with ة and when they are originally adjectives; but nouns used as adjectives; as أَرْبَع and صَفْوَان are wholly declinable.

III. All Nouns ending with an additional آء or ى; as

سُلْمَى , حُبْلَى . مَرْضَى , فُضْلَى
خَنْسَآء , حَمْرَآء , أَصْدِقَآء , صَحْرَآء

IV. Plural Nouns on the measure of the plural of plurals i. e. nouns which have after the ا of plural two letters, or three letters the middle one being ى silent, as مَفَاتِيْم , دَرَاهِم ; if ة is added to the latter then the noun is wholly declinable, as أَسَاقِفَة.

All these nouns when in construction or joined to the article take the ـِ as a sign of the genitive.

OF NOUNS WHICH ARE INDECLINABLE.

بِنَآءِ ٱلْآسْم

When nouns resemble the particle they are indeclinable. Nouns resemble the particle:

I. When they have less than three radical letters.

II. When they have the meaning of the particle or

need like it other words to complete their meaning.

III. When they take the place of the verb without being affected by it.

IV. When they have no function in the sentence مُهْمَل as وَيْهِ alas!

INDECLINABLE NOUNS. ٱلْأَسْمَآءُ ٱلْمَبْنِيَّةُ

Indeclinable Nouns are:

I. The Personal Pronouns   ٱلضَّمَائِرُ (ٱلشَّخْصِيَّةُ)

II. The Demonstrative Pronouns   أَسْمَآءُ ٱلْإِشَارَةِ

III. The Conditional Nouns   أَسْمَآءُ ٱلشَّرْطِ

IV. The Interrogative Pronouns   أَسْمَآءُ ٱلْاسْتِفْهَام

V. The Relative Pronouns   أَسْمَآءُ ٱلْمَوْصُول

VI. The Interjections   أَسْمَآءُ ٱلْأَصْوَاتِ

VII. The Names of Verbs   أَسْمَآءُ ٱلْأَفْعَال

i. e. Adverbs which perform the function of Verbs.

VIII. Some Adverbs   بَعْضُ ٱلظُّرُوفِ

These nouns always resemble particles and are therefore always indeclinable. Nouns which sometimes resemble particles are only at such times indeclinable; these are:

I. Nouns directly addressed by
the vocative   ٱلْمَقْصُودُ بِٱلنِّدَآءِ

II. The subject of the Absolute
Negative in certain states لَا ٱلنَّافِيَةُ لِلْجِنْسِ

III. The Compound Numerals from 11 to 19.

IV. Some Adverbs.

Indeclinable words should have the ـِ, but if the word is of one letter only, or if its penultimate is a silent letter, it cannot take the ـِ.

Words which are indeclinable because of their position in the sentence do not take the ـِ.

The preterite, imperative, and the aorist with the ن of assurance or ن feminine affixed to it, are indeclinable; the aorist in other forms is declinable.

Sometimes the signs of indeclension are implied; as

O Hathami يَا حَذَامِ

There is no youth with you لَا فَتَى عِنْدَكُم

DEFINITE NOUNS.

The Noun is either Definite مَعْرِفَة or Indefinite نَكِرَة.
The Definite Nouns are:

(a). The personal pronoun, (b) proper noun, (c) demonstrative pronoun, (d) relative pronoun, (e) noun made definite by the article, (f) noun in construction with a definite noun, (g) noun definitely addressed by the vocative.

SPEECH. اَلْكَلَامُ

Speech consists of sentences جُمَلٌ pl. of جُمْلَةٌ, each of which has necessarily a subject and predicate.

The subject is called اَلْمُسْنَدُ إِلَيْهِ, *that upon which the attribute leans*, that to which something is attributed, the predicate اَلْمُسْنَدُ *that which leans upon or is supported*, whilst the relation between them is called اَلْإِسْنَادُ *the act of leaning*.

The principal part of a sentence or clause (which is absolutely essential to the meaning) is called اَلْعُمْدَةُ *the support*, and the subordinate part (which may be dispensed with), as for instance the objective complement of the verb, اَلْفَضْلَةُ *that which is in excess*.

Under the term عُمْدَةٌ are included (*a*) اَلْفَاعِلُ the agent, (*b*) نَائِبُ الْفَاعِلِ the substitute for the agent, and (*c*) اَلْمُبْتَدَأُ وَ ٱلْخَبَرُ the subject and predicate; the term فَضْلَةٌ includes all other nouns in the sentence.

Sentences which begin with the subject (substantive or pronoun) are called جُمَلٌ إِسْمِيَّةٌ *Nominal Sentences*.

A nominal sentence is distinguished by the absence of a logical copula either expressed by or contained in a finite verb; but a sentence where the predicate is a verb preceding the subject, as قَامَ زَيْدٌ or one consisting of a verb which includes both subject and predicate, as مَاتَ he died, is called جُمْلَةٌ فِعْلِيَّةٌ *Verbal Sentence.*

The subject of a nominal sentence is called اَلْمُبْتَدَأُ *that with which a beginning is made,* the inchoative; and its predicate اَلْخَبَرُ *the announcement.*

The subject of a verbal sentence is called اَلْفَاعِلُ *the agent,* and its predicate اَلْفِعْلُ *the action or verb.*

A verbal sentence relates an act or event, while as a rule, a nominal sentence is descriptive of a person or thing; as اَلْمَلِكُ مَرِيْضٌ the king is ill; and in nominal sentences the مُبْتَدَأُ always implies contrast with another مُبْتَدَأُه

رَيْدٌ قَامَ وَعَمْرٌو جَلَسَ Zaid rose and Amr sat, whilst in the verbal sentence the emphasis rests solely upon the verb.

In order to avoid difficulties and misconceptions it is necessary that these terms agent and مُبْتَدَأُ be maintained.

THE NOMINATIVE CASE.

The following are in the Nominative case:

I. The Agent اَلْمَرْفُوعَاتُ اَلْفَاعِلُ.

II. The Substitute for the Agent نَائِبُ اَلْفَاعِلِ Subject of a passive verb.

III. The Subject
IV. The Predicate اَلْمُبْتَدَأُ وَ اَلْخَبَرُ.

V. The Subject اِسْم of كَان وَ أَخَوَاتِهَا.

VI. The Predicate of إِنَّ وَ أَخَوَاتِهَا and of لَا ٱلنَّافِيَة لِلْجِنْس the Absolute Negative.

VII. The Aorist when not acted upon by particles, nor followed by ن of feminine, or ن of Assurance.

VIII. Appositives or nouns in apposition to Nominatives.

THE VERBAL SENTENCE. ٱلْفَاعِلُ وَٱلْفِعْلُ

The Agent and the Verb.

The Noun is called the agent when it is preceded by the verb in the active voice.

It may be a noun إِسْم ظَاهِرٌ or a personal pronoun expressed or understood ضَمِيرٌ بَارِزٌ أَوْ مُسْتَتِرٌ.

The agent in both dual and plural of the masc. and fem. takes the verb in the singular; as

The believers came	جَاءَ ٱلْمُؤْمِنُونَ
The women spoke	تَكَلَّمَتِ ٱلنِّسَآءُ
The two men rose	قَامَ ٱلرَّجُلَانِ
The two women sat	جَلَسَتِ ٱلْمَرْأَتَانِ

The verb must have the sign of feminine when the agent is a real fem. noun singular not separated from the verb; also when the agent is a feminine personal pronoun; as

Mary feared the angel	مَرْيَمُ خَافَتْ مِنَ ٱلْمَلَاكِ

Mary understood   فَهِمَت مَرْيَمُ

In the first of these sentences مَرْيَمُ is Mubtada and خَافَت a sentence composed of the verb and the implied fem. pronoun هِيَ which refers to Mary.

The verb may or may not take the sign of fem. in the following cases:

I. Where the verb is separated from its agent in the fem.; as

Mary came to-day   جَاءَت or جَاء ٱلْيَوْمَ مَرْيَمُ

Note if إِلَّا separates them, it is best to drop the ت fem.; as

No one came but Mary   مَا جَاء إِلَّا مَرْيَمُ

II. Where the agent is not a real feminine; as

The sun rose   طَلَعَت or طَلَعَ ٱلشَّمْسُ

III. In all plurals except the reg. masc. plural; as

The believers came (fem.)   جَاءَت or جَاء ٱلْمُؤْمِنَاتُ

The men knew   عَرَفَت or عَرَفَ ٱلرِّجَالُ

The winds blew   هَبَّت or هَبَّ ٱلرِّيَاحُ

IV. Where the verb does not admit of conjugation; as

Hind is praise worthy   نِعْمَت , نِعْمَ هِنْدُ

Hind is not standing   لَيْسَت , لَيْسَ هِنْدُ وَاقِفَةً

POSITION OF THE AGENT IN THE SENTENCE.

The agent should immediately follow the verb, but in the following cases it is preceded by the object:

I. When the action of the verb is confined to the agent by إِلَّا preceded by مَا, لَا or إِنَّمَا; as

No one provides for mankind
except God مَا يَرْزُقُ ٱلخَلْقَ إِلَّا ٱللّٰهُ

Only Zaid struck Amr إِنَّمَا ضَرَبَ عَمْرًا زَيْدٌ

II. When the object is an attached pronoun and the agent a noun; as

My father loves me يُحِبُّنِي أَبِي

III. When the agent contains a pronoun which refers to the object; as

The blossom beautified the trees زَانَ ٱلشَّجَرَ زَهْرُهُ

THE AGENT PRECEDES THE OBJECT.

I. When the action is restricted to the latter by the particles إِنَّمَا or إِلَّا; as

The sailor hears nothing
but the waves لَا يَسْمَعُ ٱلْمَلَّاحُ إِلَّا ٱلْأَمْوَاجَ

II. When it is an attached pronoun; as

I honoured the king أَكْرَمْتُ ٱلْمَلِكَ

III. When it cannot be distinguished from the object by case endings or by meaning; as

This person loved that أَحَبَّ هٰذَا ذَاكَ

Jesus lived in the same age as John عَاصَرَ عِيسَى يَحْيَى

The verb may be omitted but the agent must always be either expressed or understood; as

Who came? Zaid (came) مَنْ جَاءَ ؟ (جَاءَ) زَيْدٌ

The verb is necessarily omitted when a noun in the nominative case follows a particle which is specially used with verbs; as اِذَا اِنْ.

If thou honourest the honourable one, thou wilt have gained him; and if thou honourest the base one, he will rebel

إِذَا أَنْتَ أَكْرَمْتَ ٱلْكَرِيْمَ مَلَكْتَهُ وَإِنْ أَنْتَ أَكْرَمْتَ ٱللَّئِيمَ تَمَرَّدَ

The nouns of agent, attribute, object, superiority, action, names of verbs, and nouns resembling any of these, may also have an agent.

THE SUBJECT OF A PASSIVE VERB.

نَائِبُ ٱلْفَاعِلِ

Substitute for the Agent.

The object of a passive verb is put in the nominative case; as

Thou wast struck	ضُرِبْتَ
No one was struck but thyself	مَا ضُرِبَ إِلَّا أَنْتَ
The thief was imprisoned	سُجِنَ ٱللِّصُّ

If, however, the object is not found in the sentence the noun of action or an adverbial or prepositional phrase stands for the agent, and must be made definite by (1) being qualified or (2) being in construction or (3) being a proper noun or (4) being numbered; as

(1). A just judgment was decreed قُضِيَ قَضَاءٌ عَدْلٌ

(2). The place of the prince was occupied جَلَسَ مَكَانُ آلَا مِيْرِ

(3). Zaid was passed by مُرَّ بِزَيْدٍ

(4). The Sabbath was kept حُفِظَ ٱلسَّبْتُ

Many sayings were spoken قِيْلَ أَقْوَالٌ

The noun of action, adverb, and preposition must be مُتَصَرِّف i. e. capable of having different functions in the sentence, unlike

وَاوُ ٱلْقَسَمِ ,عِنْدَ ,سُبْحَانَ

The Agent is omitted:

(a). Because unknown or well-known or unimportant; as

The house was robbed سُرِقَ ٱلْبَيْتُ

The bell was rung قُرِعَ ٱلْجَرَسُ

The world was created خُلِقَتِ ٱلدُّنَيا

(b). Brevity of speech, rhyme or measure in poetry, or concealment.

When a verb has two or more objects in the active voice, the first takes the place of the agent in the passive voice; as

Zaid was clad in a coat كُسِيَ زَيْدٌ جُبَّةً

Amr clothed Zaid with a coat كَسَا عَمْرُو زَيْدًا جُبَّةً

I informed the men that the prince was coming أَخْبَرْتُ ٱلنَّاسَ ٱلْأَمِيْرَ قَادِمًا

The men were informed that the prince was coming أُخْبِرَتِ ٱلنَّاسُ ٱلْأَمِيْرَ قَادِمًا

10

THE NOMINAL SENTENCE. اَلْمُبْتَدَأُ وَٱلْخَبَرُ

اَلْمُبْتَدَأَ *that which begins* or stands at the head of a sentence is the noun اِسْم or subject of a nominal sentence and is put in the nominative case on account of the absence of any word governing it.

It is originally a substantive مَوْصُوف *that which admits of description* forming the subject of the sentence. It is also an adjective صِفَة forming the predicate of the sentence when it occurs after a negative or interrogative particle, in which case it takes an agent instead of a خَبَر predicate.

The term مَوْصُوف comprises common and proper nouns, the nouns of time and place, and nouns of instrument. The term صِفَة comprises the nouns of agent, object, adjective resembling the agent, and the nouns of superiority and excess.

EXAMPLES OF SUBJECT AND PREDICATE.

اَلْمُبْتَدَأُ وَالْخَبَرُ

	اَلْخَبَرُ	اَلْمُبْتَدَأُ
Study is pleasant	لَذِيْذٌ	اَلدَّرْسُ
Are you forsaking my gods, O Abraham	أَنْتَ عَنْ آلِهَتِي يَا إِبْرَهِيْمُ	أَرَاغِبٌ
Zaid his father is a learned man	أَبُوْهُ عَالِمٌ	زَيْدٌ
God provides for us	يَرْزُقُنَا	اَللّٰهُ
The patient how is he this morning?	كَيْفَ أَصْبَحَ	اَلْمَرِيْضُ
My friend let him come	لِيَأْتِ	صَدِيْقِي
The age is two days, a day for you and a day against you	يَوْمَانِ	اَلدَّهْرُ
	لَكَ	يَوْمٌ
	عَلَيْكَ	وَيَوْمٌ
The orator is on the platform	فَوْقَ آلْمِنْبَرِ	اَلْخَطِيْبُ
Men continue in their follies whilst the mill stone of death grinding	فِي غَفَـلَاتِهِمْ	اَلنَّاسُ
	تَطْحَنُ	وَرَحَى اَلْمَنِيَّةِ
Examples of	اَلْمُبْتَدَأُ	اَلْخَبَرُ
To every disease there is a remedy	دَوَآءٌ	لِكُلِّ دَآءٍ
The beloved of my beloved is beloved to my heart	حَبِيْبٌ إِلَى قَلْبِي حَبِيْبُ حَبِيْبِي	

THE PREDICATE.

The predicate completes the meaning of the subject. It must be indefinite and follow the subject.

It may be:

I. مُفْرَد that is a singular, dual, or plural noun; as

The two boys are coming   اَلْغُلَامَانِ قَادِمَانِ

The believers are happy   اَلْمُوْمِنُوْنَ سُعَدَاءُ

Knowledge is useful   اَلْعِلْمُ نَافِعٌ

II. جُمْلَة a sentence. This sentence may be:

1). خَبَرِيَّة Enunciative.

(a) Nominal اِسْمِيَّة, (b) verbal فِعْلِيَّة, (c) conditional شَرْطِيَّة; as

(a). The man his son is rich   اَلرَّجُلُ اِبْنُهُ غَنِيٌّ

(b). The man is praying   اَلرَّجُلُ يُصَلِّي

(c). The king, if you obey him, will honour you   اَلْمَلِكُ إِنْ أَطَعْتَهُ يُكْرِمْكَ

2). جُمْلَة إِنْشَائِيَّة Inceptive, expressing volition or beginning.

(a) imperative, (b) interrogative, (c) prohibitive.

(a). Zaid let him stand   زَيْدٌ لِيَقِفْ

(b). Zaid is he standing?   زَيْدٌ هَلْ هُوَ قَائِمٌ

(c). You there is no welcome for you   أَنْتُمْ لَا مَرْحَبًا بِكُمْ

III. شِبْهُ الْجُمْلَة. An adverbial or prepositional phrase.

The believers are in Paradise   اَلْمُوْمِنُوْنَ فِي الْجَنَّةِ

The angels are with God   اَلْمَـلَائِكَةُ عِنْدَ ٱللّٰهِ

An adverbial phrase expressing time cannot be the predicate of a concrete noun. We cannot say

The man is to-day   اَلرَّجُلُ ٱلْيَوْمَ

The house is to-morrow   اَلْبَيْتُ غَدًا

but we may say

The prayer is to-day   اَلصَّلٰوةُ ٱلْيَوْمَ

The departure is on the morrow   اَلرَّحِيْلُ غَدًا

When the predicate is an adverbial or prepositional phrase, a verb or adjective implying simple existence is understood, and this verb or adjective forms the predicate; as

The war (will be) to-morrow   اَلْحَرْبُ (تَكُوْنُ) غَدًا

The king (is) upon his throne   اَلْمَلِكُ (كَائِنٌ) عَلَى عَرْشِهِ

The predicate must always be connected with the subject by a رَابِطٌ *binder*. This may be:

(*a*). A personal or demonstrative pronoun; as

Zaid I know him   زَيْدٌ اَعْرِفُهُ

The garment of piety, that is
better   لِبَاسُ ٱلتَّقْوٰى ذَالِكَ خَيْرٌ

(*b*). A simple repetition of the subject, or the subject may be included in the predicate; as

The day of judgment: what
is the day of judgment?   يَوْمُ ٱلدِّينِ مَا يَوْمُ ٱلدِّينِ

Zaid is a good man of men   نِعْمَ ٱلرَّجُلُ زَيْدٌ

here رَجُل is defined by the article أَلْجِنْسِيَّة and there-fore includes all men, of whom Zaid is one.

The رَابِط is unnecessary:

(*a*). When the predicate is a primitive noun; as

Zaid is my brother   زَيْدٌ أَخِي

but if the primitive noun has the meaning of a derived noun it must have the رَابِط; as

Zaid is a lion (i. e. brave)   (زَيْدٌ أَسَدٌ (شُجَاعٌ

Zaid that is a brother (friend)   (زَيْدٌ ذَاكَ أَخٌ (صَدِيْقٌ

(*b*). When the predicate is a repetition of the sub-ject; as

The fact is, (هُوَ = أَلْأَمْرُ) God is one   هُوَ ٱللّٰهُ أَحَدٌ

My belief is, God is my sufficiency   إِعْتِقَادِي ٱللّٰهُ حَسْبِي

In such a sentence as

Zaid is a lover of Amr   زَيْدٌ عَمْرٌو مُحِبُّهُ هُوَ

the رَابِط must be expressed, otherwise ambiguity will arise as to who loves and who is loved.

AGREEMENT OF SUBJECT AND PREDICATE.

The predicate, when it contains a pronoun referring to the subject, agrees in number and gender with the subject; as

Miriam is good   مَرْيَمُ صَالِحَةٌ

God does (هُوَ) what He wills   ٱللّٰهُ يَفْعَلُ مَا يَشَاءُ

The two brothers are sitting (هُمَا)   ٱلْأَخَوَانِ جَالِسَانِ

The prophets هُمْ are holy ٱلْأَنْبِيَاءُ قِدِّيسُونَ

The men هُمْ arose ٱلرِّجَالُ قَامُوا

but when there is no such pronoun there may or may not be agreement; as

Knowledge is of two kinds ٱلْعِلْمُ عِلْمَانِ

Declinable nouns are of two kinds ٱلْأَسْمَاءُ ٱلْمُعْرَبَةُ قِسْمَانِ

The subject should be definite and precede the predicate مَعْرِفَةٌ مُقَدَّمَةٌ, but it may be indefinite:

I. When it is preceded (*a*) by a negative or an interrogative particle; or (*b*) by an adverbial or a prepositional phrase as خَبَر; as

(*a*). I have not a book مَا كِتَابٌ لِي

Is anything impossible هَلْ شَيْ غَيْرُ مُسْتَطَاعٍ

(*b*). To every good horse there is a fall لِكُلِّ جَوَادٍ كَبْوَةٌ

II. When it is qualified or an adjective, or has the signification of an adjective; as

One who prays and performs not is as a bow without a string دَاعٍ بِلَا عَمَلٍ كَقَوْسٍ بِلَا وَتَرٍ

A believer is better than an infidel مُؤْمِنٌ خَيْرٌ مِنْ كَافِرٍ

Something (great) made him good مَا أَحْسَنَهُ

III. When it is in construction; as

The conscience of a man in his guide ضَمِيرُ ٱلْإِنْسَانِ دَلِيلُهُ

An hour's righteousness is better than a thousand years' worship بِرُّ سَاعَةٍ خَيْرٌ مِنْ عِبَادَةِ أَلْفِ سَنَةٍ

IV. When it expresses condition, or is an answer to a question; as

He who comes to me will find rest مَنْ يَأْتِ إِلَيَّ يَسْتَرِحْ

Who has come to you? مَنْ جَاءَ عِنْدَكَ

A man (has come to me) رَجُلٌ (جَاءَ عِنْدِي)

V. When it is (a) an inclusive expression or (b) denotes separation into kinds; as

(a). All die كُلٌّ يَمُوتُ

A date tree is better than a fig tree نَخْلَةٌ خَيْرٌ مِنْ تِينَةٍ

(b). One day is against us and

another for us فَيَوْمٌ عَلَيْنَا وَ يَوْمٌ لَنَا

VI. When it expresses supplication or imprecation; as

A curse upon Satan لَعْنَةٌ عَلَى ٱلشَّيْطَانِ

Peace upon you سَلَامٌ لَكُمْ

VII. When it is joined by a conjunction to (a) a definite noun, (b) an adjective, or (c) a qualified noun; as

(a). A man and his friend

hold converse رَجُلٌ وَصَدِيقُهُ يَتَحَدَّثَا دَتَّانِ

A book and the Bible are lost كِتَابٌ وَٱلتَّوْرَاةُ مَفْقُودَانِ

(b). A man and a wise man are

travelling رَجُلٌ وَعَالِمٌ سَائِحَانِ

(c). A man and a strong

lion strive together رَجُلٌ وَأَسَدٌ قَوِيٌّ يُصَارِعَانِ

VIII. If it follow إِذَا (ٱلْفَجَائِيَّةُ), لَوْلَا, وَ (ٱلْحَالُ) or كَمْ (ٱلْخَبَرِيَّةُ).

I entered and behold a
thief in the house   دَخَلْتُ فَإِذَا سَارِقٌ فِي ٱلْبَيْتِ

Had it not been for love I would
have become weary   لَوْلَا مَحَبَّةٌ لَكَلَلْتُ

I went forth whilst a star
was shining   خَرَجْتُ وَنَجْمٌ قَدْ أَضَاء

How many she-camels you have   كَمْ نَاقَةً لَكَ

The Predicate may be definite when it is to the person addressed as an indefinite noun; as

This is my brother   هٰذَا أَخِي
said to one who does not know him.

Also when the noun is made definite by the article; as

This is the horse   هٰذَا ٱلْحِصَانُ
said to a man to whom the horse was mentioned.

THE SUBJECT PRECEDES THE PREDICATE

I. When both are either definite or indefinite; as

My brother is my friend   أَخِي صَدِيقِي

A book is better   كِتَابٌ أَفْضَلُ

God is the creator   ٱللّٰهُ ٱلْخَالِقُ

II. When the predicate is a verb containing a pronoun in the nominative case referring to the subject; as

Love suffereth long and is kind   ٱلْمَحَبَّةُ تَتَأَنَّى وَتَرْفُقُ

III. When the predicate is restricted by إِنَّمَا or by إِلَّا after the negatives مَا and لَا; as

Victory is only to those who are patient

إِنَّمَا ٱلْفَوْزُ لِلصَّابِرِيْنَ

Paradise is not except for the good (lit.)

مَا ٱلْجَنَّةُ إِلَّا لِلصَّالِحِيْنَ

IV. When the لِ, ٱلْإِبْتِدَآءِ of assurance is prefixed to the subject; as

Of a truth thou art Lord

لَأَنْتَ سَيِّدٌ

V. When the subject expresses (*a*) condition, (*b*) interrogation, or (*c*) when it is in construction with either of these; as

(*a*). Whomsoever I looked for I did not find

أَيَّ طَلَبْتُهُ لَمْ أَجِدْهُ

(*b*). Who is present

مَنْ حَاضِرٌ

(*c*). Whose son is in the house

إِبْنُ مَنْ فِي ٱلْبَيْتِ

THE PREDICATE PRECEDES THE SUBJECT

I. When the مُبْتَدَأٌ is indefinite and the خَبَرٌ is (*a*) an adverbial or (*b*) a prepositional phrase; as

(*a*). I have a pen

عِنْدِي قَلَمٌ لِي قَلَمٌ

(*b*). Between prodigality and miserliness there is a medium

بَيْنَ تَبْذِيْرٍ وَبُخْلٍ رُتْبَةٌ

To everything which inflicts an injury however trifling there is pain (lit.)

لِكُلِّ مَا يُؤْذِيْ وَلَوْ قَلَّ أَلَمٌ

II. When the subject contains a pronoun referring to the predicate; as

The pleasure of the eye is its
beloved (lit. filling)   مِلْءُ عَيْنٍ حَبِيبُهَا

In the house is its owner   فِي ٱلدَّارِ صَاحِبُهَا

III. When the subject is restricted by إِنَّمَا or by إِلَّا with the negatives مَا and لَا.

There is no guide but God   مَا هَادٍ إِلَّا ٱللّٰهُ

Only God is forgiving   إِنَّمَا ٱلْغَافِرُ ٱللّٰهُ

IV. When it has the chief place in the sentence; as

Whose son are thou?   إِبْنُ مَنْ أَنْتَ

Where is the way?   أَيْنَ ٱلطَّرِيقُ

SUPPRESSION OF SUBJECT AND PREDICATE.

Either subject or predicate may be omitted in such sentences as

Who is with you? Zaid (is
with me)   مَنْ عِنْدَكَ زَيْدٌ (عِنْدِيْ)

How is Zaid? (Zaid) is well   كَيْفَ زَيْدٌ (زَيْدٌ) صَحِيحٌ

Also after إِذَا expressing suddenness; as

I went forth and behold!
the lion (standing)   خَرَجْتُ فَإِذَا ٱلْأَسَدُ (وَاقِفًا)

The snake, the snake, (is here)!   أَلْحَيَّةُ ٱلْحَيَّةُ (هُنَا)

A gazelle, a gazelle!   (هٰذَا) غَزَالٌ غَزَالٌ

(This is) the first chapter   (هٰذَا) ٱلْأَصْحَاحُ ٱلْأَوَّلُ

The subject must be omitted in the following places:

I. Where the qualifying adjective is used as a predicate to an omitted subject أَلنَّعْتُ ٱلْمَقْطُوعُ; as

I saw a man (he is) a generous man

رَأَيْتُ رَجُلًا (هُوَ) كَرِيْمٌ

II. After verbs of praise or blame; as

Good the man (the praised) Abdullah

نِعْمَ ٱلرَّجُلُ (أَلْمَمْدُوْحُ) عَبْدُ ٱللّٰهِ

Evil the man (the blamed) Mohammed

بِئْسَ ٱلرَّجُلُ (أَلْمَذْمُوْمُ) مُحَمَّدٌ

III. When the predicate is a noun of action taking the place of the verb; as

(My patience is) excellent patience

(صَبْرِي) صَبْرٌ جَمِيْلٌ

(His love is) a great love

(مَحَبَّتُهُ) مَحَبَّةٌ عَظِيْمَةٌ

IV. When the predicate is an oath, the subject must be omitted, and conversely when the subject is an oath, the predicate must be omitted; as

I swear by my conscience that I will do this

فِي ذِمَّتِي (يَمِيْنٌ) لَأَفْعَلَنَّ كَذَا

I swear by thy life there is no one remaining upon earth

لَعَمْرُكَ (قَسَمِي) لَيْسَ فَوْقَ ٱلْأَرْضِ بَاقٍ

The Predicate is omitted (a) after لَوْلَا when it signifies simple existence; as

Had Zaid not been present I must have perished

لَوْلَا زَيْدٌ (حَاضِرٌ) لَهَلَكْتُ

but it cannot be omitted when anything but mere existence is implied; as

Had Zaid not acted graciously

I would have perished   لَوَلَا زَيْدٌ مُحْسِنٌ لَهَلَكْتُ

(b) after , having the meaning of with; as

Every man and his work   كُلُّ رَجُلٍ وَعَمَلُهُ (مُقْتَرِنَانِ)

The Subject may have more than one predicate; as

The dog is sagacious (and) faithful   أَلْكَلْبُ نَبِيْهٌ أَمِيْنٌ

here the conjunction may be used.

The predicate may be introduced by ف when the subject is (a) a relative pronoun, (b) an indefinite noun qualified by a sentence, or (c) an adverbial or prepositional phrase; as

A man outrunning gains

the prize   رَجُلٌ يَسْبُقُ فَيَكْسِبُ ٱلْجَائِزَةَ

THE ADJECTIVE. ٱلْمُبْتَـدَأُ ٱلصّفَةُ

This is the singular adjective preceded by an interrogative or negative particle and has for its nominative a noun or a detached pronoun which forms the subject of the sentence. This noun is the agent and takes the place of the predicate; as

Are you ready?   هَلْ مُسْتَعِدٌّ أَنْتَ

here مُسْتَعِدٌّ is the adjective and أَنْتَ the pronoun in the nominative case.

158

This sentence admits of two grammatical explanations (a) مُسْتَعِدٌّ is the مُبْتَدَأُ and أَنْتَ is the agent which takes the place of the خَبَر, (b) مُسْتَعِدٌّ is the predicate and أَنْتَ is the subject with the order reversed.

When without the particle of interrogation or negation the sentence is of the first kind, as the adjective is always the predicate and the noun the subject.

if the noun is dual or plural, the adjective is the subject; as

Are the two men standing?	هَلْ قَائِمٌ ٱلرَّجُلَانِ
Are thy sons beloved?	هَلْ مَحْبُوبٌ بَنُوكَ

The صِفَة has the action of the verb, and this action is strengthened when the صِفَة is preceded by particles which are originally peculiar to verbs. The إِسْم which follows the صِفَة is therefore called the agent.

WORDS WHICH AFFECT THE SUBJECT AND PREDICATE. ٱلنَّوَاسِخُ

from نَسَخَ *to cancel.*

ٱلنَّوَاسِخُ are certain verbs and particles which precede the subject and predicate and change the declension and meaning of the latter.

The Verbs are:

ٱلْأَفْعَالُ ٱلنَّاقِصَةُ	كَانَ وَأَخَوَاتُهَا	Abstract Verbs.
أَفْعَالُ ٱلْمُقَارَبَةِ	كَادَ وَأَخَوَاتُهَا	Approximate Verbs.

ظَنَّ وَأَخَوَاتُهَا	أَفْعَالُ ٱلْقُلُوبِ Verbs denoting a Mental Process.
صَيَّرَ وَأَخَوَاتُهَا	أَفْعَالُ ٱلتَّحْوِيْلِ Verbs of Change.
أَعْلَمَ وَأَخَوَانُهَا	Verbs which take three Objects.

The Particles are:

ٱلْمُشَبَّهَاتُ بِلَيْسَ	Particles which resemble لَيْسَ
لَا ٱلنَّافِيَةُ لِلْجِنْسِ	the Absolute Negative
إِنَّ وَأَخَوَاتُهَا	إِنَّ and Sisters.

Some of these verbs take the subject and predicate as their objects, viz.

أَعْلَمَ وَأَخَوَاتُهَا   صَيَّرَ وَأَخَوَاتُهَا   ظَنَّ وَأَخَوَاتُهَا

Some take the subject as their إِسْم *noun* and the predicate as their خبر (predicate), viz.

كَانَ وَأَخَوَاتُهَا	لَا ٱلنَّافِيَةُ لِلْجِنْسِ
كَادَ وَأَخَوَاتُهَا	إِنَّ وَأَخَوَاتُهَا
ٱلْمُشَبَّهَاتُ بِلَيْسَ	

As regards government they are divided into three classes:

I. Those which put the subject in the nominative, and the predicate in the accusative, viz.

ٱلْمُشَبَّهَاتُ بِلَيْسَ   كَادَ وَأَخَوَاتُهَا   كَانَ وَأَخَوَاتُهَا

II. Those which put the إِسْم in the accusative and the predicate in the nominative, viz.

إِنَّ وَأَخَوَاتُهَا   لَا ٱلنَّافِيَةُ لِلْجِنْسِ

III. Those which put the subject and predicate in
the accusative as their objects:

ظَنَّ وَأَخَوَاتُهَا   صَيَّرَ وَأَخَوَاتُهَا   أَعْلَمَ وَأَخَوَاتِهَا

كَانَ وَأَخَوَاتُهَا

	To be	كَانَ
I. Conjugated	To become	صَارَ
throughout	To be or do something in the morning	أَصْبَحَ
and form	„ „ „ „ „ before noon	أَضْحَى
derived	„ „ „ „ „ in the day	ظَلَّ ¹)
nouns.	„ „ „ „ „ in the evening	أَمْسَى
	„ „ „ „ „ in the night	بَاتَ

To continue: —

II. Used	He did not cease	مَا زَالَ
in preterite	He did not leave off	مَا بَرِحَ
and aorist	He desisted not from	مَا انْفَكَّ
only.	He relinquished not	مَا فَتِئَ

III. Preterite	As long as	مَا دَامَ
only.	Not	لَيْسَ

---

1) These verbs are commonly used without reference to the special
times implied in their meanings; so that أَصْبَحَ أَمْسَى أَضْحَى have
the meaning of صَارَ to become; ظَلَّ بَاتَ signify a longer duration
of time.

EXAMPLES.

The earth was without form and void	كَانَتِ ٱلْأَرْضُ خَرِبَةً وَخَالِيَةً
The time became near	صَارَ ٱلْوَقْتُ قَرِيبًا
He, who overcomes, may be overcome	قَدْ يُصِيمُ ٱلْغَالِبُ مَغْلُوبًا
The horseman became a captive	أَضْحَى ٱلْفَارِسُ أَسِيرًا
The army remained in readiness	ظَلَّتِ ٱلْجُنْدُ مُسْتَعِدَّةً
My friend became distant (space)	أَمْسَى صَدِيقِي بَعِيدًا
The camel-driver has kept on driving fast	قَدْ بَاتَ ٱلْحَادِيْ يَزْجُرُهَا
The beloved one will not cease to be loved	لَا يَزَالُ ٱلْحَبِيبُ حَبِيبًا
I did not cease to live in Jerusalem	لَمْ أَبْرَحْ سَاكِنًا فِيْ أُوْرْشَلِيْمَ
He will not cease to be angry	لَا يَنْفَكُّ يَغْضَبُ
He will not cease to interfere in our affairs	مَا فَتِئَ يَتَدَاخَلُ فِيْ أُمُورِنَا
Walk in the light, as long as the light is with you	أُسْلُكُوا فِي ٱلنُّوْرِ مَا دَامَ ٱلنُّوْرُ لَكُمْ
A highwayman is not a hero	لَيْسَ مَنْ يَقْطَعُ طُرْقًا بَطَلَا

11

ٱلْأَفْعَالُ ٱلنَّاقِصَةُ are called كَادَ وَأَخَوَاتُهَا and كَانَ وَأَخَوَاتُهَا
incomplete verbs because they require more than the
subject to complete their meaning.

The conjugated forms of these verbs have the same
action as the preterite.

كَانَ only may take a verb in the preterite as predicate in which case it may be preceded by قَدْ; the
remainder require the verb to be in the aorist; as

Zaid had departed كَانَ زَيْدٌ قَدِ ٱنْطَلَقَ

The predicate may precede a verb which is conjugated throughout; but with the other verbs the order
must be preserved.

The إِسْم with the verb follows the rules of the agent
with its verb in all respects; that is, the verb takes
its إِسْم in the nominative and its خَبَر in the accusative; as

Zaid was standing كَانَ زَيْدٌ قَائِمًا

Zaid beat Amr ضَرَبَ زَيْدٌ عَمْرًا

The إِسْم with the predicate follows the same rules
as the subject and predicate ٱلْمُبْتَدَأُ وَٱلْخَبَرُ of a
nominal sentence; as

No one was standing except Zaid مَا كَانَ قَائِمًا إِلَّا زَيْدٌ

All these verbs except لَيْسَ, مَا دَامَ and مَا فَتِئَ may
be used as perfect verbs when their meaning is made
complete by the agent; as

Zaid existed كَانَ زَيْدٌ   Zaid spent the night بَاتَ زَيْدٌ

What we have done we have done قَدْ كَانَ مَا كَانَ مِنَّا

The particle of negation مَا which precedes زَالَ, بَرِحَ,

فَتِئَ, إِنْفَكَّ may be replaced by (a) لَا ٱلدُّعَـآءِ *supplication,*

(b) لَا ٱلنَّهْي *prohibition* or (c) ٱلاِسْتِفْهَامُ ٱلاِنْكَارِيُّ:

(a). May you ever be blessed لَا زِلْتَ مُبَارَكًا

(b). Do not cease to be patient لَا تَزَلْ صَابِرًا

(c). Will the lad continue ignorant هَلْ يَبْرَحُ ٱلْغُلَامُ جَاهِلًا

Any particle, verb, or noun having the meaning of
the negative may be substituted for مَا; as

Zaid does not cease to be generous زَيْدٌ غَيْرُ زَائِلٍ كَرِيمًا

The judge does not cease to judge لَيْسَ يَنْفَكَّ ٱلْقَاضِي يَقْضِي

The مَا which precedes دَامَ is the مَصْدَرِيَّة زَمَنِيَّة.

I will not accompany you

as long as I live لَا أُصَحِبُكَ مَا دُمْتُ حَيًّا

Note: There are other verbs which are incomplete
with a subject alone; the are made to follow كَانَ; as

To go in the morning غَدَا   To go in the evening رَاحَ

To return عَادَ, رَجَعَ, إِرْتَدَّ   To become آضَ

Zaid returned disappointed عَادَ زَيْدٌ خَائِبًا

Like مَا زَالَ are مَا رَامَ and مَا وَنَى.

After the conditional particles إِنْ and لَـوْ, كَـانَ and

its إِسْم may be omitted; as

The witness, if he is alone, is

as nothing ٱلْشَّاهِدُ إِنْ فَـرْدًا عَدَمٌ

Seek, even though it be

a ring of iron التَمِسْ وَلَوْ خَاتَمًا مِنْ حَدِيْدٍ

The apocopated form of كَانَ when occurring in the middle of a sentence and not joined to a pronoun may drop the ن; as

Be not afraid لَا تَكُ خَائِفًا

APPROXIMATE VERBS. أَفْعَالُ ٱلْمُقَارِبَةِ

1 and 2 may have an aorist. To be on the point of being or doing		كَادَ
		أَوْشَكَ
Express approximation	لِلْمُقَارِبَةِ	كَرِبَ
		عَسَى
Express hope or desire	لِلرَّجَاءِ	
		إِخْلَوْلَقَ
		شَرَعَ
		أَنْشَأَ
		جَعَلَ
		إِنْبَرَى
		طَفِقَ
Express beginning	أَفْعَالُ ٱلشُّرُوعِ	أَخَذَ
		قَامَ
		إِبْتَدَأَ
		عَلِقَ
		هَبَّ

These are called approximate verbs because they begin with كَادَ *about to be or do.*

EXAMPLES.

His breathing was about to cease

كَادَت أَنْفَاسُهُ أَنْ تَنْقَطِعَ

The crops were about to dry up

أَوْشَكَتِ ٱلزُّرُوعُ أَنْ تَيْبَسَ

The heart was about to melt with longing

كَرِبَ ٱلْقَلْبُ يَذُوبُ شَوْقًا

May God relieve our difficulties

عَسَى ٱللّٰهُ أَنْ يَفْرِجَ كُرُوبَنَا

The heavens appeared as though they would rain

إِخْلَوْلَقَتِ ٱلسَّمَاءُ أَنْ تُمْطِرَ

The wise man began to relate his story

شَرَعَ ٱلْعَالِمُ يَقُصُّ قِصَّتَهُ

Zaid began to read

أَنْشَأَ زَيْدٌ يَقْرَأُ

The poet began to recite

جَعَلَ ٱلشَّاعِرُ يُنْشِدُ

The runner began to run

إِنْبَرَى ٱلسَّاعِي يَجْرِي

The preacher began to preach

طَفِقَ ٱلْوَاعِظُ يَعِظُ

The men began to question one another

أَخَذَ ٱلنَّاسُ يَنَسَآءَلُونَ

The bird began to sing

قَامَ ٱلطَّيْرُ يُغَرِّدُ

My friend began to expect me

إِبْتَدَأَ صَدِيقِي يَنْتَظِرُنِي

The traveller began to go about the country

عَلِقَ ٱلسَّائِحُ يَجُولُ ٱلْبِلَادَ

The merchant began to offer his goods for sale

هَبَّ ٱلتَّاجِرُ يَعْرِضُ بَضَائِعَهُ

Al these verbs govern in the same way as كَانَ; i. e. they take an إِسْم in the nominative and a predicate in the accusative. كَادَ and أَوْشَكَ may have an aorist and at times a noun of agent; the remainder are not conjugated. إِخْلَوْلَقَ, أَوْشَكَ, عَسَى, كَادَ may take أَنْ before the predicate. The predicate of all these verbs must be in the aorist having as its agent a pronoun referring to the إِسْم.

إِخْلَوْلَقَ, أَوْشَكَ, عَسَى are sometimes treated as perfect verbs and take for their agent the noun of action composed of أَنْ and the verb following it; as

عَسَى زِيَارَتُكَ = عَسَى أَنْ تَزُورَنَا   I hope you will visit us

إِخْلَوْلَقَ نُزُولُهُ = أَلْمَطَرُ إِخْلَوْلَقَ أَنْ يَنْزِلَ   Rain was about to fall

Sometimes عَسَى takes as its nominative the pronoun in the accusative case; as

عَسَاكَ أَنْ تَأْتِي   May you come

The كَ is in the place of تَ in عَسَيْتَ.

The predicate may precede the إِسْم; as

كَادَ يَمُوتُ زَيْدٌ   Zaid almost died

PARTICLES WHICH RESEMBLE. لَيْسَ

مَا. لَا. إِنْ. لَاتَ

The particle مَا governs as لَيْسَ when the negation and order are preserved; as

مَا زَيْدٌ قَائِمًا   Zaid is not standing

but if we say

No one but Zaid is standing   مَا قَائِمٌ إِلَّا زَيْدٌ

or Zaid is only standing   مَا زَيْدٌ إِلَّا قَائِمٌ

or Zaid is not standing   مَا قَائِمٌ زَيْدٌ

the مَا does not govern because the first example is a positive assertion, and in the second and third the order is reversed.

لَا governs as لَيْسَ and follows the rules of مَا except that its subject and predicate must be indefinite; as

There is not a man present alone   لَا رَجُلَ حَاضِرًا

This negatives the individual only; so that the sentence may mean that there are two or more men present; it is therefore called ٱلنَّافِيَةُ لِلْوَحْدَة.

When مَا and لَا have the same government as لَيْسَ they are called ٱلْحِجَازِيَّتَيْنِ.

إِنْ governs as لَيْسَ and follows the rules of مَا.

I am not standing   إِنْ أَنَا قَائِمًا

A man is not dead by the mere ending of his natural life   إِنِ ٱلْمَرْءُ مَيْتًا بِٱنْتِهَاءِ حَيُوتِهِ

لَاتَ governs as لَيْسَ when its predicate is a noun of time and its إِسْم is not mentioned; as

It is not the time for study   لَاتَ (ٱلْوَقْتُ) وَقْتَ دَرْسٍ

لَاتَ takes the same word for its إِسْم as the predicate; so that the word mentioned indicates what is omitted.

PARTICLES WHICH RESEMBLE VERBS.

اَلْحُرُوفُ ٱلْمُشَبَّهَةُ بِٱلْاَفْعَالِ

إِنَّ أَنَّ *certainly, surely, verily*; express assurance.

كَأَنَّ *like, as if*; has the meaning of resemblance when the predicate is a primitive noun, but of doubt when the predicate is a derived noun.

لَكِنَّ *but, yet, nevertheless*; is used to correct the opinion formed from the previous sentence.

لَيْتَ *would that*; expresses a wish for what is impossible or difficult of attainment.

لَعَلَّ *perhaps, per chance, if haply*; expresses expectation. These particles resemble verbs in having (*a*) at least three letters, (*b*) ـَ on their final letter, (*c*) the meaning and government of verbs; but in order to distinguish them from verbs their government is reversed.

Surely God is forgiving, merciful إِنَّ ٱللَّهَ لَغَفُورٌ رَحِيمٌ

here the subject has ـَ instead of ـُ

Verily the time is nigh إِنَّ ٱلْوَقْتَ قَرِيبٌ

I knew that study would increase knowledge عَلِمْت أَنَّ ٱلْمُطَالَعَةَ تَزِيْدُ ٱلْمَعْرِفَةَ

As if Zaid were a lion كَأَنَّ زَيْدًا أَسَدٌ

Amr is rich but he is a miser عَمْرٌو غَنِيٌّ لَكِنَّهُ بَخِيْلٌ

I wish that youth would
return   لَيْتَ ٱلشَّبَابَ يَعُوْدُ

Fear God, if haply ye
may find mercy   إِتَّقُواْ ٱللَّهَ لَعَلَّكُمْ تُرْحَمُوْنَ

The particles إِنَّ and أَنَّ are really the same.

They are written with ـ when governed; as

Amr informed me that
Zaid is dead   أَخْبَرَنِـي عَمْرٌو أَنَّ زَيْدًا مَيِّتٌ

إِنَّ is found in the following places:

I. The beginning of a sentence.

II. After a relative pronoun.

III. Introducing an answer to an oath having لَ prefixed to the predicate.

IV. Introducing a statement following قَالَ and its
derivatives; as

He said that he was ready   قَالَ إِنَّهُ مُسْتَعِدٌّ

V. Beginning a جُمْلَةٌ حَالِيَّةٌ a sentence expressing
state or condition; as

I visited him, and am
assured of his generosity   زُرْتُهُ وَإِنِّي مُتَيَقِّنٌ بِكَرَمِهِ

VI. After ظَنَّ وَأَخَوَاتُهَا when their predicate is preceded by لَ.

I knew that Zaid was
really standing   عَلِمْتُ إِنَّ زَيْدًا لَقَائِمٌ

VII. After أَلَا.

Am I not a traveller?   أَلَا إِنَّنِي سَائِمٌ

VIII. After حَيْثُ.

I sat where Zaid was sitting جَلَسْتُ حَيْثُ إِنَّ زَيْدًا جَالِسٌ

IX. Beginning a sentence which is predicate to a concrete noun; as

Zaid surely is a generous man زَيْدٌ إِنَّهُ كَرِيمٌ

In the following places إِنَّ or أَنَّ may be used:

I. After إِذَا expressing suddenness; as

I wenth forth and, behold!

the tiger was standing خَرَجْتُ وَإِذَا أَنَّ ٱلنَّمِرَ وَاقِفٌ

II. Where it begins the answer to an oath whose predicate is not introduced by لَ; as

I swore that I would go حَلَفْتُ إِنِّي أَذْهَبُ

III. After ف of reward فَاءُ ٱلجَزَاءِ; as

Who comes to me will

have honour مَنْ يَأْتِ إِلَيَّ فَإِنَّ لَهُ ٱلكَرَامَةَ

IV. After a subject which is a common saying; as

The best saying, God is one خَيْرُ ٱلقَوْلِ أَنَّ ٱللَّهَ وَاحِدٌ

أَنَّ and its sentence must be convertible into a noun of action in construction with its إِسْم; as

Your faithfulness pleases me يُعْجِبُنِي أَنَّكَ صَادِقٌ = صِدْقُكَ

إِنَّ may take the لَ before its predicate when it has its true position in the sentence and also before the subject مُبْتَدَأ when the order is reversed; as

Surely Zaid is standing إِنَّ زَيْدًا لَقَائِمٌ

مَا may be affixed to these particles, in which case

with the exception of لَيْتَ they cease to govern; as

Zaid only is standing اِنَّمَا زَيْدٌ قَائِمٌ

With these particles the predicate may precede the
subject when the former is an adverbial or prepositional phrase; as

Would that I had a friend لَيْتَ لِي صَدِيْقًا

When a second noun occurring after the predicate
is joined by a conjunction to the اِسْم of اِنَّ or أَنَّ, لَكِنَّ
it may take either the nominative or accusative case;
as اِنَّ زَيْدًا قَائِمٌ وَعَمْرًا or عَمْرٌو.

THE ABSOLUTE NEGATIVE. لَا ٱلنَّافِيَةُ لِلْجِنْسِ

The Negative Particle لَا denies the existence of a
thing absolutely; as

There is no man good لَا رَجُلَ صَالِحٌ

It governs in the same manner as اِنَّ taking an اِسْم
in the accusative and a predicate in the nominative;
both the اِسْم and predicate must be indefinite and the
لَا introduce the اِسْم.

The اِسْم is either (a) in construction, (b) governing
another word, (c) followed by a preposition or adverb
which completes its meaning, or (d) a single word
مُفْرَد. In the first three cases لَا governs like اِنَّ, in
the last, the اِسْم is indeclinable and takes the sign of
the accusative which it had when declinable; as

(*a*). I have not a lead pencil لَا قَلَمَ رَصَاصٍ عِنْدِي

(*b*). There is no climber of
the mountain in the way لَا صَاعِدًا جَبَلًا فِي ٱلطَّرِيقِ

Here صَاعِدًا governs جَبَلًا.

(*c*). There is no man upon
the house top sleeping لَا رَجُلًا فَوْقَ ٱلسَّطْحِ نَائِمٌ

(*d*). There is no infidel who
shall enter heaven لَا كَافِرَ يَدْخُلُ ٱلجَنَّةَ

The reg. fem. plural may take the ـِ or ـُ. *or* ـَ

There are no female believers
in the town لَا مُؤْمِنَاتِ فِي ٱلْمَدِيْنَةِ

or لَا مُؤْمِنَاتٍ

If the لَا is repeated and its conditions are observed
we may have any of the following five forms:

I. There is no power and strength save in God لَا حَوْلَ وَلَا قُوَّةٍ إِلَّا بِٱللهِ

II.   ,, ,, ,,   ,,   ,,   ,,   ,, ,, ,, لَا حَوْلٌ وَلَا قُوَّةٌ إِلَّا بِٱللهِ

III. ,, ,, ,,   ,,   ,,   ,,   ,, ,, ,, لَا حَوْلَ وَلَا قُوَّةٌ إِلَّا بِٱللهِ

IV. ,, ,, ,,   ,,   ,,   ,,   ,, ,, ,, لَا حَوْلُ وَلَا قُوَّةٌ إِلَّا بِٱللهِ

V. ,, ,, ,,   ,,   ,,   ,,   ,, ,, ,, لَا حَوْلَ وَلَا قُوَّةً إِلَّا بِٱللهِ

In the first example each negative is regarded as
introducing a separate sentence; in the second the
repetition of the negative is regarded as preventing its
characteristic action; in the third the first negative
governs and the second is regarded as joined to the
sentence composed of لَا with its إِسْم and خَبَر which

is virtually in the nom. case. In the fourth example
the first لَا is regarded as not governing because of
repetition; the second governs because it is regarded
as introducing a new sentence. The fifth example is
seldom used.

If the noun is (*a*) separated from لَا or if it is (*b*)
definite, the لَا ceases to govern and must be repeated; as

(*a*). There is not a man and
not a woman in the house   لَا فِي ٱلدَّارِ رَجُلٌ وَلَا ٱمْرَأَةٌ

(*b*). Neither Zaid nor Amr
is with us   لَا زَيْدٌ عِنْدَنَا وَلَا عَمْرٌو

The predicate of لَا may be omitted; as

No harm لَا بَأْسَ   Zaid (came) not another جَاءَ زَيْدٌ لَا غَيْرَ

The adjective qualifying the إِسْم may take the ـَ,
ـُ or ـٌ when the إِسْم and adjective are مُفْرَدَاتٌ individual words not separated from one another. Otherwise it takes ـٌ or ـَ.

The Hemzeh of Interrogation may be prefixed to لَا
without affecting its government.

ظَنَّ وَأَخَوَاتُهَا

VERBS DENOTING A MENTAL PROCESS

أَفْعَالُ ٱلْقُلُوبِ

	To see	رَأَى
	To know	عَلِمَ
	To find	أَلْفَى
These express Certainty	To know	دَرَى
	To find	وَجَدَ
	Learn	تَعَلَّمَ
	To think	ظَنَّ
	To reckon	جَعَلَ
	To suppose	زَعَمَ
	To reckon	عَدَّ
These express Doubt	To suppose	حَجَى حَجَا
	To reckon	حَسِبَ
	To imagine	خَالَ
	Grant	هَبْ

EXAMPLES.

I see (that) men are
heedless
  أَرَى ٱلنَّاسَ غَـافِلِيْنَ

  Know (that) love is the
greatest virtue
  إِعْلَمِ ٱلْمَحَبَّةَ أَفْضَلَ ٱلْفَضَائِلِ

Zaid found Amr generous	أَلْفَى زَيْدٌ عَمْرًا كَرِيْمًا
Do you know who is with us?	أَتَدْرِي مَن عِنْدَنَا
I find a friend is needful	أَجِدُ ٱلصَّدِيْقَ لَازِمًا
Learn (that) men are different	تَعَلَّمِ ٱلنَّاسَ أَنْوَاعًا
I thought the thief was a guest	ظَنَنْتُ ٱلسَّارِقَ ضَيْفًا
You have made the night as day	جَعَلْتَ ٱللَّيْلَ نَهَارًا
Do you suppose (that) Zaid loves you	أَتَزْعَمُ زَيْدًا يُحِبُّكَ
Men count knowledge the most profitable of things	عَدَّ ٱلنَّاسُ ٱلْعِلْمَ أَنْفَعَ ٱلْأُمُورِ
Do you reckon (that) the pupils are in the school?	أَتَحْسِبُ ٱلتَّلَامِيْذَ فِي ٱلْمَدْرَسَةِ
Do not imagine (that) Zaid is your friend	لَا تَخَلْ زَيْدًا صَدِيْقَكَ
Grant that you are absent	هَبْ أَنَّكَ غَائِبٌ

When these verbs precede the subject and predicate they take them as their objects; but when they come between they may or may not have their special government. If however they follow their objects they govern.

Some of them are conjugated throughout; others are defective or not conjugated at all.

تَعَلَّمْ and هَبْ are only used in the imperative.

رَأَى to see (by dreams) follows these verbs in taking a double accusative, and also قَالَ to say when it means to think, but only when in the second person aorist, and immediately following an interrogative particle; as

Do you say that rain in the summer is harmful? أَتَقُولُ ٱلْمَطَرَ فِي ٱلصَّيْفِ مُضِرًّا

If the particles لَا إِنْ مَا of negation, ل، جَوَابُ ٱلْقَسَمِ, لَوْ ل, of condition, كَمِ ٱلْخَبَرِيَّةُ and particles of ٱلِٱبْتِدَاء interrogation come between one of these verbs and its objects, the verb does not govern, as these particles are regarded as having the chief function in the sentence.

These verbs are reflexive; the agent and the object may be two personal pronouns referring to the same person; as

I see myself ill أَرَانِي مَرِيْضًا

Either one or both objects may be omitted when the meaning is known; as

Do you think that Zaid is standing أَتَظُنُّ زَيْدًا قَائِمًا

I think that (Zaid is standing) أَظُنُّ

صَيَّرَ وَأَخَوَانُهَا

VERBS DENOTING CHANGE.

أَفْعَالُ ٱلتَّحْوِيْلِ

To leave	غَادَرَ	To make	صَيَّرَ
,, ,,	تَرَكَ	,, ,, and reckon	جَعَلَ
To make, give	وَهَبَ	To take as	تَخَذَ
To change into	رَدَّ	,, ,, ,,	إِتَّخَذَ

These verbs are all conjugated except وَهَبَ.

They govern like ظَنَّ i. e. they take the subject and predicate as their objects, and exert their characteristic action independently of their position in the sentence.

EXAMPLES.

I made the clay into earth-enware	صَيَّرْتُ ٱلطِّيْنَ خَزَفًا
Zaid made the branch into a bow	جَعَلَ زَيْدٌ ٱلغُصْنَ قَوْسًا
I took him as a friend	تَخَذْتُهُ صَدِيْقًا
I used the stick as a crutch	إِتَّخَذْتُ ٱلعَصَا عُكَّازًا
I left him sick	غَادَرْتُهُ مَرِيْضًا
I left him standing	تَرَكْتُهُ قَائِمًا
May I be your ransom	وَهَبَنِي فِدَاكَ
It changed the heat into cold	رَدَّ ٱلحَرَّ بَرْدًا

VERBS WHICH TAKE THREE OBJECTS.

أَعْلَمَ وَأَخَوَاتِهَا

To inform	أَخْبَرَ	To make to know	أَعْلَمَ
„ „	خَبَّرَ	To make to see (mentally)	أَرَى (أُرْأَى)
To relate	حَدَّثَ	To inform beforehand	أَنْبَأَ
		„ „ „	نَبَّأَ

أَرَى and أَعْلَمَ are conjugated throughout; the remaining five are mostly used in the passive voice. Particles may be introduced before the second and third objects; as

I was informed that the
physician was not present   أُنْبِئْتُ مَا ٱلطَّبِيبُ حَاضِرٌ

The first object is the نَائِبُ ٱلْفَاعِلِ and the sentence which follows the particle is in the accusative عِوَضٌ ٱلْمَفْعُولَيْنِ (instead of the two objects).

If we say:

I knew that Zaid was coming   عَلِمْتُ أَنَّ زَيْدًا قَادِمٌ

or, I shewed him that the rain
was beneficial   أَرَيْتُهُ أَنَّ ٱلْمَطَرَ مُفِيدٌ

أَنَّ with its إِسْم and predicate takes the place of the two objects in the first example, and that of the second and third objects in the second, so that they are thus virtually in the accusative فِي مَحَلِّ نَصْبٍ.

EXAMPLES.

I made him know that knowledge is profitable	أَعْلَمْتُهُ ٱلْعِلْمَ نَافِعًا
God caused men to see that Job was patient	أَرَاى ٱللّٰهُ ٱلنَّاسَ أَيُّوبَ صَابِرًا
The children of Israel were foretold that Christ would come	أُنْبِئَ بَنُو إِسْرَائِيلَ ٱلْمَسِيحَ قَادِمًا
I was informed that my friend was absent	نُبِّئْتُ صَدِيقِي غَائِبًا
I informed him that my love is great	أَخْبَرْتُهُ مَحَبَّتِي عَظِيمَةً
The men were informed that the locusts were distant	خُبِّرَ ٱلنَّاسُ ٱلْجَرَادَ بَعِيدًا
Amr informed his brother that he is sick	حَدَّثَ عَمْرُو أَخَاهُ أَنَّهُ مَرِيضٌ

THE ACCUSATIVE CASE. ٱلنَّصْبُ

The following take the accusative case ٱلْمَنْصُوبَاتُ

I. The Absolute Object ٱلْمَفْعُولُ ٱلْمُطْلَقُ

II. The Objective Complement ٱلْمَفْعُولُ بِهِ

III. The Vocative ٱلْمُنَادَى

IV. The Adverbial Accusative of Time and Place ٱلْمَفْعُولُ فِيهِ

V. The Adverbial Accusative of Cause or
  Reason   اَلْمَفْعُولُ لَهُ

VI. The Object following و of Association   اَلْمَفْعُولُ مَعَهُ

VII. That which is Excepted   اَلْمُسْتَثْنَى

VIII. The Adverbial Accusative of State or
   Condition   اَلْحَالُ

IX. The Specification   اَلتَّمْيِيزُ

X. The Predicate of   خَبَرُ كَانَ وَكَادَ وَآلْمُشَبَّهَاتِ بِلَيْسَ

XI. The Subject of   إِسْمُ أَنَّ وَلَا آلنَّا فِيَةٍ لِلجِنْسِ

XII. The Aorist when preceded by the
   Accusative Particles   نَوَاصِبُ آلفِعْلِ

XIII. The Appositives or words in
   Apposition to Accusatives   تَوَابِعُ آلْمَنْصُوبَات

These are called فَضَلَاتٌ and are used either objec-
tively or adverbially.

The transitive verb governs its object in the accusative case. When, however, the object follows a preposition connecting it with the verb, the presence of
the preposition puts the object in the genitive.

THE ABSOLUTE OBJECT. اَلْمَفْعُولُ آلْمُطْلَقُ

The Absolute Object is so called because it has not
a preposition attached to its name, limiting or defining
its action, like the other مَفَاعِيْل.

It expresses simple action of the verb, and is originally the noun of action of the same verb; as

He surely killed قَتَلَ قَتْلًا   He surely beat ضَرَبَ ضَرْبًا

I greatly approved it   إِسْتَحْسَنْتُهُ آسْتِحْسَانًا عَظِيمًا

This noun of action must follow:

(*a*). A strong verb, not such as نِعْمَ ,مَاأَحْسَنَ ,كَانَ ,كَادَ

(*b*). Another noun of action, or (*c*) an adjective expressing accidental qualities; as

(*a*). I loved him with a great love أَحْبَبْتُهُ حُبًّا عَظِيمًا

(*b*). I wondered at thy

striking Zaid severely عَجِبْتُ مِنْ ضَرْبِكَ زَيْدًا ضَرْبًا شَدِيدًا

(*c*). Zaid is very accomplished زَيْدٌ فَاضِلٌ فَضْلًا

THE ABSOLUTE OBJECT IS OF TWO KINDS:

(I). أَلْمُؤَكِّدُ *that which assures*, is the noun of action of the same verb and simply strengthens its meaning thereby removing the idea of metaphor. This noun of action is always in the singular; as

I assuredly killed him قَتَلْتُهُ قَتْلًا

(II). أَلْمُبَيِّنُ *that which makes manifest*. This noun of action gives more meaning than the verb itself, and is used to express number and form; it may be made dual or plural; as

He ran swiftly رَكَضَ رَكْضًا سَرِيعًا   I squatted تَقَعَّدْتُ ٱلْقُرْفُصَاءِ

I took two steps خَطَوْتُ خَطْوَتَيْنِ   I sat upright جَلَسْتُ جُلُوسًا مُسْتَقِيمًا

The Absolute Object is originally the noun of action

of the same verb; but the following may take its place
نُوَّابُ ٱلْمَفْعُولِ ٱلْمُطْلَقِ.

1. The noun of action of another verb having a
similar meaning; as

I rejoiced greatly ⁧فَرِحْتُ ٱبْتِهَاجًا⁩

2. The noun of action of the same verb but on a
different measure; as

I washed myself ⁧تَغَسَّلْتُ ٱغْتِسَالًا⁩

3. ⁧إِسْمُ ٱلْمَصْدَرِ⁩ which has the signification of the noun
of action; as

I prayed ⁧صَلَّيْتُ صَلَاةً⁩

4. ⁧كُلٌّ وَبَعْضٌ⁩ when in construction with a noun of
action; as

I loved him greatly ⁧أَحْبَبْتُهُ كُلَّ ٱلْمَحَبَّةِ⁩

5. A demonstrative pronoun; as

I read that sort of reading ⁧قَرَأْتُ تِلْكَ ٱلْقِرَاءةِ⁩

6. An adjective; as

I ran with all my might ⁧رَكَضْتُ أَشَدَّ ٱلرَّكْضِ⁩

7. Number; as

I struck him three blows ⁧ضَرَبْتُهُ ثَلَاثَ ضَرَبَاتٍ⁩

8. Form; as

I sat in a squatting posture ⁧تَعَدْتُ ٱلْقُرْفُصَاء⁩

9. Instrument; as

I beat him with a whip ⁧ضَرَبْتُهُ سَوْطًا⁩

10. The pronoun of a noun of action; as

I loved him with such
love as I did not love others أَحْبَبْتُهُ مَحَبَّةً لَمْ أُحِبَّهَا غَيْرَهُ

11. مَا and أَيُّ which imply interrogation; as

Speak what you wish مَا شِئْتَ تَـكَـلَّمْ

The verb is necessarily implied when the noun of
action takes its place; as

(Go) slowly (أَمْهِلْ) مَهْلًا

I heard and I obeyed سَمِعْتُ سَمْعًا, أَطَعْتُ طَاعَةً, سَمْعًا وَطَاعَةً

THE OBJECTIVE COMPLEMENT. أَلْمَفْعُولُ بِهِ

The Objective Complement receives the action of the
verb. The verb must therefore be transitive and in this
respect differs from the other مَفَاعِيل whose verbs may
be either transitive or intransitive. If the verb is not
originally transitive it is made so by a preposition; as

I rode the mare رَكِبْتُ ٱلْفَرَسَ

I sat in a chair جَلَسْتُ عَلَى كُرْسِيٍّ

I clothed him with a beautiful garment أَلْبَسْتُهُ ثَوْبًا جَمِيلًا

I informed him that you were present أَخْبَرْتُهُ أَنَّكَ حَاضِرٌ

I brought a book أَتَيْتُ بِكِتَابٍ

THE VOCATIVE. أَلْمُنَادَى

The object addressed أَلْمُنَادَى is a part of the objective complement.

The vocative particles take the place of the implied verb to call نَادَى, أُنَادِي *I call*.

If the noun addressed is definite مَعْرِفَة and single مُفْرَد it becomes indeclinable, and takes the sign of the nominative, but when neither definite nor single it is put in the accusative; as

يَا مُحَمَّدُ O Mohammed!   يَا رَجُلاً O Man!

When the noun addressed is in construction with أَلْمُتَكَلِّمِ ي and does not end with a weak letter, the ي may be changed into ا; as

O my brother!   يَا أَخَا for يَا أَخِي

In أَبْ and أُمّ the ي may be changed into تِ; as

O my father يَا أَبَتِ   O my mother يَا أُمَّتِ

If the word إِبْن follows the vocative the noun addressed takes the ◌َ in place of the ◌ُ; as يَا زَيْدَ بْنَ عَمْرٍو

O Zaid son of Amr.

If the noun addressed has the article, the word أَيُّ or أَيَّة with هَا ٱلتَّنْبِيه, is introduced between the particle and the noun; in this case the noun takes the ◌ُ.

If the noun is a derived one it is regarded as an adjective and if primitive it is بَدَل; as

O you generous one   يَا أَيُّهَا ٱلْكَرِيْمُ

O Man   يَا أَيُّهَا ٱلرَّجُلُ

Sometimes the noun addressed follows the demonstrative pronoun instead of أَيُّهَا; as

O (you) this man يَا هٰذَا ٱلرَّجُلَ

The word God although possessing the article may be addressed, as يَا ٱللّٰهُ O God! also يَا ٱللّٰهُمَّ or أَللّٰهُمَّ.

The vocative particle or the noun addressed may be omitted; as

(O) Joseph hear my saying يُوسُفُ ٱسْمَعْ قَوْلِي

O (people) worship يَا ٱسْجُدُوا

The Vocative Particles are:

أ for a near object.

آ, أَيْ, هيَا, أَيَا for a distant object.

يَا for both near and distant objects.

THE ADVERBIAL ACCUSATIVE OF TIME AND PLACE.

ٱلْمَفْعُولُ فِيهِ

This expresses the time and place of the action of the verb, and is so called because the nouns have the meaning of فِي in; as

I prayed (in) to day صَلَّيْتُ (فِي) ٱليَوْمَ

I sat aside جَلَسْتُ (فِي) نَاحِيَةً

The noun of time whether definite or indefinite is put in the accusative; as

I came yesterday جِئْتُ ٱلْبَارِحَةَ

I travelled for a time سَافَرْتُ مُدَّةً

The noun of place when indefinite is put in the accusative; as

I looked east and west,
north and south   تَطَلَّعْتُ شَرْقًا وَغَرْبًا شِمَالًا وَجَنُوْبًا

When the noun of place is definite the preposition فِي is introduced; as

I prayed in the mosque   صَلَّيْتُ فِي ٱلْمَسْجِدِ

The place of the adverb may be taken by (*a*) the noun of action, (*b*) demonstrative pronoun, (*c*) adjective, (*d*) numeral, (*e*) بَعْضٌ and كُلٌّ; as

(*a*). I awoke at sunrise (time of)   إِسْتَيْقَظْتُ طُلُوعَ ٱلشَّمْسِ

I sat near the table   جَلَسْتُ قُرْبَ ٱلْمَائِدَةِ

(*b*). I ran there   رَكَضْتُ هُنَاكَ

(*c*). I fasted a little   صُمْتُ قَلِيْلًا

(*d*). I journeyed three days   سَافَرْتُ ثَلَثَةَ أَيَّامٍ

(*e*). I watched the whole night
or (part of it)   سَهِرْتُ كُلَّ ٱللَّيْلِ (بَعْضَهُ)

The adverb is of two kinds:

I. مُتَصَرِّفٌ which may have different functions in a sentence, as the word يَوْم in the following sentences.

To-day is Friday   ٱلْيَوْمُ ٱلْجُمَعَةُ   I rode to-day   رَكِبْتُ ٱلْيَوْمَ

II. غير مُتَصَرِّفٍ which is always an adverb; as

In front of	أَمَامُ	Where	حَيْثُ
Behind	خَلْفُ	At	عِنْدَ
After	بَعْدُ	Before	قَبْلُ
Where	أَيْنَ	Above	فَوْقُ

These adverbs may take the preposition مِنْ before

them, with the exception of مَتَى which takes both إِلَى
and حَتَّى, and اَيْنَ and حَيْثُ which take إِلَى; as

Until when will you not return? إِلَى مَتَى لَا تَرْجِعُ

How long, O Lord, how long? حَتَّى مَتَى يَا رَبُّ حَتَّى مَتَى

Whither are you going? إِلَى آيْنَ أَنْتَ ذَاهِبٌ

He went wherever he wished ذَهَبَ إِلَى حَيْثُ شَاءَ

The following adverbs are always indeclinable:

Yesterday	أَمْسِ	When	مَتَى	When	لَمَّا
Where	أَيْنَ	When	إِذَا	Here	هُنَا
Where	حَيْثُ	When	إِنْ	With	مَعَ
There	هُنَاكَ	There	هُنَالِكَ	Where	أَيَّانَ
Now	أَلْآنَ	Where	أَنَّى	At all, never	قَطُّ

Some adverbs become indeclinable when in construction
with a sentence beginning with a verb in the preterite; as

He came when Zaid came جَاءَ حِيْنَ جَاءَ زَيْدٌ

THE ADVERBIAL ACCUSATIVE OF CAUSE
OR REASON. أَلْمَفْعُوْلُ لَهُ

This expresses the cause of the action. It must be
a noun of action but not of the same verb, and agree
with the verb in respect to agent and time, and also
be indefinite; as

I fled from fright هَرَبْتُ خَوْفًا

I visited him from love   زُرْتُهُ حُبًّا

here خَـوْف expresses the cause of flight; it is a noun of action although not of the same verb, and agrees with the verb to flee as to its agent, because the one who fled is the one who feared; it is also indefinite. If any of these conditions are not fulfilled, the noun of action must be introduced by one of the particles of causation; as

I fled on account of fear   هَرَبْتُ لِلْخَوْفِ

I went to him for water   قَصَدْتُهُ لِلْمَآءِ

I visited you to-day for your
honouring me yesterday   زُرْتُكَ ٱلْيَوْمَ لِإِكْرَامِكَ لِي ٱلْبَارِحَةَ

The Particles of Causation are مِنْ فِي بِ لِ.

Sometimes ٱلْمَفْعُولُ لَهُ is itself the cause of the action and must then be a noun of action of a verb denoting a mental process; as

The Messiah died from love to us   مَاتَ ٱلْمَسِيْحُ حُبًّا لَنَا

At other times the verb is the cause of the action and then ٱلْمَفْعُول لَهُ may be the noun of action of any verb; as

I beat him to correct him   ضَرَبْتُهُ تَأْدِيْبًا لَهُ

If the مَفْعُوْل لَهُ is made definite by the article, it may be put in the accusative; as

I fled from fear   هَرَبْتُ ٱلْخَوْفَ

Also if in construction it may be put in the accusative; as

I fled fearing slaughter هَرَبْتُ خَوْفَ ٱلْقَتْلِ

but it is better to use the preposition.

THE OBJECT IN RELATION TO WHICH SOMETHING IS DONE. ٱلْمَفْعُولُ مَعَهُ

This object follows و having the meaning of *with*.

The و is called وَاوُ ٱلْمَعِيَّةِ or وَاوُ ٱلْمُصَاحَبَةِ the و *of association.*

The و must not have the meaning of the conjunction; as

I travelled in the morning سَافَرْتُ وَٱلصَّبْحَ

Zaid went along the road مَشَى زَيْدٌ وَٱلطَّرِيْقَ

Here the و cannot be the conjunction because it does not join the word صُبْح to the pronoun, as the noun cannot be joined to an attached pronoun except the latter be repeated; as

I came, together with Zaid جِئْتُ أَنَا وَزَيْدًا

The مَفْعُول مَعَهُ is also found after كَيْفَ and مَا of interrogation; as

How art thou, together with Zaid كَيْفَ أَنْتَ وَزَيْدًا

What has thou to do with thy brother? مَا لَكَ وَأَخَاكَ

THAT WHICH IS EXCEPTED. ٱلْمُسْتَثْنَى

The particles of exception are إِلَّا غَيْرِ سِوَى عَدَا خَلَا حَاشَا

That which is excepted is either (*a*) of the same kind as the noun preceding, and is called مُتَّصِل *joined*, or

(b) of a different kind and called مُنْقَطِعْ *severed from, cut off*; as

(a). The people came except Zaid جَاءَ ٱلْقَوْمُ إِلَّا زَيْدًا

(b). The army returned except

a cannon رَجَعَ ٱلْجَيْشُ إِلَّا مَدْفَعًا

ٱلْمُسْتَثْنَى بِـإِلَّا

When the preceding sentence is affirmative and complete in meaning, that which is excepted is put in the accusative; as

The trees yielded fruit except

a fig-tree أَثْمَرَتِ ٱلشَّجَرُ إِلَّا تِينَةً

When the preceding sentence is negative and complete in meaning, that which is excepted may be put in the accusative or be made بَدَل and take the case of the preceding word; as

I fear no one except God لَا أَخَافُ أَحَدًا إِلَّا ٱللَّهَ

No one came except Zaid مَا جَاءَ أَحَدٌ إِلَّا زَيْدًا أَوْ زَيْدٌ

When the part excepted precedes the whole or is of a different kind it is put in the accusative; as

No one came except Zaid مَاجَاءَ إِلَّا زَيْدًا أَحَدٌ

No one returned from

the army except a horse مَا رَجَعَ مِنَ ٱلْجَيْشِ إِلَّا حِصَانًا

When the sentence is negative and incomplete, that which is excepted completes the sentence and is declined according to its regent; as

Only Zaid came   مَا جَاءَ إِلَّا زَيْدٌ

I saw Zaid only   مَا رَأَيْتُ إِلَّا زَيْدًا

I passed by Zaid only   مَا مَرَرْتُ إِلَّا بِزَيْدٍ

غَيْرٍ وَسِوَى

غَيْرٍ وَسِوَى are put in construction with the noun excepted and themselves take the same case as the noun when excepted after إِلَّا; as

The people came except Zaid   جَاءَ ٱلْقَوْمُ غَيْرَ زَيْدٍ

i. e. if إِلَّا were used instead of غَيْرِ Zaid would be in the accusative; therefore غَيْرَ is in the accusative.

No one came but Zaid   مَا جَاءَ غَيْرُ زَيْدٍ

عَدَا خَلَا حَاشَا

These words may be regarded as verbs or prepositions. When verbs they govern that which is excepted in the accusative, as مَفْعُول بِهِ and their agents are necessarily implied pronouns; as

The men read except Amr   قَرَأَ ٱلْقَوْمُ عَدَا عَمْرًا

When preceded by مَا they cannot be regarded as prepositions; but when used as prepositions they govern as prepositions; as

I saw the children except Fareed   رَأَيْتُ ٱلْأَوْلَادَ خَلَا فَرِيْدٍ

Sometimes لَا يَكُوْن and لَيْسَ are used as particles

of exception; that which is excepted being خَبَر and the إِسْم an implied pronoun.

بَيْدَ is used in the same manner as غَيْر but is restricted to ٱلْاِسْتِثْنَاء ٱلْمُنْقَطِع. It is always in the accusative and in construction with أَنَّ and its sentence; it cannot be used as an adjective.

THE ADVERBIAL ACCUSATIVE OF STATE
OR CONDITION. ٱلْحَالُ

This shows the state of the agent or the object at the time of the action of the verb. It must be an indefinite derived adjective expressing a transitory condition and coming after a complete sentence; and is therefore a فَضْلَة; as

The prince came riding	جَاءَ ٱلْأَمِيْرُ رَاكِبًا

The object may be any of the مَفَاعِيل; as

I rode the horse saddled	بِهِ رَكِبْتُ ٱلْفَرَسَ مُسْرَجًا
I struck severely	مُطْلَق ضَرَبْتُ ٱلضَّرْبَ شَدِيْدًا
I fasted the whole month	فِيْهِ صُمْتُ ٱلشَّهْرَ كَامِلًا
I fled for fear only	لَهُ هَرَبْتُ لِلخَوْفِ مُجَرَّدًا
I walked along the Nile while it overflowed	مَعَهُ مَشَيْتُ وَٱلنّيْلَ فَائِضًا

The subject or object of the action to which the حَال refers صَاحِبُ ٱلْحَالِ should be definite and precede the حَال. If the صَاحِبُ ٱلْحَال is indefinite the حَال must come first; as

A man came riding جَاءَ رَاكِبًا رَجُلٌ

When the حَـال is definite it must be treated as if indefinite; as

The prince came alone جَاءَ ٱلْأَمِيرُ وَحْدَهُ (مُنْفَرِدًا)

The حَال may be a primitive noun when (*a*) convertible into a derivative noun, and also when it expresses *b*) order (*c*) division or (*d*) price; as

(*a*). I sold him, hand to hand بِعْتُهُ مُقَابَضَةً = بِعْتُهُ يَدًا بِيَدٍ

(i. e. for ready money)

I spoke to him face to face كَلَّمْتُهُ فَمًا لِلْفَمِ (مُشَافَهَةً)

(*b*). Enter, man by man أُدْخُلُوا رَجُلًا رَجُلًا

(*c*). I taught him nahu, chapter by chapter عَلَّمْتُهُ ٱلنَّحْوَ بَابًا بَابًا

(*d*). I bought the cloth for a majēdee a yard إِشْتَرَيْتُ ٱلْجُوخَ ٱلذِّرَاعَ بِرِيَالٍ

When the حَـال follows two definite nouns each of which may be صَاحِبُ ٱلْحَال it is best to ascribe it to the noun which directly precedes it; as

I met Zaid riding لَقِيتُ زَيْدًا رَاكِبًا

but if we wish to ascribe it to the pronoun we must say;

I met Zaid whilst I was riding لَقِيتُ رَاكِبًا زَيْدًا

In such a sentence as

I walking met Zaid riding   لَقِيْتُ زَيْدًا مَاشِيًا رَاكِبًا

it is better to ascribe the first حَال to the subject and the second to the object.

The حَال may be an indicative sentence or quasi sentence; as

Zaid came running   جَاءَ زَيْدٌ يَرْكُضُ

Zaid died, and his son a minor   مات زَيْدٌ وَٱبْنُهُ قَاصِرٌ

I entered the house, and there

was a lion in it   دَخَلْتُ ٱلْبَيْتَ وَفِيْهِ أَسَدٌ

The حَــال must be connected with its noun by a رَابِط *binder* and this may be:

I. An implied pronoun; as

I came running جِئْتُ أَرْكُضُ (أَنَا is in the verb).

I bought the grapes a rotal of them for a dirham

إِشْتَرَيْتُ ٱلْعِنَبَ ٱلرَّطْلُ (مِنْهُ) بِدِرْهَمٍ

II. وَاوُ ٱلْحَالِ , و .

I journeyed while the men were

sleeping   سَافَرْتُ وَٱلنَّاسُ نِيَامٌ

III. وَاوُ ٱلْحَالِ with a pronoun; as

Zaid came with his hand

upon his head   جَاءَ زَيْدٌ وَيَدُهُ عَلَى رَأْسِهِ

IV. قَدْ with و introducing the preterite in the affirmative; as

I came when the sun had risen   جِئْتُ وَقَدْ طَلَعَتِ ٱلشَّمْسُ

THE SPECIFICATION. اَلتَّمْيِيزُ

اَلتَّمْيِيزُ is the primitive noun which explains what would otherwise have been indefinite; this indefiniteness has respect either to ذَاتٌ substance, or نِسْبَةٌ relation.

I. تَمْيِيزُ ٱلنِّسْبَةِ limits or defines the predicate; as

Zaid is honourable in respect to birth   كَرُمَ زَيْدٌ مَوْلِدًا

How noble a man is Zaid!   مَا اكْرَمَ زَيْدًا رَجُلًا

Zaid has more relatives than Amr   زَيْدٌ أَكْثَرُ مِنْ عَمْرٍو أَقَارِبَ

II. تَمْيِيزُ ٱلذَّاتِ explains what is indefinite in respect to number, weight, measure, quantity, similarity, disimilarity or area; as

He has twenty she-camels   لَهُ عِشْرُونَ نَاقَةً

I bought a rotal of butter, and a saa of wheat, and two miles of land   ٱشْتَرَيْتُ رَطْلًا زُبْدًا وَصَاعًا قَمْحًا وَمِيلَيْنِ أَرْضًا

I have a handful of flour,

and the like of it of rice   عِنْدِي حَفْنَةٌ طَحِينًا وَمِثْلُهَا رُزًّا

The noun which is specified must not be deprived of any of the signs of declension.

اَلذَّاتِ may be put in construction with the تَمْيِيزُ and the تَمْيِيزُ may be put in the genitive by مِنْ; as

I have a shekel of silver   عِنْدِي شَاقِلُ فِضَّةٍ

We planted the land with trees   غَرَسْنَا ٱلْأَرْضَ مِنَ ٱلشَّجَرِ

I have a ring of gold   لِيَ خَاتَمٌ مِنْ ذَهَبٍ

THE GENITIVE CASE. اَلْجَرُّ

The Genitive Case is peculiar to the Noun.

The nouns in the genitive case, اَلْـمَـجْـرُورَاتُ, are of two kinds:

I. Those governed by prepositions اَلدَّاخِلَةُ عَلَيْهَا حُرُوفُ ٱلْجَرِّ.

II. Those which are the complement in the case of two nouns in construction اَلْمُضَافُ إِلَيْهِ.

I. PREPOSITIONS. حُرُوفُ ٱلْجَرِّ

The prepositions are: عِنْدَ ,لِ ,بِ ,عَلَى ,فِي ,إِلَى ,مِنْ, حَاشَا ,عَدَا ,خَلَا ,كَيْ ,مُنْذُ ,مُذْ ,حَتَّى ,رُبَّ ,تَ ,وَ ,كَ and some authorities say لَعَلَّ ,مَتَى.

Chief meanings of the prepositions

مِنْ with pronominal suffixes مِنْهُ ,مِنْكَ ,مِنَّا ,مِنِّي.

Meanings.

from	I came forth from the house	خَرَجْتُ مِنَ ٱلْبَيْتِ
some of	I took some of the dirhams	أَخَذْتُ مِنَ ٱلدَّرَاهِمِ
„ „	He drank some of the water	شَرِبَ مِنَ ٱلْمَآءِ
of	I have a ring of gold	لِي خَاتَمٌ مِنْ ذَهَبٍ

on account of	He died from fear	مَاتَ مِنَ ٱلْخَوْفِ
by	He entered by the door	دَخَلَ مِنَ ٱلْبَابِ
to	Draw nigh to me	إِقْتَرِبْ مِنِّي
from	I knew the truth from falsehood	عَرَفْتُ ٱلْحَقَّ مِنَ ٱلْبَاطِلِ
than	The sea is larger than the land	ٱلْبَحْرُ أَكْبَرُ مِنَ ٱلْبَرِّ
at all	No one at all came	مَا جَاءَ مِنْ رَجُلٍ
rather than	Are ye contented with the life of this world rather than the next	هَلْ رَضِيتُمْ بِٱلْحَيٰـوةِ ٱلدُّنْيَا مِنَ ٱلْآخِرَةِ

because of	مِنْ جَرَى ,مِنْ جَرَّاءِ	about	مِنْ أَمْرِ
from the presence	مِنْ قِبَلِ	without	مِنْ دُونِ ,مِنْ غَيْرِ
of this sort	مِنْ هٰذَا ٱلْقَبِيلِ	before	مِنْ قَبْلُ
the next day	مِنَ ٱلْغَدِ	from this time	مِنْ ذِي قِبَلٍ
on account of	مِنْ أَجْلِ	at once	مِنْ سَاعَتِهِ ,مِنْ وَقْتِهِ
by itself	مِنْ ذَاتِهِ	behind him	مِنْ وَرَائِهِ
by habit	مِنْ عَادَةٍ	must	لَا بُدَّ مِنْ
from his youth	مِنْ شَبَابِهِ	a little	شَيْءٌ مِنْ
to-morrow	مِنْ غَدٍ	the same day	مِنْ يَوْمِهِ
at night	مِنَ ٱللَّيْلِ		

إِلَى with pronominal suffixes إِلَيَّ, إِلَيْكَ, إِلَيْهِ.

until	I fasted until sunset	صُمْتُ إِلَى ٱلْمَغْرِبِ
,,	He ate until he was satisfied	أَكَلَ إِلَى ٱلشَّبَعِ
to	I went to the market	ذَهَبْتُ إِلَى ٱلسُّوقِ
unto	Come unto me	تَعَالَوْا إِلَيَّ
beside	I sat beside the guest	جَلَسْتُ إِلَى ٱلضَّيْفِ
comparison	I like truth more than gain	ٱلصِّدْقُ أَحَبُّ إِلَيَّ مِنَ ٱلرِّبْحِ
addition	Add this to that	أَضِفْ هٰذَا إِلَى ذَاكَ
multiplication	Three times five	ثَلْثَةٌ فِي خَمْسَةٍ

how long	إِلَى مَتَى, إِلَى كَمْ	As long as God pleases	إِلَى مَا شَاءَ ٱللّٰهِ
until	إِلَى أَنْ	Get you gone!	إِلَيْكَ عَنِّي
and so on	إِلَى غَيْرِ ذٰلِكَ	referred to	ٱلْمُشَارُ إِلَيْهِ
et cetera	إِلَى آخِرِهِ (الخ)		

فِي with pronominal suffixes فِيَّ, فِيْكَ, فِيْهِ.

It is used as an adverb of time or place.

in	I sat in the house	جَلَسْتُ فِي ٱلْبَيْتِ
,,	He was born in summer	وُلِدَ فِي ٱلصَّيْفِ
,,	I came in the evening	جِئْتُ فِي ٱلْمَسَاءِ
with	The prince rode with his host	رَكِبَ ٱلْأَمِيرُ فِي جُنْدِهِ
on account of	He was killed because of his crime	قُتِلَ فِي ذَنْبِهِ

among	There is not a learned man among them	مَا فِيْهِمْ عَالِمٌ
in my power	فِي يَدِي	It has nothing to do with it	لَيْسَ فِي شَيٍّ مِنْ ذٰلِكَ
in my knowledge	فِي عِلْمِي		
in the proper time	فِي حِيْنِهِ	Leave what you are about	دَعْ مَا أَنْتَ فِيْهِ
in the past	فِيْمَا مَضَى		
immediately	فِي ٱلْحَالِ	None among them is generous	مَا فِيْهِمْ كَرِيْمٌ
about	فِي أَمْرٍ		
meanwhile	فِي أَثْنَاءِ ذٰلِكَ		

عَلَى with pronominal suffixes عَلَيَّ, عَلَيْكَ, عَلَيْهِ.

upon, on	He sat upon his throne	جَلَسَ عَلَى عَرْشِهِ
on account of	Thank God for His mercy	أُشْكُرُوا ٱللّٰهَ عَلَى رَحْمَتِهِ
at	The army entered at an unexpected time	دَخَلَ ٱلْجَيْشُ عَلَى حِيْنِ غَفْلَةٍ
to	And we preferred some to others	وَفَضَّلْنَا بَعْضَهُمْ عَلَى بَعْضٍ
„	I preferred study to sleep	إِخْتَرْتُ ٱلدَّرْسَ عَلَى ٱلنَّوْمِ
against	He went out against him	خَرَجَ عَلَيْهِ
„	He owes a debt I owe thee a debt	لَكَ عَلَيَّ دَيْنٌ عَلَيْهِ دَيْنٌ
„	You ought to do this	عَلَيْكَ أَنْ تَعْمَلَ هٰذَا

on	On this condition عَلَى هٰذَا ٱلشَّرْطِ	After this manner عَلَى هٰذَا ٱلنَّمَطِ

With caution عَلَى حَذَرٍ	At a time of عَلَى حِيْنٍ	
as much as عَلَى قَدْرٍ	by means of عَلَى يَدٍ	
aside عَلَى جَانِبٍ	by all means عَلَى كُلِّ أَحْوَالٍ	
I covenant ٱلْعَهْدُ عَلَيَّ	and so on قِسْ عَلَى	
certainly عَلَى كُلِّ حَالٍ	in a manner عَلَى وَجْهِ	
by heart عَلَى ظَهْرِ ٱلْقَلْبِ	according عَلَى حَسَبِ	
in his time عَلَى عَهْدِهِ	though عَلَى أَنْ	
according to their saying عَلَى قَوْلِهِمْ	to repent نَدِمَ عَلَى	
to enter upon أَقْبَلَ عَلَى	to fall upon the face خَرَّ عَلَى	
to induce, attack حَمَلَ عَلَى	to be pleased with رَضِيَ عَلَى	
to be informed وَقَفَ عَلَى	to disapprove أَنْكَرَ عَلَى	
to appoint, invest أَقَامَ عَلَى		

He did it in spite of his old age   فَعَلَهُ عَلَى كِبْرِ سِنّهِ

ب with pronominal suffixes   بِهِ, بِكَ, بِي.

making neuter verbs active	I brought him	أَتَيْتُ بِهِ
,,	He took him	ذَهَبَ بِهِ
,,	He came with his people	جَاءَ بِأَهْلِهِ
in	I dwelt in Jaffa	سَكَنْتُ بِيَافَا
,,	Go in peace	إِذْهَبْ بِسَلَامٍ

with	I struck him with a sword	ضَرَبْتُهُ بِسَيْفٍ
on account of	He was imprisoned for stealing	سُجِنَ بِسَرِقَةٍ
by	By grace we are saved	بِـٱلنِّعْمَةِ نَحْنُ مُخَلَّصُونَ
for	An eye for an eye	عَيْنٌ بِعَيْنٍ	This for that	هٰذَا بِذَاكَ
,,	A rotal for a dirham	رَطْلٌ بِدِرْهَمٍ
swearing	By thy head	بِرَأْسِكَ	By God	بِـٱللّٰهِ

| unjustly | بِغَيْرِ ٱلْحَقِّ | without | بِلَا بِغَيْرٍ |
| because | بِمَا أَنَّ | so that | بِحَيْثُ |

It is best for you in some way or other

ٱلْأَوْلَى بِكَ , ٱلْأَجْدَرُ بِكَ   بِوَجْهٍ مِنَ ٱلْوُجُوهِ

to dwell in a place   سَكَنَ , حَلَّ , نَزَلَ بِـٱلْمَكَانِ

You are more deserving   ٱلْأَحْرَى بِكَ

لِ with pronominal suffixes لِي, لَكَ, لَهُ.

ownership	Zaid has property	لِزَيْدٍ مَالٌ
,,	Paradise is for the righteous	ٱلْجَنَّةُ لِلصَّالِحِينَ
,,	Majesty belongs to God	ٱلْعَظَمَةُ لِلّٰهِ
,,	Praise belongs to God	ٱلْحَمْدُ لِلّٰهِ
purpose	I came for study	جِئْتُ لِلدَّرْسِ
,,	Build for destruction	ٱبْنُوا لِلْخَرَابِ

of or for	Saviour the world	مُخَلِّص لِلْعَالَم
strengthening	He does what he wishes	هُوَ فَعَّالٌ لِمَا يُرِيْدُ
admiration	What a learned man you are	يَا لَكَ مِنْ عَالِم
,,	What a horseman	يَا لَهُ مِنْ فَارِس
swearing	By your life	لَعَمْرُكَ
because of	لِسَبَب He is concerned in, or has power	لَهُ يَدٌ
called	يُقَالُ لَهُ He is well versed in	لَهُ ٱلْيَدُ ٱلطُّوْلَى فِي
instantly لِسَاعَتِهِ لِوَقْتِهِ	I thank you	لَكَ مِنِّي ٱلشُّكْرُ

for the length of time since لِطُولِ عَهْدِهِ ب	you shall have what you like لَكَ مِنِّي مَا تُحِبُّ
It is better or best for you ٱلْأَوْفَقُ لَكَ	because it لِأَنَّهُ
I owe Mr. عَلَيَّ لِفُلَان	to speak to قَالَ لَهُ

عَنْ with pronominal suffixes عَنِّي, عَنَّا, عَنْكَ, عَنْهُ.

at	Sit at my right hand	إِجْلِسْ عَنْ يَمِيْنِي
from	He did it with a good will	فَعَلَهُ عَنْ نَفْسٍ رَاضِيَةٍ
,,	Go from me, Satan	إِذْهَبْ عَنِّي يَا شَيْطَانُ
by or near	He travelled past the town	سَافَرَ عَنِ ٱلْمَدِيْنَةِ

for	One soul shall not make satisfaction for another	لَا تَجْزِي نَفْسٌ عَنْ نَفْسٍ شَيْئًا
on account of	Pay instead of me	إِدْفَعْ عَنِّي
„	May God reward you for me	جَزَاكَ ٱللَّهُ عَنِّي
„	He only came because he was called	لَمْ يَأْتِ إِلَّا عَنْ دَعْوَةٍ
about	He asked me about your name	سَأَلَنِي عَنِ ٱسْمَكَ
source	He acquired knowledge from him	أَخَذَ ٱلْعِلْمَ عَنْهُ
above	God is exalted above the worlds	تَعَالَى ٱللَّهُ عَنِ ٱلْعَالَمِينَ
to	May God be gracious unto him	رَضِيَ ٱللَّهُ عَنْهُ
„	They were killed to the last man	قُتِلُوا عَنْ آخِرِهِمْ

He died aged seventy	مَاتَ عَنْ سَبْعِينَ سَنَةً
He died leaving a son	مَاتَ عَنِ ٱبْنٍ
After a little	عَنْ or عَمَّا قَلِيلٍ
by the agency of	عَنْ يَدٍ
He did it without intention	عَمِلَهُ عَنْ غَيْرِ قَصْدٍ
To quote	أَنْقَلَ عَنْ
To relate a narrative as heard from another	حَدَّثَ عَنْ

كَ

resemblance: Zaid is like a lion   زَيْدٌ كَأَسَدٍ

as, as if, as though   كَأَنْ

swearing: By God وَٱللّٰهِ   By your father وَأَبِيكَ

تَ

تَ *by*, is only used with the words رَبُّ, ٱلرَّحْمٰنُ, ٱللّٰهُ
for swearing; as

Lord, The Merciful, God   تَاللّٰهِ ,تَٱلرَّحْمٰنِ ,تَرَبِّي

رَبَّ *many a*

Many a generous man will travel   رُبَّ رَجُلٍ كَرِيمٍ يُسَافِرُ

مُذْ, مُنْذُ *since, when*, the word governed by these
signifies past time; as

I have not seen him since

Friday last   مَا رَأَيْتُهُ مُنْذُ يَوْمِ ٱلْجُمَعَةِ

I have not seen him to-day   مَا رَأَيْتُهُ مُذْ ٱلْيَوْمِ

From everlasting   مُنْذُ ٱلْأَزَلِ

كَيْ *in order that*; as

Man works in order that

he may live   ٱلْإِنْسَانُ يَشْتَغِلُ كَيْ يَعِيشَ

I came that I might see you   جِئْتُ كَيْ أَنْظُرَكَ

خَلَا ,عَدَا ,حَاشَا *see the particles of exception.*

مَتَى has the force of مِنْ when used as a preposition.

لَوْلَا if followed by a pronoun is regarded by some
authorities as a preposition; as

Had it not been for you I would not

have stayed لَوْلَاكَ لَمْ أَبْقَ

لِ ,بِ ,عَـلَـى ,عَـنْ ,فِي ,إِلَى ,مِنْ *are used with both*

nouns and pronouns.

رُبَّ ,تَ ,وَ ,كَ ,مَتَى ,حَاشَ ,عَدَا ,خَلَا ,كَي ,مُنْذُ ,مُذ ,حَتَّى

are not used with personal pronouns.

رُبَّ governs an indefinite but qualified noun.

The noun is virtually in the nominative because it

is مُبْتَـدَأٌ and the predicate is the verb in the preterite

which follows; as

Many a generous man visited us رُبَّ رَجُلٍ كَرِيمٍ زَارَنَا

When مَا is affixed it ceases to act as a preposition.

رُبَّ though omitted still governs after the particles

وَ ,فَ ,بَلْ.

حَتَّى *until, as far as, even*; as

I ate the fish even its head أَكَلْتُ ٱلسَّمَكَةَ حَتَّى رَأْسِهَا

I watched until the dawn (i. e.

the whole night) سَهِرْتُ حَتَّى ٱلْفَجْرِ

إِلَى *implies motion to*; as

I ate the fish to its head أَكَلْتُ ٱلسَّمَكَةَ إِلَى رَأْسِهَا

مُذ ,مُنْذُ govern nouns of time; they may be prepo-

sitions or adverbs; adverbs when the following noun

is in the nominative; also when they are followed by

verbs; as

I have not seen him since he came مَا رَأَيْتُهُ مُنْذُجَاءَ

I have not spoken to him for

two days   لَمْ أُكَلّمْهُ مُذْ يَوْمَانِ

كَيْ: when this particle governs the مَا of interrogation

the ا of the مَا may be replaced by ه; as

for what   كَيْمَ or كَيْمَهْ or كَيْمَا

The ى of عَلَى and إِلَى become ي when they govern

pronouns; as إِلَيْكَ to you عَلَيْهِ upon it.

ل has ـِ with all pronouns except يَآءُ ٱلْمُتَكَلّمِ; with

other nouns and the ي it has ـَ.

ب takes ـِ, ت, ك take ـَ.

مُذْ is changed into مُذ when it governs a noun be-

ginning with هَمْزَةُ ٱلْوَصْلِ; عَنْ takes ـَ and مِـنْ takes ـَ

(before the article however ـِ); as

From the roof	مِنَ ٱلسَّطْحِ	from among	مِنْ بَيْنِ
from the house	مِنَ ٱلْبَيْتِ	below	مِنْ تَحْتِ
from above	مِنْ فَوْقِ	around	مِنْ حَوْلِ
before	مِنْ قَبْلِ	after	مِنْ بَعْدِ
from	مِنْ عِنْدِ	from behind	مِنْ وَرَاءِ
during this day	مُذُ ٱلْيَوْمِ	„ „	مِنْ خَلْفِ

Certain of the prepositions are used as nouns, being

put in construction with the noun which follows them,

and are themselves generally governed by other pre-

positions; as

From my right hand   مِنْ عَنْ يَمِيْنِي

I took the book from
the table أَخَذْتُ ٱلْكِتَابَ مِنْ عَلَى ٱلْمَائِدَةِ

The prepositions may be omitted before أَنَّ and أَنْ; as

I commanded him to do so أَمَرْتُهُ (بِ) أَنْ يَفْعَلَ كَذَا;

the sentence introduced by أَنْ is then in the accusative.

The preposition may be omitted after a conjunction
which connects a word to another governed by the
same preposition; as

I passed by Zaid and Amr مَرَرْتُ بِزَيْدٍ وَعَمْرٍو

Prepositions and adverbs are always dependent upon
a verb or quasi verb.

When the verb or that which takes its place signifies
simple existence, it is omitted; as

My brother is with my
father in Jerusalem أَخِي عِنْدَ أَبِي فِي أُوْرْشَلِيْمَ

but if it signifies more than mere existence, it is expressed; as

My brother lived in Jaffa أَخِي سَكَنَ فِي يَافَا

This omission is peculiar to the خَبَر, نَعْت and حَال.

The verb, or the word resembling it, may be implied
in the first three; in the صِلَة the verb alone is implied.

NOUNS IN CONSTRUCTION. أَلْاِضَافَةُ

from أَضَافَ *to add, ascribe or attribute.*

The antecedent is called أَلْمُضَاف *that which is ascribed;*
the complement أَلْمُضَاف إِلَيْهِ *that to which ascription is made.*

When a noun is so connected in thought with a following word or clause that the two make up one idea, the first is said to be in construction, as in:

Son of the king	إِبْنُ ٱلْمَلِكِ	All creatures	كُلُّ ٱلْمَخْلُوقَاتِ
The wisdom of God	حِكْمَةُ ٱللّٰهِ	Those who fear God	خَائِفُو ٱللّٰهِ
The sleep of death	رُقَادُ ٱلْمَوْتِ	Holy of Holies	قُدْسُ ٱلْأَقْدَاسِ
The company of believers	جَمَاعَةُ ٱلْمُؤْمِنِيْنَ	The book of God	كِتَابُ ٱللّٰهِ

The antecedent must be stripped of (*a*) the ن of tanween, (*b*) the ن of dual, (*c*) the ن of plural, and (*d*) the article, and is then declined according to its position in the sentence; as

The prince's boy came	جَاءَ غُلَامُ ٱلْأَمِيْرِ
I saw the king's two sons	رَأَيْتُ ٱبْنَيِ ٱلْمَلِكِ
I passed by the lovers of Zaid	مَرَرْتُ بِمُحِبِّيْ زَيْدٍ

A noun with a suffix being in construction and definite, does not take the article; as

My generous son — إِبْنِي ٱلْكَرِيْمُ

The complement is always in the genitive.

REAL CONSTRUCTION. ٱلْإِضَافَةُ ٱلْحَقِيقِيَّةُ

This kind of construction has the force of an implied preposition. This preposition is فِي when the second noun is used as an adverb of time or place; as

The prayer of the morning — صَلٰوةُ (فِي) ٱلصُّبْحِ

The believers of Gaza   مُؤْمِنُو (فِي) غَزَّةَ

This preposition is مِن when the second noun denotes the material of the first; as

A silver cup   كَأْسُ فِضَّةٍ

In other cases the preposition لِ is implied; as

The servant of the king   خَادِمُ ٱلْمَلِكِ (لِلْمَلِكِ)

When the second noun is definite, the first also becomes definite; and when indefinite, the first is specialized; as

The brother of Zaid أَخُو زَيْدٍ   A garment of silk ثَوْبُ حَرِيرٍ

The second of the two nouns may give the gender to the first; as

The mercy of God is nigh   رَحْمَةَ ٱللّٰهِ قَرِيبٌ

Some of his fingers were cut off   قُطِعَتْ بَعْضُ أَصَابِعِهِ

A second kind of إِضَافَة is found which consists in having the form of construction without the meaning ٱلْإِضَافَةُ ٱللَّفْظِيَّةُ *verbal construction.*

The first noun is always a derived adjective, viz. the noun of agent, or the noun of object with the present or future signification, or the noun of attribute; as

A beater of Zaid   ضَارِبُ زَيْدٍ

The beloved one of the king   مَحْبُوبُ ٱلْمَلِكِ

One who is of good stature   حَسَنُ ٱلْقَامَةِ

This part of إِضَافَة is only for ٱلتَّخْفِيف *lightening* as ضَارِبُ زَيْدٍ instead of ضَارِبٌ زَيْدًا .

The article may precede the first noun, when the second noun has it prefixed; as

He that loves good ﺍَﻟْﻤُﺤِﺐُّ ﺍﻟْﺨَﻴْﺮِ

If the first noun is in the dual form or is the regular masc. plural it may take the article whether the second has it or not; and also when the second noun is in construction with another noun which has the article; as

The two who are of many cunning devices ﺍَﻟْﻜَﺜِﻴْﺮَﺍ ﺍﻟْﺤِﻴَﻞِ

Those who hate Zaid ﺍَﻟْﻤُﺒْﻐِﻀُﻮﺍ ﺯَﻳْﺪٍ

The striker of the man's lad ﺍَﻟﻀَّﺎﺭِﺏُ ﻏُﻼَﻡِ ﺍﻟﺮَّﺟُﻞِ

Certain nouns require always to be put in construction. This construction may be (a) in form and meaning or (b) in meaning although not in form.

The first are such nouns as ﻋِﻨْﺪَ by, ﻟَﺪُﻥ in presence of; the second are such as ﺑَﻌْﺾ some of, ﻛُﻞّ all of; as

All die (every one dies) ﻛُﻞُّ ﺃَﺣَﺪٍ ﻳَﻤُﻮْﺕُ for ﻛُﻞُّ ﻳَﻤُﻮْﺕُ

I know some of them ﺃَﻋْﺮِﻑُ ﺑَﻌْﻀَﻬُﻢ for ﺃَﻋْﺮِﻑُ ﺑَﻌْﻀًﺎ

Certain adverbs; as ﺇِﺫَﺍ when, ﺇِﻥْ when, ﺣَﻴْﺚُ where, are put in construction always with sentences, in which case the latter are convertible into sing. nouns; as

I went where you commanded me ﺫَﻫَﺒْﺖُ ﺣَﻴْﺚُ ﺃَﻣَﺮْﺗَﻨِﻲ

The following adverbs are indeclinable when the second noun though omitted is implied, and they take the ُ.

| Behind | ﺧَﻠْﻒ | first | ﺃَﻭَّﻝ | after | ﺑَﻌْﺪ |
| in front | ﺃَﻣَﺎﻡ | according | ﺣَﺴْﺐ | before | ﻗَﺒْﻞ |

below	تَحْت	left	شِمَال	right	يَمِيْن
below	دُوْن	above	فَوْق		
I came before	جِئْتُ قَبْلُ				

The adverbs take ــَـ when in construction with a
noun expressed or implied; as

Who came first, you or Zaid   مَن جَاء قَبْلًا أَنْتَ أَمْ زَيْدٌ

I came before Zaid   جِئْتُ قَبْلَ زَيْدٍ

When not in construction they take the ــٌـ.

I came beforehand   جِئْتُ قَبْلًا

Some useful Adverbs are:

towards, about	نَحْوَ	yes, certainly	أَجَلْ
by, by the side of	إِزَاءٍ	yes	جَيْرِ
opposite, in front		ever	قَطُّ
of	تِجَاهَ, تِلْقَاءِ, قُبَالَةَ	thus	كَذَا
between	بَيْنَ	likewise	كَذَالِكَ
in the middle	وَسْطَ	not at all	كَلَّا, أَلْبَتَّةَ
near	قُرْبَ	gratis	مَجَّانًا
as far as	بُعْدَ	left (hand)	شِمَال
the distance of	مَسَافَةَ	around	حَوْلَ
before	قُدَّامَ	after	غِبَّ بَعْدُ
in front	أَمَامَ		

Words and expressions used adverbially:

| to morrow | غَدًا | yesterday | أَلْبَارِحَةَ |
| to-day | أَلْيَوْمَ | before yesterday | قَبْلُ أَمْسِ |

now	أَلآنَ	early	بَاكِرًا
after an hour	بَعْدَ سَاعَةٍ	late	مُتَأَخِّرًا
after a day	بَعْدَ يَوْمٍ	formerly	سَابِقًا
firstly	أَوَّلًا	lately	مُوَخَّرًا
lastly	أَخِيرًا	also	أَيْضًا
sometimes	أَحْيَانًا	slowly	رُوَيْدًا رُوَيْدًا
many times	مِرَارًا	little by little	شَيْئًا فَشَيْئًا
always	دَائِمًا	every morning	صَبَاحَ مَسَاء
oftentimes, generally	غَالِبًا	and evening	
never, not at		by day	نَهَارًا
all	أَبَدًا أَصْلًا قَطْعًا	by night	لَيْلًا
especially, above		at one time,	
all	خُصُوصًا, لَا سِيَّمَا	once	طَوْرًا ... وَتَارَةً
together	مَعًا	at another,	
very, exceedingly	جِدًّا	again	تَارَةً ... وَطَوْرًا
wholly, in		inside	دَاخِلًا
general	عُمُومًا, بِالإِجْمَالِ	outside	خَارِجًا
all	جَمِيعًا	inwardly	بَاطِنًا
quickly, soon		outwardly	ظَاهِرًا
عَاجِلًا, سَرِيعًا, عَلَى الفَوْر		vainly	بَاطِلًا
presently	حَالًا, فِي الحَالِ	by force	غَصْبًا, جَبْرًا
slowly	مَهْلًا	in spite	رَغْمًا عَنْ
suddenly	بَغْتَةً	being obliged	اِضْطِرَارًا

legally	شَرْعًا	to the left	شِمَالًا
truly	حَقًّا, بِالْحَقِيقَةِ	to the right	يَمِينًا
aside	جَانِبًا, عَلَى جَانِبٍ	much	كَثِيرًا
instead of	بَدَلًا مِنْ, عِوَضًا عَنْ	little	قَلِيلًا
certainly		eagerly	رَغْبَةً
	عَلَى كُلِّ حَالٍ, مِنْ كُلِّ بُدٍّ	eternally	أَبَدًا
by all means	عَلَى كُلِّ أَحْوَالٍ	with a good will	حُبًّا وَكَرَامَةً
every place and time	فِي كُلِّ مَكَانٍ وَزَمَانٍ	welcome	أَهْلًا وَسَهْلًا
undoubtedly	لَا مَحَالَةَ	ever, never	قَطُّ
in the meantime	فِي أَثْنَاءِ ذَالِكَ	with aversion	كَرْهًا
may it do you good	هَنِيئًا مَرِيئًا	only	فَقَطْ
obediently	سَمْعًا وَطَاعَةً		

THE APPOSITIVES. اَلتَّوَابِعُ

The Appositive follows the declension of the noun to which it stands in apposition by way of description or designation.

It is of five kinds:

I. اَلنَّعْتُ The Adjective.

II. عَطْفُ ٱلْبَيَانِ The Explanatory Apposition.

III. اَلتَّوْكِيدُ The Corroborative.

IV. اَلْبَدَلُ The Substitution.

V. عَطْفُ ٱلنَّسَقِ The Connexion of Sequence.

THE ADJECTIVE. أَلنَّعْت

أَلنَّعْت is the تَابِع which qualifies the preceding noun أَلْمَتْبُوع. It is originally a derived adjective i. e. a noun of agent, object, attribute or superiority: but it may be:

(*a*). A masdar but not مِيْمِيّ of a triliteral verb in the masc. sing.; as

A just man   رَجُلٌ عَدْلٌ

(*b*). A demonstrative or relative pronoun qualifying a definite noun; as

This man came   جَاءَ ٱلرَّجُلُ هٰذَا

Give me the book which is on the table   أَعْطِنِي ٱلكِتَابَ ٱلَّذِي عَلَى ٱلْمَائِدَةِ

(*c*). ذُو *possessing*; as

I love a pious man   أُحِبُّ رَجُلًا ذَا تَقْوَى

(*d*). A noun of relation أَلْمَنْسُوب; as

I am an Arab   أَنَا رَجُلٌ عَرَبِيٌّ

(*e*). A common noun إِسْمُ جِنْسٍ when the latter can be regarded as an adjective; as

This is Zaid the lion (the brave)   هٰذَا زَيْدٌ ٱلْأَسَدُ

(*f*). An indicative sentence or phrase qualifying an indefinite noun; as

This is a horse I like   هٰذَا حِصَانٌ أُحِبُّهُ

All these must admit of being changed into an adjective.

If the noun is definite the adjective makes clearer the definiteness; as

Zaid the merchant came ‏جَاءَ زَيْدٌ ٱلتَّاجِرُ‏

If the noun is indefinite, it is specialized by the adjective; as

A little boy opened the door ‏وَلَدٌ صَغِيرٌ فَتَحَ ٱلبَابَ‏

The adjective may denote (*a*) praise, (*b*) blame or (*c*) assurance; as

(*a*). In the name of the most

merciful God ‏بِسْمِ ٱللّٰهِ ٱلرَّحْمٰنِ ٱلرَّحِيمِ‏

(*b*). I seek the protection of God from Satan the

vile one ‏أَعُوذُ بِاللّٰهِ مِنَ ٱلشَّيْطَانِ ٱلرَّجِيمِ‏

(*c*). Yesterday which is past ‏أَمْسِ ٱلدَّابِرُ‏

‏ٱلنَّعْتُ‏ is of two kinds:

I. ‏ٱلنَّعْتُ ٱلحَقِيقِيُّ‏ qualifies the noun which it follows; as

This is a profitable book ‏هٰذَا كِتَابٌ مُفِيدٌ‏

II. ‏ٱلـنَّـعْـتُ ٱلـسَّـبَـبِـيُّ‏ qualifies the noun which it precedes; as

This book is profitable: its

subject ‏هٰذَا كِتَابٌ مُفِيدٌ مَوْضُوعُهُ‏

‏ٱلنَّعْتُ ٱلحَقِيقِيُّ‏ agrees with the noun preceding it in being definite, or indefinite, and in number, gender, and case as;

I saw two accomplished men   رَأَيْتُ رَجُلَيْنِ فَاضِلَيْنِ

The accomplished woman came   جَاءتِ ٱلْمَرْأَةُ ٱلْفَاضِلَةُ

A good man, the good man   رَجُلٌ صَالِحٌ, ٱلرَّجُلُ ٱلصَّالِحُ

Firm Mountains   جِبَالٌ رَاسِيَةٌ

ٱلنَّعْتُ ٱلسَّبَبِيّ agrees with the preceding noun as to definiteness or indefiniteness and, with what follows it in gender; as

These are the two men,

whose mother is good   هٰذَانِ ٱلرَّجُلَانِ ٱلْحَسَنَةُ أُمُّهُمَا .

These are the two men whose children are many

هٰذَانِ ٱلرَّجُلَانِ ٱلْكَثِيْرُونَ أَوْلَادُهُمَ

When two adjectives qualify a noun, the conjunction may or may not be used; as

This is a learned man and intelligent   هٰذَا رَجُلٌ عَالِمٌ وَنَبِيْهٌ

When a noun in the dual or plural is followed by different adjectives in the sing. number the conjunction must be used; as

Three men came a scribe, a poet and a lawyer

جَاءَ ثَلْثَةُ رِجَالٍ كَاتِبٌ وَشَاعِرٌ وَفَقِيْهٌ

The adjective may be separated from its noun when the meaning of the latter is obvious; as

Truly this is a great oath if you had known

إِنَّهُ لَقَسَمٌ لَوْ تَعْلَمُوْنَ عَظِيْمٌ

Our God is a God really generous   إِلَهُنَا إِلَهٌ حَقِيْقَةً كَرِيـمٌ

but if the noun is vague in meaning the adjective must follow it; as

I saw this generous person رَأَيْتُ هٰذَا ٱلْكَرِيْمَ

لَا *not*, and إِمَّا *either*, when separating adjectives from their nouns must be repeated with the و; as

This is a day not hot and
not cold هٰذَا يَوْمٌ لَاحَارٌّ وَلَا بَارِدٌ

To every soul there is a time of death; either near
at hand or distant لِكُلِّ نَفْسٍ أَجَلٌ إِمَّا قَرِيْبٌ وَإِمَّا بَعِيْدٌ

The adjective may be regarded as a new expression
when it forms the predicate of an implied مُبْتَدَأٌ in
which case it is called ٱلنَّعْتُ ٱلْمَقْطُوعُ; as

I passed by a man, (he is) a tall man مَرَرْتُ بِرَجُلٍ طَوِيْلٌ

When a noun has two or more adjectives one of
them being مَقْطُوعٌ this one comes last; as

I saw a man learned, a
poet, an old man رَأَيْتُ رَجُلًا عَالِمًا شَاعِرًا شَيخٌ

Zaid beat Amr, the two poets ضَرَبَ زَيْدٌ عَمْرًا ٱلشَّاعِرَانِ

When one adjective qualifies two nouns in different
cases and the regents are different the adjective must
be مَقْطُوع; as

I honoured Zaid and I beat Amr, the two poets
أَكْرَمْتُ زَيْدًا وَضَرَبْتُ عَمْرًا ٱلشَّاعِرَانِ

THE EXPLANATORY APPOSITION. عَطْفُ ٱلْبَيَانِ

This is the تَابِع which is more definite than the
مَتْبُوع *the noun which is qualified*.

It is a definite and primitive noun but has the character of an adjective, and agrees in number and gender with the noun it qualifies; as

The man came, Zaid   جَاءَ الرَّجُلُ زَيْدٌ

A sentence may thus be put in apposition to another; as

He called upon his Lord, he said; O Lord have mercy on me   دَعَا رَبَّهُ قَالَ رَبِّ ٱرْحَمْنِي

THE CORROBORATION. اَلتَّوْكِيْدُ

اَلتَّوْكِيْدُ is the تَابِع which corroborates.

It is either (a) تَوْكِيْدٌ لَفْظِيٌّ *verbal corroboration*, the repetition of the word itself; as

Zaid, Zaid came   جَاءَ زَيْدٌ زَيْدٌ   No, No   لَا لَا

Zaid, died died   زَيْدٌ مَاتَ مَاتَ

or (b) تَوْكِيْدٌ مَعْنَوِيٌّ *corroboration in meaning*, the use of the words نَفْس عَيْن after the مَتْبُوع which are put in construction with the pronoun of the noun corroborated; as

Zaid himself came   جَاءَ زَيْدٌ نَفْسُهُ

نَفْس must precede the عَيْن when they are mentioned together and the preposition بِ may be prefixed to them. When the noun is dual it is best to put نَفْس or عَيْن in the plural, أَنْفُس, أَعْيُن, and in construction with the pronoun of the noun; as

The two women themselves came جَاءَتِ ٱلْمَرْأَتَانِ أَنْفُسُهُمَا

An indefinite noun does not admit of this kind of corroboration. When an attached pronoun in the nom. case needs corroboration it must be repeated in a separate form; as

I came myself جِئْتُ أَنَا نَفْسِي

instead of جِئْتُ نَفْسِي

In the sentence, I passed by him مَرَرْتُ بِهِ بِهِ the attached pronoun must be repeated with the preposition.

The إِسْم of أَنَّ must be repeated; as

Surely Zaid, surely Zaid is

standing إِنَّ زَيْدًا إِنَّ زَيْدًا قَائِمٌ

Corroboration may also take place by the use of synonyms; as

He threw the book, he threw it أَلْقَى ٱلْكِتَابَ رَمَاهُ

Yes, certainly نَعَم جَيْرِ

and by the following words تَوْكِيدُ ٱلشُّمُول

all جَمِيع   all أَجْمَع   all كُلّ

all قَاطِبَة   all بَأْسِر كَافَّة   both كِلْتَا   both كِلَا

These are put in construction with the pronoun of the noun to which they refer; as

The people came, all of them جَاء ٱلْقَوْمُ كُلُّهُمْ

I saw the two women, both

of them رَأَيْتُ ٱلْمَرْأَتَيْنِ كِلْتَيْهِمَا

كِلَا masc. كِلْتَا fem. *both*, when in construction with

a noun have vowels implied upon the ‍ I as signs of declension; as

Both the men came   جَا كِلَا ٱلرَّجُلَيْنِ

I saw both the men   رَأَيْتُ كِلَا ٱلرَّجُلَيْنِ

but when in construction with the pronoun of the noun to which they refer they have the ordinary declension of the dual; as

I passed by the two girls, both of them   مَرَرْتُ بِٱلِٱبْنَتَيْنِ كِلْتَيهِمَا

أَجْمَعُ، أَكْتَعُ، أَبْتَعُ، أَبْصَعُ any or all of these may follow أَجْمَعُ is made fem. and plural and generally follows كُلّ.

كُلّ is common to both singular and plural; as

The army came, all of it   جَاءَ ٱلجَيْشُ كُلُّهُ

The men came, all of them   جَاءَ ٱلقَوْمُ كُلُّهُمْ

The separate pronoun in the nominative case may be used as تَوْكِيْد to any attached pronoun; as

I came   جِئْتُ أَنَا   I saw thee   رَأَيْتُكَ أَنْتَ

I passed by him, him   مَرَرْتُ بِهِ هُوَ

THE SUBSTITUTION. ٱلْبَدَلُ

ٱلْبَدَلُ is the تَابِع which is substituted for the noun which it follows; it is of five kinds:

(a). بَدَلُ ٱلْكُلِّ *substitution of the whole for the whole*; as

The man came Zaid   جَاءَ ٱلرَّجُلُ زَيْدٌ

Amr thy brother came   جَاءَ عُمْرُو أَخُوكَ

(*b*). بَدَلُ ٱلْبَعْضِ *substitution of the part for the whole*; as

I ate the fish, the half of it   أَكَلْتُ ٱلسَّمَكَةَ نِصْفَهَا

(*c*). بَدَلُ ٱلْآشْتِمَالِ *the comprehensive substitution* indicating something inherent in the preceding word; as

I love Zaid, his name   أُحِبُّ زَيْدًا إِسْمَهُ

(*d*). بَدَلُ ٱلْغَلَطِ وَٱلنِّسْيَانِ *substitution of error and forgetfulness*; as

I rode the mare, the she-camel   رَكِبْتُ ٱلْفَرَسَ ٱلنَّاقَةَ

I saw Zaid, Amr   رَأَيْتُ زَيْدًا عَمْرًا

(*e*). بَدَلُ ٱلتَّفْصِيلِ *substitution denoting separation*; as

In the book are two chapters, a chapter on etymology and a chapter on syntax

فِي ٱلْكِتَابِ فَصْلَانِ فَصْلٌ فِي ٱلصَّرْفِ وَفَصْلٌ فِي ٱلنَّحْوِ

In the second and third kinds the بَدَل must be in construction with the pronoun of the noun preceding.

When the regent governs the genitive is repeated; as

I passed by a man, by Zaid   مَرَرْتُ بِرَجُلٍ بِزَيْدٍ

A verb may be substituted for a verb when they agree in tense; or a sentence for a sentence. In the sentence جَاءَ أَخُوكَ زَيْدٌ thy brother Zaid came Zaid may be either بَدَلٌ or عَطْفُ بَيَانٍ. If Zaid shews which brother came it is عَطْفُ بَيَانٍ but if it is only substituted for the words أَخُوكَ it is بَدْلٌ.

THE CONNEXION OF SEQUENCE. عَطْفُ ٱلنَّسَقِ

This "contextual" apposition is produced by the use of the conjunctions. The conjunctions may join two words or two sentences; as

His saying is truth and right	قَوْلُهُ صِدْقٌ وَحَقٌّ
God giveth life and taketh it	ٱللّٰه يُحْيِي وَيُمِيتُ
Life and death are in the hand of God	ٱلْحَيَوةُ وَٱلْمَوْتُ بِيَدِ ٱللّٰهِ
and the world and what is in it are His	وَٱلْكَوْنُ وَمَا فِيْهِ لَهُ

It is better to join a noun with a noun and a verb with a verb, and one sentence with another; the verbs of the two sentences being of the same mood and tense.

The conjunctions are:

II. Disjunctive.		I. Conjunctive.	
but	لٰكِنْ	and	وَ
not	لَا	and then	فَ
but rather, or rather	بَلْ	then	ثُمَّ
or, or rather	أَمْ	even	حَتَّى
or	أَوْ		
either, or	إِمَّا		

وَ is used without reference to order or time; as

I led armies and fed guests	قُدْتُ ٱلصُّفُوفَ وَقُتُّ ٱلضُّيُوفَ

فَ denotes (a) sequence and (b) consequence; as

(a). The men entered and then the children	دَخَلَ ٱلرِّجَالُ فَٱلْأَوْلَادُ

I read it page by page   قَرَأْتُ وَجْهًا فَوَجْهًا

(b). He reviled me and I struck him   شَتَمَنِي فَضَرَبْتُهُ

Depart from me Satan for   إِذْهَبْ عَنِّي يَا شَيْطَانُ فَإِنَّكَ

It is also used to join the conditional clause with that expressing the result of the condition; as

If ye love me keep my commandments

إِنْ كُنْتُمْ تُحِبُّونِي فَاحْفَظُوا وَصَايَايَ

and after أ of interrogation; as

Do you also not understand   أَفَأَنْتُمْ أَيْضًا غَيْرُ فَاهِمِينَ

and as the correlative of أَمَّا; as

But ye have known me   أَمَّا أَنْتُمْ فَقَدْ عَرَفْتُمُونِي

ثُمَّ denotes succession extending over a longer period than ف; as

God humbled me then he exalted me   حَطَّنِي اللّٰهُ ثُمَّ رَفَعَنِي

حَتَّى joins two common nouns together provided that the latter expresses part of the former; as

The pilgrims came even those on foot   قَدِمَ الْحُجَّاجُ حَتَّى الْمُشَاةُ

The people died even the prophets   مَاتَ النَّاسُ حَتَّى الْأَنْبِيَاءُ

لـكـن without the و prefixed, is always used after a negative or prohibitive sentence; as

Zaid did not come but Amr   مَاجَاءَ زَيْدٌ لَكِنْ عَمْرٌو

لَا denotes simple negation and is always used after affirmation or command; as

The man came and not another	جَاءَ ٱلرَّجُلُ لَا غَيْرُهُ
Take the bow and not the sword	خُذِ ٱلْقَوْسَ لَا ٱلسَّيْفَ

بَلْ is used after any of these sentences; as

The man or rather the child died	مَاتَ ٱلرَّجُلُ بَلِ ٱلْوَلَدُ

Do not fear your enemy but

rather your brother   لَا تَخَفْ عَدُوَّكَ بَلْ أَخَاكَ

أَمْ is used after the أَ of interrogation; as

Did you hold up the heavens or your fathers?

أَأَنْتُمْ رَفَعْتُمُ ٱلسَّمَوَاتِ أَمْ آبَاؤُكم

When not preceded by the أَ it means *or rather*; as

Did you create man or rather have you given him

reason?   هَلْ خَلَقْتُمُ ٱلْإِنْسَانَ أَمْ هَلْ أَعْطَيْتُمُوهُ ٱلْعَقْلَ

أَوْ denotes choice or division; as

Take a dirham or a dinar	خُذْ دِرْهَمًا أَوْ دِينَارًا
Be good or evil	كُنْ صَالِحًا أَوْ شِرِّيرًا

إِمَّا *either, or*, is always followed by another إِمَّا with

وَ prefixed; as

Speech is either prose or verse	ٱلْكَلَامُ إِمَّا نَثْرٌ وَإِمَّا شِعْرٌ

لَا وَلَا *neither, nor*

Neither this nor that is mine	لَا هٰذا يَخُصُّنِي وَلَا ذَاكَ

The detached pronoun must be introduced and the

regent of the genitive repeated in such sentences; as

I came and Zaid	جِئْتُ أَنَا وَزَيْدٌ

He sat between Zaid and

between Amr   جَلَسَ بَيْنَ زَيْدٍ وَبَيْنَ عَمْرٍو

THE MOODS OF THE VERB. إِعْرَابُ ٱلْفِعْلِ وَبِنَاؤُهُ

The aorist like the noun admits of declension; i. e. its final vowel may undergo certain changes to express the moods. These changes are produced by the action of certain particles. These particles are of two kinds:

I. Those which change the final vowel of the aorist ـُ into ـَ to express the subjunctive mood.

II. Those which apocopate the final vowel of the aorist to express the conditional and imperative moods.

The aorist is in the indicative mood when its final letter is vowelled with ـُ, or, as we may say, when not governed by the particles of نَصْب *accusative*, or جَزْم *apocopation*.

I. THE SUBJUNCTIVE MOOD. نَوَاصِبُ ٱلْفِعْلِ

The subjunctive mood is governed by the particles أَنْ, لَنْ, إِذَنْ and by كَيْ with لِ prefixed to prevent its being a preposition, and occurs only in subordinate clauses.

أَنْ *that*, as I wish to accompany you أُرِيْدُ أَنْ أُصَاحِبَكَ.

لَنْ = (أَنْ لَا = أَنْ لَا يَكُوْنُ) *it will not happen that*, *never*; as

He did not enter it and shall never enter it لَمْ يَدْخُلْهَا وَلَنْ يَدْخُلَهَا

إِذَنْ *then, in that case,* in answer to the question "what if".

| What if I believe God | إِنْ آمَنْتُ بِٱللّٰهِ |
| then thou shalt enter Paradise | إِذَنْ تَدْخُلَ ٱلجَنَّةَ |

كَيْ *in order*; as

| Learn in order that you may teach | تَعَلَّمُوا لِكَيْ تُعَلِّمُوا |

أَنْ is called ٱلْمَصْدَرِيَّةِ because with the verb it governs it is equivalent in meaning to the masdar of that verb; as

| I hope to assist you | أَرْجُو أَنْ أُسَاعِدَكَ , مُسَاعَدَتَكَ |

أَنْ has the meaning of longing or desire for something ٱلطَّمَعُ, and its verb can neither have a future signification nor follow another verb expressing certainty.

أَنْ may be omitted in the following cases:

(*a*). After the preposition لِ , ٱلتَّعْلِيلِ expressing the cause of an event; as

| I came to study | جِئْتُ لِلدَّرْسِ , جِئْتُ لِأَدْرُسَ |

(*b*). After a conjunction connecting a verb and noun; as

| I prefer flight and to be safe | أُفَضِّلُ ٱلْهَرَبَ وَأَسْلَمَ |

أَنْ although not expressed may affect the declension of the aorist; this ellipse is to be assumed in the following cases:

(*a*). After كَيْ a preposition which has not the لِ; as

| He sat in order that he might rest | جَلَسَ كَيْ يَسْتَرِيْحَ |

(*b*). After حَتَّى a preposition

I asked him to come ‏دَعَوْتُهُ حَتَّى يَأْتِيَ‎

(c). After ‏أَوْ‎ which has the meaning of ‏إِلَى‎ or ‏إِلَّا‎ *till, lest,* or *else*; as

Beat the thief till he confesses ‏إِضْرِبِ ٱللِّصَّ أَوْ يُقِرَّ‎

Sit, or else the prince will rise ‏إِجْلِسْ أَوْ يَقُومَ ٱلْأَمِيْرُ‎

(d). After ‏ل‎, ‏أَلْجَحُودُ‎ *denial*

This ‏ل‎ is prefixed to the predicate of ‏كَانَ‎ when it is in the negative, thereby strengthening the negation, as

God surely will not

torment the good ‏مَا كَانَ ٱللَّهُ لِيُعَذِّبَ ٱلصَّالِحِيْنَ‎

(e). After ‏فَ‎, ‏أَلـسَّـبَـبُ‎ *expressing result or effect,* and ‏و‎, ‏أَلْمُصَاحَبَةُ‎ *association,* following negation or request; as

I. Negation:

Zaid did not visit me that I

might honour him ‏لَمْ يَزُرْنِي زَيْدٌ فَأُكْرِمَهُ‎

The sheik is not present

that we might ask him ‏لَيْسَ ٱلشَّيْخُ حَاضِرًا وَنَسْأَلَهُ‎

II. Request.

Under request the following are included:

I. Command. II. Prohibition. III. Interrogation. IV. Exhortation. V. Threatening. VI. Wishing. VII. Hoping.

I. Strive and you will derive benefit ‏جِدَّ فَتَنَالَ ٱلْخَيْرَ‎

II. Do not speak or you will make a slip ‏لَا تَتَكَلَّمْ فَتَزِلَّ‎

III. Where are you going that I

may follow you ‏أَيْنَ تَذْهَبُ فَأَتْبَعَكَ‎

IV. Will you not study and
please your teacher   أَلَا تَدْرُسْ فَتُرْضِيَ مُعَلِّمَكَ

V. Why do you not believe and be safe   هَلَّا تُؤْمِنُ وَتَأْمَنَ

VI. Would that you were a
learned man to profit us   لَيْتَكَ عَالِمٌ وَتُفِيْدَنَا

VII. Perhaps I may go to Jerusalem then I will
visit you   لَعَلِّي أَذْهَبُ إِلَى ٱلْقُدْسِ وَأَزُوْرَكَ

II. THE CONDITIONAL AND IMPERATIVE MOODS.

جَوَازِمُ ٱلْفِعْلِ

The particles which apocopate the final vowel of the
aorist are of two kinds:

I. Those which apocopate the final vowel of one
verb only.

II. Those which apocopate the final vowel of two verbs.

I. These are لَمْ, لَمَّا, لِ, لَا .

لَمْ, لَمَّا *not, not yet*, are always used before the aorist
and give it the signification of the preterite; as

He did not come and then he came   لَمْ يَأْتِ ثُمَّ جَاءَ

I plucked the fruit when it
was not yet ripe   قَطَعْتُ ٱلثَّمَرَ وَلَمَّا يَنْضُجْ

The conditional particle إِنْ may precede لَمْ but not
لَمَّا, and the verb which follows لَمَّا but not that which
follows لَمْ may be dropped.

لِ *let*, and لَا *not*, give the aorist a future signification.

ل is used imperatively and in prayer; as

May God bless us لِيُبَارِكْنَا ٱللّٰهُ

Let every one know لِيَعْلَمْ كُلُّ وَاحِدٍ

لَا is used for prohibition ٱلنَّهْيُ, and prayer; as

Do not be angry with us لَا تَغْضَبْ عَلَيْنَا

Do not kill لَا تَقْتُلْ

ل when preceded by فَ or وَ may drop its ؟; as

May our God bless us فَلْيُبَارِكْنَا إِلٰهُنَا

II. Particles which apocopate the aorist of two Verbs

حَيْثُمَا, إِذْمَا, أَنَّى, أَيَّانَ, أَيْنَ, مَتَى, أَيٌّ, مَهْمَا, مَا, مَنْ, إِنْ
كَيْفَمَا and إِذَا in poetry.

These, with the exception of إِنْ, إِذَا, and مَا when it signifies time, are all regarded as nouns and are all except أَيٌّ indeclinable.

إِنْ *if*; as

If you seek you will find إِنْ تَطْلُبْ تَجِدْ

مَنْ *whosoever*; as

Whosoever cometh to me I will not cast out

مَنْ يُقْبِلْ إِلَيَّ لَا أُخْرِجْهُ خَارِجًا

مَا and مَهْمَا *whatsoever*; as

Whatsoever good you do God knoweth it

وَمَا تَفْعَلُوا مِنْ خَيْرٍ يَعْلَمْهُ ٱللّٰهُ

Whatsoever you bring us we will not believe

مَهْمَا تَأْتِنَا بِهِ لَا نُؤْمِنْ

أَيٌّ or أَيَّمَا *whosoever, whatsoever, whichsoever*; as

By whatsoever you call upon Him He has the most
excellent names أَيَّمَا تَدْعُوا فَلَهُ ٱلْأَسْمَآء ٱلْحُسْنَى

إِنْ مَا and أَيَّانَ, مَتَى مَا or مَتَى *whenever*; as

Whenever you meet us you die
with fear مَتَى تَلْقَنَا تَمُتْ رُعْبًا

Whenever you come to us you
will find good أَيَّانَ تَأْتِنَا تَلْقَ خَيْرًا

حَيْثُمَا and أَيْنَمَا or أَيْنَ *wherever*; as

Wherever you are death will
overtake you أَيْنَمَا تَكُونُوا يُدْرِكُّمُ ٱلْمَوْتُ

Wherever you go God will award you success
حَيْثُمَا تَذْهَبْ يُقَدِّرْ لَكَ ٱللّٰهُ نَجَاحًا

أَنَّى *wherever, whenever*; as

Wherever you are I will be أَنَّى تَكُنْ أَكُنْ

كَيْفَ. كَيْقَمَا *however*; as

However you sit I will sit كَيْفَمَا تَجْلِسْ أَجْلِسْ

Those of the particles which express time or place
are adverbs; the remainder may be (*a*) the subject, (*b*)
the objective complement or (*c*) the absolute object, as

(*a*). He who seeks finds مَنْ يَطْلُبْ يَجِدْ

(*b*). Whomsoever you love I will love أَيًّا تُحِبَّ أُحِبَّ

(*c*). Whatever walk you walk I
will follow أَيَّ سَيْرٍ تَسِرْ أَتْبَعَكَ

All these particles stand at the head of the sentence.

مَا must be affixed to اِنْ and حَيْثُ, but not to مَنْ, مَا, مَهْمَا or اَنَّى; it may or may not follow the other particles.

كَيْفَمَا can only be used when the verbs have the same root.

The first verb which is introduced by these particles is called فِعْلُ ٱلشَّرْطِ *the conditional verb*, protasis, and the second جَوَابُ ٱلشَّرْطِ *the answer to the condition*, apodosis, both are deprived of their final vowels on account of their dependence one upon the other.

فِعْلُ ٱلشَّرْطِ must be indicative and admit of conjugation, and not be preceded by س or سَوْفَ or قَدْ; جَوَابُ ٱلشَّرْطِ must always follow the conditional verb, and be preceded by ف when it is (*a*) a neuter verb, or (*b*) denotes request or (*c*) is preceded by س, قَدْ, مَا or لَنْ of negation, or (*d*) is a nominal sentence.

A nominal sentence may be introduced by اِذَا, *as well*, and if it is in the aorist affirmative or preceded by لَا the ف may be introduced; in these instances, the verb is in the nominative (not apocopated) and the sentence is فِي مَحَلِّ جَزْمٍ because it is the answer to the conditional verb.

When the verbs of both clauses are in the aorist or the first only is in the aorist, apocopation takes place; but when the first verb is in the preterite and the second in the aorist, the latter may or may not be apocopated.

If the ف is omitted, the second verb may be apocopated, in which case it is regarded as an answer to an implied verb of condition; as

Visit me and I will honour you   زُرْنِي أُكْرِمْكَ

as though written

Visit me and if you visit me

I will honour you   زُرْنِي وَإِنْ تَزُرْنِي أُكْرِمْكَ

The conditional verb has the form of the preterite and a future signification.

If the verb ends with a weak letter or ن masc. plur. or fem. sing. this is dropped   لَمْ تَفْعَلِي, لَمْ يَفْعَلُوا.

THE CONDITIONAL PARTICLES.

أَمَّا, لَوْ, لَوْلَا, لَومَا, لَمَّا

أَمَّا *but, but as for*, takes ف as its correlative; it is followed by a noun or pronoun; as

But as for me I shall die   أَمَّا أَنَا فَأَمُوتُ

As for the poor man it is

he who has no sense   أَمَّا ٱلْفَقِيرُ فَمَنْ لَا عَقْلَ لَهُ

لَوْ *if*, denotes condition with reference to past time, and signifies the non-existence of the result because of the non-existence of the condition, حَرْفُ ٱمْتِنَاعٍ لِٱمْتِنَاعٍ; it must be followed by a verb; as

Had God pleased he would have guided you all in
the right way لَوْ شَاءَ ٱللّٰهُ لَهَدَاكُمْ أَجْمَعِيْنَ

When followed by the aorist form of the verb the
past tense is signified; لَ is commonly used as its correlative. It always changes the statement of the verb,
if negative into affirmative and vice versa; as

Had he come to me I would have

honoured him لَوْ جَاءَنِي لَأَكْرَمْتُهُ

Had he not known he would

not have been responsible لَوْ لَمْ يَعْلَمْ لَمْ يُطَالَبْ

لَوْلَا and لَوْمَا (لَوْ with لَا and مَا) *were it not for, had
it not been for,* are conditional particles used with the
subject, the predicate of which is usually omitted; لَ is
generally used as their correlative; as

Had it not been for God we would

have perished لَوْلَا ٱللّٰهُ لَهَلَكْنَا

It is called حَرْفُ ٱمْتِنَاعٍ لِوُجُودٍ a particle denoting the
impossibility of one thing because of the existence of
another.

لَمَّا *when,* is an adverb expressing condition with
reference to past time and is only used with the preterite; as

When he brought you safe to the land you turned
away فَلَمَّا نَجَّاكُمْ إِلَى ٱلْبَرِّ أَعْرَضْتُمْ

It is called حَرْفُ وُجُودٍ لِوُجُودٍ a particle denoting the
existence of one thing because of the existence of another.

TENSES OF THE VERB. أَزْمِنَةُ ٱلْفِعْل

The Arabic Verb expresses the state rather than the time of an action or event. The state may be complete, a finished act; or incomplete, an unfinished act.

There are two forms of the verb to express these states, the preterite ٱلْمَاضِي *the past*, and the aorist ٱلْمُضَارِعُ *resembling*.

THE PRETERITE.

The Preterite includes:

I. All Past Tenses of other languages; the particular time of an action or event is to be inferred from the context or some accompanying particle; as

Many of his disciples went back

رَجَعَ كَثِيرُونَ مِنْ تَـلَامِيْذِهِ إِلَى ٱلْوَرَاءِ

Of a truth we have placed the gift of prophecy among the descendants of Jacob لَقَدْ جَعَلْنَا ٱلنُّبُوَّةَ فِي نَسْلِ يَعْقُوْبَ

The particle قَـدْ لِلتَّحْقِيْقِ assures the action of the verb and necessarily limits the preterite to a time actually past.

To express the pluperfect كَانَ is used with the preterite; as

Amr had sat كَانَ عَمْرُو قَدْ جَلَسَ

II. The Present Tense with such verbs as بَاعَ to sell, إِشْتَـرَى to buy, when used at the time of selling or buying; as

I sell you the camel for two pounds   بِعْتُكَ ٱلْجَمَلَ بِلِيْرَتَيْنِ

These verbs are called   عُقُوْدُ ٱلْإِنْشَـاءِ

III. The Future Tense when it is (a) دُعَـآءٌ, a prayer or curse; as

May God who is exalted above all have mercy upon you   } رَحِمَكَ ٱللّٰهُ تَعَالَى

May God preserve your existence   أَدَامَ ٱللّٰهُ بَقَاءَكُم

May God curse thee   لَعَنَكَ ٱللّٰهُ

(b). After the negative لا following an oath; as

By God I will not visit you until you visit me   } وَٱللّٰهُ لَا زُرْتُكَ حَتَّى تَزُوْرَنِي

(c). A condition or an answer to a condition; as

If you seek you will find   إِنْ طَلَبْتَ تَجِدْ

THE AORIST.

The Aorist indicates:

I. Present or Future Tense.

It is limited to the Present Tense when preceded by (a) لِ ٱلْإِبْتِدَآءِ, (b) the negative مَا or إِنْ, (c) the verb لَـيْـسَ; as

The days are really passing   إِنَّ ٱلْأَيَّامَ لَتَمُرُّ

The ignorant one does not know his good from his evil   } ٱلْجَـاهِلُ لَيْسَ يَعْلَمُ خَيْرَهُ مِنْ شَرِّهِ

It is limited to the Future Tense when preceded by

(a). The particles سَ a near future or سَـوْفَ a remote future; as

The new moon will become a full moon سَيَصِيرُ ٱلْهِلَالُ بَدْرًا

Your Lord will give to you and you will be satisfied. سَوْفَ يُعْطِيكَ رَبُّكَ فَتَرْضَى

(b). Particles of نَصْب; as

I long to see you أَشْتَاقُ لِأَنْ أَرَاكَ

(c). Particles of Expectation أَدَاةُ ٱلتَّوَقُّع; as

Perchance I may come لَعَلِّي آتِي

(d). لَوْ or قَدْ; as If you know لَوْ تَعْلَمُونَ

(e). When it expresses دُعَاء a prayer or curse; as

May God help you يُسَاعِدُكَ ٱللّٰهُ

(f). When it expresses condition or is an answer to a condition; as

Whosoever studies will acquire learning مَنْ يَدْرُسْ يَحْفَظْ

II. Past Tense when preceded by لَمْ or لَمَّا particles of جَزْم; as

I did not hear لَمْ أَسْمَعْ

The day did not break لَمْ يَطْلَعِ ٱلنَّهَارُ

III. An idiomatic use of the aorist is seen in such phrases as

Zaid drinks wine زَيْدٌ يَشْرَبُ ٱلْخَمْرَ i. e. is in the habit of.

The negro bears the heat ٱلزِّنْجِيُّ يَحْتَمِلُ ٱلْحَرَّ i. e. is able to.

IV. At times no special tense is indicated by the aorist; as

Zaid reads زَيْدٌ يَقْرَأُ

V. كَانَ with the aorist expresses the imperfect tense of the Greek and Latin languages.

THE NEGATIVE PARTICLES. أَدَوَاتُ ٱلنَّفْيِ

The negative particles are: لَمْ, لَنْ, إِنْ, لَاتَ, لَا, مَا; لَيْسَ, لَمَّا; of these لَيْسَ is a verb.

لَنْ, لَمَّا, لَمْ precede the aorist only.

لَيْسَ *not*, is used only with nouns, adverbs and prepositions; as

The army is not prepared لَيْسَ ٱلْجَيْشُ مُسْتَعِدًّا

لَمْ (*did*) *not* لَمَّا (*did*) *not yet*, are used with the aorist and give it the signification of the past tense; they differ in that لَمْ is a simple negative, whilst لَمَّا negatives till a special time; as

The guest arose and had not eaten قَامَ ٱلضَّيْفُ وَلَمَّا يَأْكُلْ

لَنْ *never*, gives the aorist a future signification; as

He will never see death لَنْ يَرَى ٱلْمَوْتَ

إِنْ, *not*, does not precede the future tense.

لَا *not, no*, is a general negative for all tenses.

THE PARTICLES سَ, سَوْفَ and قَدْ

When these precede the aorist they give it a future signification.

سَوْف is called حَرْف تَسْوِيف from سَوَّف to *delay*.

س is called حَرْف تَوْسِيْع or حَرْف تَنْفِيْس *widening*.

قَدْ is called حَرْف ٱلتَّوَقُّع *particle of expectation*.

قَدْ precedes a verb in the indicative mood; with the preterite it expresses certainty; with the aorist doubt; as

We have believed قَدْ آمَنَّا

The liar may sometimes speak
the truth قَدْ يَصْدُقُ ٱلْكَذُوبُ

THE LETTER نُوْن

The نُوْن is of five kinds:

I. نُوْن ٱلتَّوْكِيْد *assurance*, which is annexed for emphasis to the aorist when this has a future signification. It is either

(*a*). Silent, or (*b*) Doubled; as

(*a*). Worship thou God أُسْجُدَنْ لِلّٰهِ

(*b*). Keep the commandments of
thy God إِحْفَظَنَّ وَصَايَا إِلٰهِكَ

II. نُوْن ٱلتَّنْوِيْن *the nunation*.

III. نُوْن ٱلإِنَاتِ *the* ن *of the feminine gender* viz.

(*a*) the personal pron. plural (*b*) sign of fem. plural; as

(*a*). The women knew and know ٱلنّسَآءَ عَلِمْنَ وَيَعْلَمْنَ

(*b*). Ye women knew أَنْتُنَّ عَلِمْتُنَّ

IV. نُوْن ٱلْوِقَايَةِ *protection*, also called نُوْن ٱلْعِمَادِ; it separates the verb from the آيَ, ٱلْمُتَكَلِّمُ and so prevents its final vowel from being changed into =.

It is also used with the particles that resemble verbs, the prepositions مِنْ and عَنْ, the إِسْمُ ٱلْفِعْلِ and the particle لَدُنْ.

V. نُوْنُ زَائِدَة *pleonastic*.

(*a*). نُوْنُ ٱلْإِعْرَابِ which is found in the five verbs; as

All men know him كُلُّ ٱلنَّاسِ يَعْرِفُونَهُ

(*b*). نُوْنُ of dual, رَجُلَانِ Two men.

(*c*). نُوْنُ of plural مُؤْمِنُوْنَ Believers.

VERBS OF WONDER. أَفْعَالُ ٱلتَّعَجُّبِ

These are on two measures:

I. مَا أَفْعَلَ.

II. أَفْعِلْ بِ.

I. The مَا is an indefinite noun qualified by an implied adjective expressing greatness; as

How generous is Zaid مَا أَكْرَمَ زَيْدًا

How handsome he is مَا أَحْسَنَهُ

مَا is the مُبْتَدَآء and أَكْرَمَ the verb of wonder with its agent implied مُسْتَتِرٌ وُجُوبًا referring to the مَا; and the sentence forms the predicate of مَا Zaid is the object in the accusative.

II. أَفْعِلْ بِ (the form is imperative).

241

The thing wondered at (أَلْمُتَعَجَّبُ مِنْهُ) is put in the genitive by بِ and is the agent of the verb.

How noble he is أَكْرِمْ بِهِ   How noble is Zaid أَكْرِمْ بِزَيْدٍ

These verbs cannot be conjugated; they follow the rules of the noun of superiority.

كَانَ signifying past time is sometimes introduced after مَا without having an اِسْمٌ or خَبَرٌ; as

How wise he was   مَا كَانَ أَحْكَمَهُ

VERBS OF PRAISE AND BLAME.
أَفْعَالُ ٱلْمَدْحِ وَٱلذَّمّ

These are four in number, namely

نِعْمَ   حَبَّذَا   for praise

بِئْسَ   سَاءَ   for blame.

The agent must either have the article or be in construction with a noun which has it; or be an implied pronoun, in which case the indefinite noun is put in the accusative as تَمْيِيزٌ

He is a good man is Zaid   نِعْمَ رَجُلًا زَيْدٌ

In the verb حَبَّذَا, compounded of ذَا and حَبَّ, ذَا is the agent and remains the same for all numbers and genders. The agent of نِعْمَ بِئْسَ and سَاءَ may take the dual, plural or feminine; as

She is a good woman is Hind   نِعْمَت ٱلْمَرْأَةُ هِنْدُ

They are bad men Zaid and Amr   بِئْسَ ٱلرَّجُلَانِ زَيْدٌ وَعَمْرٌو

16

Evil are the people the infidels سَاءَ ٱلْقَوْمُ ٱلْكَــافِرُونَ

The man is good that praised one Zaid نِعْمَ الرَّجُلُ زَيْدٌ

That which is praised or blamed is mentioned immediately after the agent. It is put in the nominative case either as مُبْتَدَأٌ مُوَخَّرٌ in which case the verb with its agent forms the predicate, or as the predicate when the subject is the implied words of praise or blame; as

Good is the man (the praised one) Zaid نِعمَ ٱلرَّجُلِ (ٱلْمَمْدُوْحُ) زَيْدٌ

Other words for praise or blame are on the measure فَــعُــلَ.

A noble man is Zaid شَرُفَ ٱلرَّجُلُ زَيْدٌ

ٱلْٱشْتِغَالُ Diversion from the original object.

In the sentence زَيْدٌ ضَرَبْتُـهُ Zaid is in reality the object of ضَرَبَ but the verb governs the pronoun ه in the accusative as object and Zaid as it stands at the head of the sentence is put in the nominative as مُبْتَدَأٌ. Zaid may, however, be put in the accusative as the objective complement, by assuming the ellipse of another verb.

If the word Zaid is preceded by a particle peculiar to verbs, as إِنْ, it is put in the accusative but if by those peculiar to nouns it is put in the nominative; as

If you honour Zaid he will honour you إِنْ زَيْدًا أَكْرَمْتَهُ يُكْرِمْكَ

I went out and behold they

were beating Zaid خَرَجْبُ وَإِذَا زَيْدٌ يَضْرِبُونَهُ

This also occurs in the case of the agent; as

If Zaid rises I will rise إِنْ زَيْدٌ قَامَ أَقُمْ

Zaid is the agent to an omitted verb.

DERIVED NOUNS WHICH GOVERN AS VERBS.

The nouns of agent, excess and object govern as verbs:

(*a*). When they have the article prefixed.

(*b*). When they are preceded by a particle of interrogation or negation; as

Is Zaid beating Amr أَضَارِبٌ زَيْدٌ عَمْرًا

(*c*). When they have the present or future signification and are 1) خَبَر or 2) نَعْت or 3) حَال; as

1). Zaid is riding a horse زَيْدٌ رَاكِبٌ فَرَسًا

2) I saw a man riding a horse رَأَيْتُ رَجُلًا رَاكِبًا فَرَسًا

3) Zaid came riding a horse جَاءَ زَيْدٌ رَاكِبًا فَرَسًا

The noun of object takes the نَائِبُ ٱلْفِعْل substitute for the agent; as

Is your finger wounded هَلْ مَجْرُوحٌ أُصْبُعُكَ

The noun of agent of a transitive verb takes both an object and an agent, whilst that of an intransitive verb takes an agent only; as

Zaid is not doing good مَا صَانِعٌ زَيْدٌ خَيْرًا

The object of the noun of agent is in the accusative; as

I was pleased by Zaid's riding

of the horse أَعْجَبَنِي رُكُوبُ زَيْدٍ ٱلْفَرَسَ

The noun of attribute may govern as a verb; as

Zaid is fair of face زَيْدٌ حَسَنٌ وَجْهُهُ

The noun of superiority also governs as a verb but its agent is expressed only when the noun itself is convertible into a verb; as

There is no man to whom study is more beneficial

than Zaid لَا رَجُلَ أَنْفَعُ لَهُ ٱلدَّرْسُ مِنْ زَيْدٍ

جُمُودُ ٱلْفِعْلِ from جَمُدَ to *harden.*

The verb is either مُتَصَرِّفٌ conjugated throughout as to tenses, voices, and derivative nouns, or جَامِدٌ indeclinable. The verb is indeclinable when it resembles the particle in meaning, as لَيْسَ which has the meaning of لَا *not,* and عَسَى *perhaps,* which has the meaning of لَعَلَّ.

Some verbs are only indeclinable when they have special meanings as the verbs of wonder, in which case they must immediately precede the noun they govern.

APPENDIX.

TO FOLLOW LIST OF TRILITERAL VERBS.

DERIVED FORMS OF THE DOUBLED VERB.

Noun of Object. Noun of Action with م. Noun of Place and Time.	Noun of Agent.	Noun of Unity and Species.	Noun of Action.	Passive.		Imperative.	Active.	
				Aorist.	Preterite.		Aorist.	Preterite.
مُمَدَّد	مُمَدِّد	تَمْدِيدَة	تَمْدِيد	يُمَدَّد	مُدِّد	مَدِّد	يُمَدِّد	مَدَّد
مُمَادّ	مُمَادّ	مُمَادَّة (رِحْلَة)	مُمَادّة	يُمَادّ	مُودّ	مَادّ	يُمَادّ	مَادّ
مُمَدّ	مُمِدّ	اِمْدَادَة	اِمْدَاد	يُمَدّ	أُمِدّ	أَمْدِدْ	يُمِدّ	أَمَدّ
مُتَمَدَّد	مُتَمَدِّد	تَمَدُّدَة	تَمَدُّد	يُتَمَدَّد	تُمُدِّد	تَمَدَّد	يَتَمَدَّد	تَمَدَّد
مُتَمَادّ	مُتَمَادّ	تَمَادّة	تَمَادّ	يُتَمَادّ	تُمُودّ	تَمَادّ	يَتَمَادّ	تَمَادّ
مُنْمَدّ	مُنْمَدّ	اِنْمِدَادَة	اِنْمِدَاد	يُنْمَدّ	اُنْمُدّ	اِنْمَدّ	يَنْمَدّ	اِنْمَدّ
مُمْتَدّ	مُمْتَدّ	اِمْتِدَادَة	اِمْتِدَاد	يُمْتَدّ	اُمْتُدّ	اِمْتَدّ	يَمْتَدّ	اِمْتَدّ
مُسْتَمَدّ	مُسْتَمِدّ	اِسْتِمْدَادَة	اِسْتِمْدَاد	يُسْتَمَدّ	اُسْتُمِدّ	اِسْتَمْدِد	يَسْتَمِدّ	اِسْتَمَدّ

DERIVED FORMS OF VERBS WITH INITIAL HEMZEH.

Noun of Object. Noun of Action with م. Noun of Place and Time.	Noun of Agent.	Noun of Unity and Species.	Noun of Action.	Passive.		Imperative.	Active.	
				Aorist.	Preterite.		Aorist.	Preterite.
مُؤَكَّل	مُؤَكِّل	تَأْكِيلَة	تَأْكِيل، تَأْكِلَة	يُؤَكَّل	أُكِّل	أَكِّلْ	يُؤَكِّل	أَكَّلَ
مُؤَاكَل	مُؤَاكِل	(أَحَدُهُ) مُؤَاكَلَة	مُؤَاكَلَة، إِكَال	يُؤَاكَل	أُوكِل	آكِلْ	يُؤَاكِل	آكَلَ
مُؤْكَل	مُؤْكِل	إِيكَالَة	إِيكَال	يُؤْكَل	أُوكِل	أَكِلْ	يُؤْكِل	أَكَلَ
مُتَآكَل	مُتَآكِل	تَآكُلَة	تَآكُل	يُتَآكَل	تُؤُكِل	تَآكَلْ	يَتَآكَل	تَآكَلَ
مُتَأَكَّل	مُتَأَكِّل	تَأَكُّلَة	انْتِكَال	يُتَأَكَّل	تُؤُكِّل	تَأَكَّلْ	يَتَأَكَّل	تَأَكَّلَ
مُؤْتَكَل	مُؤْتَكِل	ائْتِكَالَة	ائْتِكَال	يُؤْتَكَل	ائْتُوكِل	ائْتَكِلْ	يَأْتَكِل	ائْتَكَلَ
مُسْتَأْكَل	مُسْتَأْكِل	اسْتِئْكَالَة	اسْتِئْكَال	يُسْتَأْكَل	اسْتُؤْكِل	اسْتَأْكِلْ	يَسْتَأْكِل	اسْتَأْكَلَ

DERIVED FORMS OF VERBS WITH MEDIAL HEMZEH.

Noun of Object. Noun of Action with مَ Noun of Place and Time.	Noun of Agent.	Noun of Unity and Species.	Noun of Action.	Passive		Imperative.	Active	
				Aorist.	Preterite.		Aorist.	Preterite.
مَسْأَل	سَائِل	تَسْئِلَة	تَسْئِيل تَسْئِلَة	يُسْأَل	سُئِل	سَلْ	يَسْأَل	سَأَل
مَسَائَل	مُسَائِل	(وَاحِدَة) مُسَاءَلَة سِئَال	سِئَال مُسَاءَلَة	يُسَاءَل	سُوئِل	سَائِل	يُسَائِل	سَاءَل
مَسْأَل	مُسْئِل	إِسْآل	إِسْآل	يُسْأَل	أُسْئِل	أَسْئِلْ	يُسْئِل	أَسْأَل
مُتَسَأَّل	مُتَسَأِّل	تَسَأُّل	تَسَأُّل	يُتَسَأَّل	تُسُئِّل	تَسَأَّلْ	يَتَسَأَّل	تَسَأَّل
مُتَسَاءَل	مُتَسَائِل	تَسَاؤُل	تَسَاؤُل	يُتَسَاءَل	تُسُوئِل	تَسَاءَلْ	يَتَسَاءَل	تَسَاءَل
مُنْسَأَل	مُنْسَئِل	اِنْسِئَال	اِنْسِئَال	يُنْسَأَل	اُنْسُئِل	اِنْسَئِلْ	يَنْسَأَل	اِنْسَأَل
مُسْتَأَل	مُسْتَئِل	اِسْتِئَال	اِسْتِئَال	يُسْتَأَل	اُسْتُئِل	اِسْتَئِلْ	يَسْتَأَل	اِسْتَأَل
مُسْتَسْأَل	مُسْتَسْئِل	اِسْتِسْآل	اِسْتِسْآل	يُسْتَسْأَل	اُسْتُسْئِل	اِسْتَسْئِلْ	يَسْتَسْأَل	اِسْتَسْأَل

DERIVED FORMS OF VERBS WITH FINAL HEMZEH.

250

Noun of Object. Noun of Action with م. Noun of Place and Time.	Noun of Agent.	Noun of Unity and Species.	Noun of Action.	Passive.		Imperative.	Active.	
				Aorist.	Preterite.		Aorist.	Preterite.
مُقَرَّأ	مُقَرِّئ	تَقْرِيئَة	تَقْرِئَة	يُقَرَّأ	قُرِّئَ	قَرِّئ	يُقَرِّئ	قَرَّأ
مُقَارَأ	مُقَارِئ	مُقَارَأَة قِرَاء	مُقَارَأَة قِرَاء	يُقَارَأ	قُورِئَ	قَارِئ	يُقَارِئ	قَارَأ
مُتَقَرَّأ	مُتَقَرِّئ	تَقَرُّؤ	تَقَرُّؤ	يُتَقَرَّأ	تُقُرِّئَ	تَقَرَّأ	يَتَقَرَّأ	تَقَرَّأ
مُتَقَارَأ	مُتَقَارِئ	تَقَارُؤ	تَقَارُؤ	يُتَقَارَأ	تُقُورِئَ	تَقَارَأ	يَتَقَارَأ	تَقَارَأ
مُقْتَرَأ	مُقْتَرِئ	اِقْتِرَاء	اِقْتِرَاء	يُقْتَرَأ	اُقْتُرِئَ	اِقْتَرِئ	يَقْتَرِئ	اِقْتَرَأ
مُنْقَرَأ	مُنْقَرِئ	اِنْقِرَاء	اِنْقِرَاء	يُنْقَرَأ	اُنْقُرِئَ	اِنْقَرِئ	يَنْقَرِئ	اِنْقَرَأ
مُسْتَقْرَأ	مُسْتَقْرِئ	اِسْتِقْرَاء	اِسْتِقْرَاء	يُسْتَقْرَأ	اُسْتُقْرِئَ	اِسْتَقْرِئ	يَسْتَقْرِئ	اِسْتَقْرَأ

DERIVED FORMS OF VERBS WITH INITIAL و.

Noun of Object. Noun of Action with م. Noun of Place and Time.	Noun of Agent.	Noun of Unity and Species.	Noun of Action.	Passive		Imperative.	Active	
				Aorist.	Preterite.		Aorist.	Preterite.
مُوَعَّدٌ	مُوَعِّدٌ	تَوْعِدَةٌ	تَوْعِيدٌ تَوْعِدَةٌ	يُوَعَّدُ	وُعِّدَ	وَعِّدْ	يُوَعِّدُ	وَعَّدَ
مُوَاعَدٌ	مُوَاعِدٌ	مُوَاعَدَةٌ (وِعَادَةٌ)	مُوَاعَدَةٌ وِعَادٌ	يُوَاعَدُ	وُوعِدَ	وَاعِدْ	يُوَاعِدُ	وَاعَدَ
مُوعَدٌ	مُوعِدٌ	إيعَادَةٌ	إيعَادٌ	يُوعَدُ	أُوعِدَ	أَوْعِدْ	يُوعِدُ	أَوْعَدَ
مُتَوَعَّدٌ	مُتَوَعِّدٌ	تَوَعُّدَةٌ	تَوَعُّدٌ	يُتَوَعَّدُ	تُوُعِّدَ	تَوَعَّدْ	يَتَوَعَّدُ	تَوَعَّدَ
مُتَوَاعَدٌ	مُتَوَاعِدٌ	تَوَاعُدَةٌ	تَوَاعُدٌ	يُتَوَاعَدُ	تُوُوعِدَ	تَوَاعَدْ	يَتَوَاعَدُ	تَوَاعَدَ
مُتَّعَدٌ	مُتَّعِدٌ	اتِّعَادَةٌ	اتِّعَادٌ	يُتَّعَدُ	اتُّعِدَ	اتَّعِدْ	يَتَّعِدُ	اتَّعَدَ
مُسْتَوعَدٌ	مُسْتَوعِدٌ	اسْتِيعَادَةٌ	اسْتِيعَادٌ	يُسْتَوعَدُ	اسْتُوعِدَ	اسْتَوْعِدْ	يَسْتَوْعِدُ	اسْتَوْعَدَ

DERIVED FORMS OF THE HOLLOW VERB.

Noun of Object. Noun of Action with م. Noun of Place and Time.	Noun of Agent.	Noun of Unity and Species.	Noun of Action.	Passive — Aorist.	Passive — Preterite.	Imperative.	Active — Aorist.	Active — Preterite.
مُخَوَّف	مُخَوِّف	تَخْوِيفَة	تَخْوِيف	يُخَوَّف	خُوِّف	خَوِّف	يُخَوِّف	خَوَّف
مُخَاوَف	مُخَاوِف	مُخَاوَفَة، حِوَاف	مُخَاوَفَة، حِوَاف	يُخَاوَف	خُووِف	خَاوِف	يُخَاوِف	خَاوَف
مُخَاف	مُخِيف	إِخَافَة (إِخَاذَة)	إِخَافَة	يُخَاف	أُخِيف	أَخِف	يُخِيف	أَخَاف
مُتَخَوَّف	مُتَخَوِّف	تَخَوُّفَة	تَخَوُّف	يُتَخَوَّف	تُخُوِّف	تَخَوَّف	يَتَخَوَّف	تَخَوَّف
مُتَخَاوَف	مُتَخَاوِف	تَخَاوُفَة	تَخَاوُف	يُتَخَاوَف	تُخُووِف	تَخَاوَف	يَتَخَاوَف	تَخَاوَف
مُنْخَاف	مُنْخَاف	اِنْخِيَاف	اِنْخِيَاف	يُنْخَاف	اُنْخِيف	اِنْخَف	يَنْخَاف	اِنْخَاف
مُخْتَاف	مُخْتَاف	اِخْتِيَافَة	اِخْتِيَاف	يُخْتَاف	اُخْتِيف	اِخْتَف	يَخْتَاف	اِخْتَاف
مُسْتَخَاف	مُسْتَخِيف	اِسْتِخَافَة، أَحْدَثَة	اِسْتِخَافَة	يُسْتَخَاف	اُسْتُخِيف	اِسْتَخِف	يَسْتَخِيف	اِسْتَخَاف

DERIVED FORMS OF VERBS BEGINNING WITH ي.

Noun of Object. Noun of Action with م. Noun of Place and Time.	Noun of Agent.	Noun of Unity and Species.	Noun of Action.	Passive.		Imperative.	Active.	
				Aorist.	Preterite.		Aorist.	Preterite.
مُيَسَّر	مُيَسِّر	تَيْسِيْر تَيْسِرَة	تَيْسِيْر تَيْسِرَة	يُيَسَّر	يُسِّر	يَسِّر	يُيَسِّر	يَسَّر
مُيَاسَر	مُيَاسِر	مُيَاسَرَة (وَاحِدَة)	مُيَاسَرَة يِسَار	يُيَاسَر	يُوسِر	يَاسِر	يُيَاسِر	يَاسَر
مُوسَر	مُوسِر	إِيْسَارَة	إِيْسَار	يُوسَر	أُوسِر	أَيْسِر	يُوسِر	أَيْسَر
مُتَيَسَّر	مُتَيَسِّر	تَيَسُّرَة	تَيَسُّر	يُتَيَسَّر	تُيُسِّر	تَيَسَّر	يَتَيَسَّر	تَيَسَّر
مُتَيَاسَر	مُتَيَاسِر	تَيَاسُرَة	تَيَاسُر	يُتَيَاسَر	تُيُوسِر	تَيَاسَر	يَتَيَاسَر	تَيَاسَر
مُنْيَسَر	مُنْيَسِر	إِنْيِسَارَة	إِنْيِسَار	يُنْيَسَر	أُنْيُسِر	إِنْيَسِر	يَنْيَسِر	إِنْيَسَر
مُتَّسَر	مُتَّسِر	إِتِّسَارَة	إِتِّسَار	يُتَّسَر	أُتُّسِر	إِتَّسِر	يَتَّسِر	إِتَّسَر
مُسْتَيْسَر	مُسْتَيْسِر	إِسْتِيْسَارَة	إِسْتِيْسَار	يُسْتَيْسَر	أُسْتُوسِر	إِسْتَيْسِر	يَسْتَيْسِر	إِسْتَيْسَر

DERIVED FORMS OF VERBS WITH FINAL ي.

Noun of Object. Noun of Action with مِ. Noun of Place and Time.	Noun of Agent.	Noun of Unity and Species.	Noun of Action.	Passive.		Imperative.	Active.	
				Aorist.	Preterite.		Aorist.	Preterite.
مُغَزَّى	مُغَزِّى	تَغْزِيَةً (وَاحِدَةً)	تَغْزِيَةً	يُغَزَّى	غُزِّيَ	غَزِّ	يُغَزِّى	غَزَّى
مُغَازَى	مُغَازِى	مُغَازَاةً (وَاحِدَةً)	مُغَازَاةً، غِزَاءً	يُغَازَى	غُوزِيَ	غَازِ	يُغَازِى	غَازَى
مُغْزَى	مُغْزِى	إِغْزَاءً	إِغْزَاءً	يُغْزَى	أُغْزِيَ	أَغْزِ	يُغْزِى	أَغْزَى
مُتَغَزَّى	مُتَغَزِّى	تَغَزِّيَةً	تَغَزِّيًا	يُتَغَزَّى	تُغُزِّيَ	تَغَزَّ	يَتَغَزَّى	تَغَزَّى
مُتَغَازَى	مُتَغَازِى	تَغَازِيَةً	تَغَازِيًا	يُتَغَازَى	تُغُوزِيَ	تَغَازَ	يَتَغَازَى	تَغَازَى
مُنْغَزَى	مُنْغَزِى	اِنْغِزَاءَةً	اِنْغِزَاءً	يُنْغَزَى	اُنْغُزِيَ	اِنْغَزِ	يَنْغَزِى	اِنْغَزَى
مُغْتَزَى	مُغْتَزِى	اِغْتِزَاءَةً	اِغْتِزَاءً	يُغْتَزَى	اُغْتُزِيَ	اِغْتَزِ	يَغْتَزِى	اِغْتَزَى
مُسْتَغْزَى	مُسْتَغْزِى	اِسْتِغْزَاءَةً	اِسْتِغْزَاءً	يُسْتَغْزَى	اُسْتُغْزِيَ	اِسْتَغْزِ	يَسْتَغْزِى	اِسْتَغْزَى

DERIVED FORMS OF VERBS WITH FINAL ي.

Noun of Object. Noun of Action with م. Noun of Place and Time.	Noun of Agent.	Noun of Unity and Species.	Noun of Action.	Passive Aorist.	Passive Preterite.	Imperative.	Active Aorist.	Active Preterite.
مَخْشًى	(مُ)	(وَاحِدٌ) تَخْشِيَةٌ	تَخْشِيَةٌ	يُخْشَى	خُشِّى	خَشِّ	يُخَشِّى	خَشِّى
مُتَخَاشًى	»	(وَاحِدٌ) مُخَاشَاةٌ خِشَاءٌ	مُخَاشَاةٌ خِشَاءٌ	يُخَاشَى	خُوشِى	خَاشِ	يُخَاشِى	خَاشَى
مُخْتَشًى	»	إِخْشَاءٌ	إِخْشَاءٌ	يُخْشَى	خُشِى	أَخْشِ	يُخْشِى	أَخْشَى
مُتَخَشًّى	»	تَخْشِيَةٌ	تَخَشٍّ	يُتَخَشَّى	تُخُشِّى	تَخَشَّ	يَتَخَشَّى	تَخَشَّى
مُتَخَاشًى	»	تَخَاشٍ	تَخَاشٍ	يُتَخَاشَى	تُخُوشِى	تَخَاشَ	يَتَخَاشَى	تَخَاشَى
مُنْخَشًى	»	اِنْخِشَاءٌ	اِنْخِشَاءٌ	يُنْخَشَى	أُنْخُشِى	اِنْخَشِ	يَنْخَشِى	اِنْخَشَى
مُخْتَشًى	»	اِخْتِشَاءٌ	اِخْتِشَاءٌ	يُخْتَشَى	أُخْتُشِى	اِخْتَشِ	يَخْتَشِى	اِخْتَشَى
مُسْتَخْشًى	»	اِسْتِخْشَاءٌ	اِسْتِخْشَاءٌ	يُسْتَخْشَى	اُسْتُخْشِى	اِسْتَخْشِ	يَسْتَخْشِى	اِسْتَخْشَى

DERIVED FORMS OF VERBS WITH MEDIAL و, AND FINAL ى.

Noun of Object. Noun of Action with مـ. Noun of Place and Time.	Noun of Agent.	Noun of Unity and Species.	Noun of Action.	Passive Aorist.	Passive Preterite.	Imperative.	Active Aorist.	Active Preterite.
مُرَوَّى	مُرَوِّى (و)	تَرْوِيَة (رِواية) (وَاحِدَة)	تَرْوِيَة	يُرَوَّى	رُوِّى	رَوِّ	يُرَوِّى	رَوَّى
مُرَاوَى	مُرَاوِى	مُرَاوَاة (وَاحِدَة)	مُرَاوَاة، رِوَاء	يُرَاوَى	رُووِى	رَاوِ	يُرَاوِى	رَاوَى
مُرْوَى	مُرْوِى	إِرْوَاءَة	إِرْوَاء	يُرْوَى	أُرْوِى	أَرْوِ	يُرْوِى	أَرْوَى
مُتَرَوَّى	مُتَرَوِّى	تَرْوِيَة	تَرَوٍّ	يُتَرَوَّى	تُرُوِّى	تَرَوَّ	يَتَرَوَّى	تَرَوَّى
مُتَرَاوَى	مُتَرَاوِى	تَرَاوٍ	تَرَاوٍ	يُتَرَاوَى	تُرُووِى	تَرَاوَ	يَتَرَاوَى	تَرَاوَى
مُنْرَوَى	مُنْرَوِى	اِرْوِيَة	اِرْوِاء	يُنْرَوَى	اُرْوِى	اِرْوِ	يَنْرَوِى	اِرْوَى
مُرْتَوَى	مُرْتَوِى	اِرْتِوَاء	اِرْتِوَاء	يُرْتَوَى	اُرْتُوِى	اِرْتَوِ	يَرْتَوِى	اِرْتَوَى
مُسْتَرْوَى	مُسْتَرْوِى	اِسْتِرْوَاءَة	اِسْتِرْوَاء	يُسْتَرْوَى	اُسْتُرْوِى	اِسْتَرْوِ	يَسْتَرْوِى	اِسْتَرْوَى

DERIVED FORMS OF VERBS WITH MEDIAL ‚ AND FINAL ي.

Noun of Object. Noun of Action with م. Noun of Place and Time.	Noun of Agent.	Noun of Unity and Species.	Noun of Action.	Passive		Imperative.	Active	
				Aorist.	Preterite.		Aorist.	Preterite.
مُطَوَّى	مُطَوِّى (و)	تَطْوِيَةٌ (واحِدة)	تَطْوِيَةٌ	يُطَوَّى	طُوِّى	طَوِّ	يُطَوِّى	طَوَّى
مُطَاوَى	مُطَاوِى »	مُطَاوَاةٌ (واحِدة)	مُطَاوَاةٌ طِوَاءٌ	يُطَاوَى	طُووِى	طَاوِ	يُطَاوِى	طَاوَى
مُطْوَى	مُطْوِى »	اِطْوَاءَةٌ	اِطْوَاءٌ	يُطْوَى	أُطْوِى	أَطْوِ	يُطْوِى	أَطْوَى
مُتَطَوَّى	مُتَطَوِّى »	تَطَوِّيَةٌ	تَطَوُّ	يُتَطَوَّى	تُطُوِّى	تَطَوَّ	يَتَطَوَّى	تَطَوَّى
مُتَطَاوَى	مُتَطَاوِى »	اِنْطَوَاءَةٌ	تَطَاوُ	يُتَطَاوَى	تُطُووِى	تَطَاوَ	يَتَطَاوَى	تَطَاوَى
مُنْطَوَى	مُنْطَوِى »	اِنْطِوَاءَةٌ	اِنْطِوَاءٌ	يُنْطَوَى	اُنْطُوِى	اِنْطَوِ	يَنْطَوِى	اِنْطَوَى
مُطَّوَى	مُطَّوِى »	اِطِّوَاءَةٌ	اِطِّوَاءٌ	يُطَّوَى	اُطُّوِى	اِطَّوِ	يَطَّوِى	اِطَّوَى
مُسْتَطْوَى	مُسْتَطْوِى »	اِسْتِطْوَاءَةٌ	اِسْتِطْوَاءٌ	يُسْتَطْوَى	اُسْتُطْوِى	اِسْتَطْوِ	يَسْتَطْوِى	اِسْتَطْوَى

DERIVED VERBS.

I. فَعَّلَ

To make distant	بَعَّدَ	To found	أَسَّسَ
,, rebuke	بَكَّت	,, compose, compile	أَلَّفَ
,, inform	بَلَّغَ	,, hope	أَمَّلَ
,, wet	بَلَّلَ	,, entrust	أَمَّنَ
,, give chloroform	بَنَّجَ	,, strengthen	أَيَّدَ
,, blow a trumpet	بَوَّق	,, honour	بَجَّلَ
,, make plain, clear	بَيَّنَ	,, burn incense	بَخَّرَ
,, fulfil	تَمَّمَ	,, scatter	بَدَّدَ
,, value	ثَمَّنَ	,, change	بَدَّلَ
,, blaspheme	جَدَّفَ	,, pitch a tent	خَيَّمَ
,, row	جَذَّفَ	,, manage well	دَبَّرَ
,, try, tempt	جَرَّبَ	,, train	دَرَّبَ
,, strip	جَرَّدَ	,, destroy utterly	دَمَّرَ
,, divide	جَزَّأَ	,, winnow	ذَرَّى
,, levy troops	جَنَّدَ	,, gild	ذَهَّبَ
,, compose an elegy	أَبَّنَ	,, appoint a chief	رَأَّسَ
,, impress, influence	أَثَّرَ	,, foster	رَبَّى
,, grant a delay	أَجَّلَ	,, arrange	رَتَّبَ
,, retard	أَخَّرَ	,, cause to return	رَجَّعَ
,, call to prayer	أَذَّنَ	,, frighten	رَهَّبَ
,, date	أَرَّخَ	,, play upon a reed	زَمَّرَ

To adorn	زَيَّنَ	To give choice	خَيَّرَ
,, praise	سَبَّحَ	,, dye red	ضَرَّج
,, register	سَجَّلَ	,, embroider	طَرَّزَ
,, heat	سَخَّنَ	,, divorce	طَلَّق
,, arm	سَلَّحَ	,, cleanse	طَهَّرَ
,, surrender	سَلَّمَ	,, bless	طَوَّبَ
,, nail	سَمَّرَ	,, overshadow	ظَلَّلَ
,, permit	جَوَّزَ	,, express, to cause to	
,, gather troops	جَيَّشَ	pass over	عَبَّرَ
,, make lovable	حَبَّبَ	,, hasten	عَجَّلَ
,, adorn (speech)	حَبَّرَ	,, count	عَدَّدَ
,, sharpen, set limits	حَدَّدَ	,, torment	عَذَّبَ
,, look intently	حَدَّقَ	,, strip	عَرَّى
,, warn	حَذَّرَ	,, comfort	عَزَّى
,, get ready, bring	حَضَّرَ	,, perfume	عَطَّرَ
,, burden	حَمَّلَ	,, magnify	عَظَّمَ
,, change	حَوَّلَ	,, hang up	عَلَّقَ
,, perplex	حَيَّرَ	,, teach	عَلَّمَ
,, salute	حَيَّى	,, prolong life, build	عَمَّرَ
,, inform	خَبَّرَ	,, make general	عَمَّمَ
,, devastate	خَرَّبَ	,, accustom	عَوَّدَ
,, save, deliver	خَلَّصَ	,, name	سَمَّى
,, leaven	خَمَّرَ	,, facilitate	سَهَّلَ
,, frighten	خَوَّفَ	,, fence a field	سَيَّجَ
,, disappoint	خَيَّبَ	,, winter	شَتَّى

To strengthen	شَدَّدَ	To accede to	لَبَّى
,, exhort to patience	صَبَّرَ	,, abridge, extract	لَخَّصَ
,, correct	صَحَّحَ	,, to glorify	مَجَّدَ
,, believe	صَدَّقَ	,, refine by fire, try	مَحَّصَ
,, proclaim	صَرَّحَ	,, nurse	مَرَّضَ
,, plate	صَفَّحَ	,, rend	مَزَّقَ
,, applaud	صَفَّقَ	,, facilitate	مَهَّدَ
,, clarify	صَفَّى	,, rouse, draw attention to	نَبَّهَ
,, pray	صَلَّى		
,, determine upon	صَمَّمَ	,, rely upon	عَوَّلَ
,, compose, assort	صَنَّفَ	,, keep a festival	عَيَّدَ
,, make a noise	صَوَّتَ	,, sing (bird)	غَرَّدَ
,, paint	صَوَّرَ	,, wash	غَسَّلَ
,, summer	صَيَّفَ	,, cover	غَشَّى
,, slaughter a victim	ضَحَّى	,, sing	غَنَّى
,, fetter, to register	قَيَّدَ	,, change	غَيَّرَ
,, accuse of lying	كَذَّبَ	,, search	فَتَّشَ
,, consecrate	كَرَّسَ	,, distribute	فَرَّقَ
,, shatter	كَسَّرَ	,, explain	فَسَّرَ
,, atone	كَفَّرَ	,, prefer	فَضَّلَ
,, enshroud	كَفَّنَ	,, think upon	فَكَّرَ
,, crown	كَلَّلَ	,, kiss	قَبَّلَ
,, speak	كَلَّمَ	,, sanctify	قَدَّسَ
,, complete	كَمَّلَ	,, offer	قَدَّمَ
,, create	كَوَّنَ	,, cut into pieces	قَطَّعَ

To straighten	قَوَّمَ	To make one a ruler	وَلَّى
„ strengthen	قَوَّى	„ deliver	نَجَّى
„ prepare	هَيَّأ	„ bring down	نَزَّلَ
„ reprove	وَبَّخَ	„ scrutinize	نَقَّبَ
„ distribute	وَزَّعَ	„ revise	نَقَّحَ
„ explain	وَضَّحَ	„ cleanse	نَقَّى
„ make fit, favourable (God)	وَفَّقَ	„ embellish a book	نَمَّقَ
„ venerate	وَقَّرَ	„ threaten	هَدَّدَ
„ seal, let fall	وَقَّعَ	„ educate	هَذَّبَ
„ appoint an agent	وَكَّلَ	„ praise God	هَلَّلَ
		„ congratulate	هَنَّأ

II. فَاعَل

To struggle	جَاهَدَ	To disagree with	خَالَفَ
„ be contiguous to	جَاوَرَ	„ ward off	دَافَعَ
„ exceed limits	جَاوَزَ	„ persevere	دَاوَمَ
„ converse with	حَادَثَ	„ reproach, blame	آخَذَ
„ give careful attention to	حَافَظَ	„ be sociable with one	آنَسَ
„ summon	حَاكَمَ	„ hasten	بَادَرَ
„ try to do	حَاوَلَ	„ go forth to battle, duel	بَارَزَ
„ try to deceive	خَادَعَ	„ bless	بَارَكَ
„ contend with	خَاصَمَ	„ act in person	بَاشَرَ
„ address	خَاطَبَ	„ exaggerate	بَالَغَ
„ risk	خَاطَرَ		

To pay attention to	بَالَى	To share with	قَاسَمَ
„ swear fealty	بَايَعَ	„ endure	قَاسَى
„ dispute	جَادَلَ	„ punish	قَاصَّ
„ recompense	جَازَى	„ oppose	قَاوَمَ
„ sit in company with	جَالَسَ	„ dissemble	رَاءَى
„ show courtesy	جَامَلَ	„ review	رَاجَعَ
„ be similar	جَانَسَ	„ accompany	رَافَقَ
„ double	ضَاعَفَ	„ guard	رَاقَبَ
„ oppress	ضَايَقَ	„ try to surpass	سَابَقَ
„ pursue, chase	طَارَدَ	„ help	سَاعَدَ
„ comply with	طَاوَعَ	„ journey	سَافَرَ
„ censure	عَاتَبَ	„ live with	سَاكَنَ
„ treat with animosity	عَادَى	„ live peaceably with	سَالَمَ
„ punish	عَاقَبَ	„ equalize	سَاوَى
„ treat disease, endeavour	عَالَجَ	„ keep peace with	سَايَرَ
„ deal with	عَامَلَ	„ resemble	شَابَهَ
„ resist	عَانَدَ	„ drink with	شَارَبَ
„ covenant	عَاهَدَ	„ share „	شَارَكَ
„ help	عَاوَنَ	„ consult	شَاوَرَ
„ abandon	غَادَرَ	„ accompany	صَاحَبَ
„ compare	قَابَلَ	„ find by chance	صَادَفَ
„ be near to	قَارَبَ	„ wrestle	صَارَعَ
		„ reconcile	صَالَحَ
		„ contradict	نَاقَضَ
		„ hand	نَاوَلَ

To emigrate	هَاجَرَ	To vie for superiority	كَابَرَ
,, assault	وَاثَبَ	,, write	كَاتَبَ
,, conceal	وَارَى	,, recompense	كَافَأَ
,, poise	وَازَنَ	,, observe	لَاحَظَ
,, correspond	وَازَى	,, deal kindly	لَاطَفَ
,, persist in	وَاصَلَ	,, sport with	لَاعَبَ
,, persevere	وَاظَبَ	,, meet	لَاقَى
,, make an appoint- ment	وَاعَدَ	,, help	مَالَأً
,, agree with	وَافَقَ	,, seek to hinder	مَانَعَ
,, arrive	وَافَى	,, call	نَادَى
,, suffer	كَابَدَ	,, be hypocritical	نَافَقَ

III. أَفْعَلَ

To become rich	أَثْرَى	To count	أَحْصَى
,, bear fruit	أَثْمَرَ	,, bring	أَحْضَرَ
,, be liberal with	أَجْزَلَ	,, inform	أَخْبَرَ
,, cause to sit	أَجْلَسَ	,, be fertile	أَخْصَبَ
,, answer	أَجَابَ	,, subdue	أَخْضَعَ
,, do or say anything well	أَجَادَ	,, give	آتَى
,, protect	أَجَارَ	,, prefer	آثَرَ
,, allow	أَجَازَ	,, harm	آذَى
,, feel	أَحَسَّ	,, believe	آمَنَ
,, do good	أَحْسَنَ	,, originate	أَبْدَعَ
		,, change	أَبْدَلَ

To see	اَبْصَرَ	To quench	اَطْفَأَ
„ be slow	اَبْطَأَ	„ set free	اَطْلَقَ
„ abolish	اَبْطَلَ	„ obey	اَطَاعَ
„ remove to a distance	اَبْعَدَ	„ be dark	اَظْلَمَ
„ reserve	اَبْقَى	„ prepare	اَعَدَّ
„ be clear, manifest	اَبَانَ	„ deprive of	اَعْدَمَ
„ weary	اَتْعَبَ	„ err	اَخْطَأَ
„ perfect	اَتْقَنَ	„ break a promise	اَخْلَفَ
„ fulfil	اَتَمَّ	„ bring in, insert	اَدْخَلَ
„ satisfy (food)	اَشْبَعَ	„ submit to	اَذْعَنَ
„ shine	اَشْرَقَ	„ commit a crime	اَذْنَبَ
„ take into partner-ship	اَشْرَكَ	„ spread news	اَذَاعَ
		„ show	اَرَى
„ pity	اَشْفَقَ	„ send	اَرْسَلَ
„ be ambiguous	اَشْكَلَ	„ anchor	اَرْسَى
„ point to	اَشَارَ	„ give rest	اَرَاحَ
„ be morning	اَصْبَحَ	„ wish	اَرَادَ
„ persist	اَصَرَّ	„ quench thirst	اَرْوَى
„ rectify	اَصْلَحَ	„ resolve	اَزْمَعَ
„ afflict, be right, hit the mark	اَصَابَ	„ hasten	اَسْرَعَ
		„ squander	اَسْرَفَ
„ light	اَضَاءَ	„ submit	اَسْلَمَ
„ add, show hospi-tality	اَضَافَ	„ be or become aged	اَسَنَّ
		„ „ prolix	اَسْهَبَ
„ feed	اَطْعَمَ	„ do evil	اَسَاءَ

To sail	أَقْلَعَ	To become fatigued	أَعْيَا
,, convince	أَقْنَعَ	,, shut	أَغْلَقَ
,, abide, to raise	أَقَامَ	,, succour	أَغَاثَ
,, increase	أَكْثَرَ	,, seduce	أَغْرَى
,, honour	أَكْرَمَ	,, separate	أَفْرَزَ
,, compel	أَكْرَهَ	,, divulge	أَفْشَى
,, clothe	أَلْبَسَ	,, be successful	أَفْلَحَ
,, glue	أَلْصَقَ	,, be penniless	أَفْلَسَ
,, exclude	أَلْغَى	,, annihilate	أَفْنَى
,, inspire	أَلْهَمَ	,, approach	أَقْبَلَ
,, retain	أَمْسَكَ	,, advance boldly	أَقْدَمَ
,, be evening	أَمْسَى	,, confess	أَقَرَّ
,, consider attentively	أَمْعَنَ	,, lend	أَقْرَضَ
,, be possible	أَمْكَنَ	,, swear	أَقْسَمَ
,, inform	أَنْبَأَ	,, deposit	أَوْدَعَ
,, accomplish	أَنْجَزَ	,, lead to water, state	أَوْرَدَ
,, bring down	أَنْزَلَ	,, cause to reach	أَوْصَلَ
,, compose, begin	أَنْشَأَ	,, command	أَوْصَى
,, recite poetry	أَنْشَدَ	,, make plain	أَوْضَحَ
,, give	أَعْطَى	,, kindle	أَوْقَدَ
,, reveal	أَعْلَنَ	,, beckon	أَوْمَأَ
,, lend	أَعَارَ	,, awaken	أَيْقَظَ
,, lack	أَعْوَزَ	,, be sure	أَيْقَنَ
,, help	أَعَانَ	,, treat with justice	أَنْصَفَ
		,, grant	أَنْعَمَ

To spend	أَنْفَقَ	To present	أَهْدَى
,, deliver	أَنْقَذَ	,, despise	أَهَانَ
,, deny	أَنْكَرَ	,, make obligatory	أَوْجَبَ
,, light up	أَنَارَ	,, inspire	أَوْحَى

IV. تَفَعَّلَ

To adopt	تَبَنَّى	To regret	تَأَسَّفَ
,, be manifest	تَبَيَّنَ	,, be rooted	تَأَصَّلَ
,, follow up	تَتَبَّعَ	,, ,, sure	تَأَكَّدَ
,, be confirmed	تَثَبَّتَ	,, ,, composed(book)	تَأَلَّفَ
,, ,, educated	تَثَقَّفَ	,, suffer	تَأَلَّمَ
,, ,, renewed	تَجَدَّدَ	,, meditate	تَأَمَّلَ
,, ,, incarnate	تَجَسَّدَ	,, act with delibe-	
,, spy	تَجَسَّسَ	ration	تَأَنَّى
,, bear patiently	تَجَلَّدَ	,, be scattered	تَبَدَّدَ
,, be unveiled	تَجَلَّى	,, ,, changed	تَبَدَّلَ
,, shun	تَجَنَّبَ	,, give freely	تَبَرَّعَ
,, be petrified	تَحَجَّرَ	,, smile	تَبَسَّمَ
,, ,, moved	تَحَرَّكَ	,, consider	تَبَصَّرَ
,, verify	تَحَقَّقَ	,, amuse oneself	تَسَلَّى
,, suffer patiently	تَحَمَّلَ	,, be poisoned	تَسَمَّمَ
,, carry under the		,, ,, scattered	تَشَتَّتَ
arm	تَأَبَّطَ	,, ,, encouraged	تَشَجَّعَ
,, be polite	تَأَدَّبَ	,, ,, strengthened	تَشَدَّدَ
,, ,, founded	تَأَسَّسَ	,, long for	تَشَوَّقَ

To give alms	تَصَدَّقَ	To show pity	تَرَآَفَ
,, employ oneself in	تَصَرَّفَ	,, hope	تَرَجَّى
,, imagine	تَصَوَّرَ	,, welcome	تَرَحَّبَ
,, beseech	تَضَرَّعَ	,, watch for	تَرَقَّبَ
,, comprise	تَضَمَّنَ	,, reflect	تَرَوَّى
,, be immoderate	تَطَرَّفَ	,, marry	تَزَوَّجَ
,, act voluntarily	تَطَوَّعَ	,, be adorned	تَزَيَّنَ
,, draw bad omen from	تَطَيَّرَ	,, ,, armed	تَسَلَّمَ
,, accuse of injustice	تَظَلَّمَ	,, exercise absolute power over	تَسَلَّطَ
,, be astonished	تَعَجَّبَ	,, enjoy	تَمَتَّعَ
,, become numerous	تَعَدَّدَ	,, be glorified	تَمَجَّدَ
,, excuse oneself, be impossible	تَعَذَّرَ	,, rebel	تَمَرَّدَ
,, learn	تَعَلَّمَ	,, wallow	تَمَرَّغَ
,, compassionate	تَحَنَّنَ	,, be habituated to	تَمَرَّنَ
,, be changed	تَحَوَّلَ	,, grasp	تَمَسَّكَ
,, ,, perplexed	تَحَيَّرَ	,, be stable	تَمَكَّنَ
,, ,, educated	تَخَرَّجَ	,, flatter	تَمَلَّقَ
,, ,, afraid	تَخَوَّفَ	,, take possession, reign	تَمَلَّكَ
,, choose	تَخَيَّرَ	,, be awake to	تَنَبَّهَ
,, be trained	تَدَرَّبَ	,, ,, ascetic	تَنَسَّكَ
,, proceed gradually	تَدَرَّجَ	,, become a Christian	تَنَصَّرَ
,, be defiled	تَدَنَّسَ	,, live luxuriously	تَنَعَّمَ
,, humble oneself	تَذَلَّلَ	,, breathe	تَنَفَّسَ

To disguise oneself	تَنَكَّر	To come into existence	تَكَوَّن
„ groan, sigh	تَنَهَّد	„ be compact	تَلَبَّد
„ be diverse	تَنَوَّع	„ muffle oneself	تَلَثَّم
„ „ well brought up	تَهَذَّب	„ be soiled	تَلَطَّخ
„ deride	تَهَكَّم	„ show kindness	تَلَطَّف
„ purpose, be baptized	تَعَمَّد	„ rejoice	تَهَلَّل
„ dine	تَغَدَّى	„ rush heedlessly into	تَهَوَّر
„ take nourishment	تَغَذَّى	„ be prepared	تَهَيَّأ
„ gaze	تَفَرَّس	„ fear	تَهَيَّب
„ be dispersed	تَفَرَّق	„ go towards	تَوَجَّه
„ seek a lost object	تَفَقَّد	„ seek diligently	تَوَخَّى
„ be sanctified	تَقَدَّس	„ fall into difficulty	تَوَرَّط
„ advance	تَقَدَّم	„ lean on a pillow	تَوَسَّد
„ approach	تَقَرَّب	„ mediate	تَوَسَّط
„ be proved	تَقَرَّر	„ supplicate	تَوَسَّل
„ put on	تَقَلَّد	„ penetrate into	تَوَغَّل
„ be proud	تَكَبَّر	„ expect	تَوَقَّع
„ „ shattered	تَكَسَّر	„ lean upon	تَوَكَّأ
„ speak	تَكَلَّم	„ suspect, imagine	تَوَهَّم
		„ become easy	تَيَسَّر
		„ be sure of	تَيَقَّن

V. تَفَاعَل

To discuss together	تَحَاوَر	To dispute together	تَخَاصَم
„ inform one another	تَخَابَر	„ interfere	تَدَاخَل

To be mutually agreed	تَرَاضَى	To affect ignorance	تَجَاهَلَ
„ be closely packed	تَرَاكَمَ	„ transgress, exceed the bounds	تَجَاوَزَ
„ crowd	تَزَاحَمَ	„ love one another	تَحَابَّ
„ be exalted	تَسَامَى	„ fight one another	تَحَارَبَ
„ „ accomodating	تَسَاهَلَ	„ summon one another	تَحَاكَمَ
„ „ equal	تَسَاوَى	„ follow in regular series	تَقَاطَرَ
„ forebode ill	تَشَاءَمَ	„ intersect	تَقَاطَعَ
„ resemble one another	تَشَابَهَ	„ neglect	تَقَاعَدَ
„ quarrel	تَشَاجَرَ	„ increase	تَكَاثَرَ
„ share with	تَشَارَكَ	„ be thick, dense	تَكَاثَفَ
„ feign occupation	تَشَاغَلَ	„ „ lazy	تَكَاسَلَ
„ take counsel together	تَآمَرَ	„ meet one another	تَلَاقَى
„ discuss together	تَبَاحَثَ	„ feign sickness	تَمَارَضَ
„ exchange	تَبَادَلَ	„ feign death	تَمَاوَتَ
„ be blessed	تَبَارَكَ	„ swing	تَمَايَلَ
„ „ far apart	تَبَاعَدَ	„ commune secretly	تَنَاجَى
„ follow consecutively	تَتَابَعَ	„ contend, litigate	تَنَازَعَ
„ yawn	تَثَاءَبَ	„ take by the hand	تَنَاوَلَ
„ be heavy, sluggish	تَثَاقَلَ	„ feign sleep	تَنَاوَمَ
„ dispute together	تَجَادَلَ	„ rush to	تَهَافَتَ
„ dare	تَجَاسَرَ	„ neglect	تَهَاوَنَ
		„ conceal oneself	تَوَارَى

To be equal to	تَوَازَى	To feign blindness, ignorance	تَعَامَى
„ „ humble	تَوَاضَعَ	„ covenant	تَعَاهَدَ
„ consult together	تَشَاوَرَ	„ help one another	تَعَاوَنَ
„ accompany	تَصَاحَبَ	„ rival in glory	تَفَاخَرَ
„ shake hands with	تَصَافَحَ	„ become important, formidable	تَفَاقَمَ
„ be reconciled	تَصَالَحَ		
„ fight one another	تَضَارَبَ	„ draw near to	تَقَارَبَ
„ exceed the rights	تَطَاوَلَ	„ divide with	تَقَاسَمَ
„ be scattered	تَطَايَرَ	„ demand payment	تَقَاضَى
„ feign	تَظَاهَرَ	„ agree upon	تَوَاطَأَ
„ engage in	تَعَاطَى	„ agree together	تَوَافَقَ
„ be exalted	تَعَالَى	„ be dilatory	تَوَانَى
„ deal with one another	تَعَامَلَ		

VI. اِنْفَعَلَ

To be forsaken	اِنْخَذَلَ	To be healed	اِنْدَمَلَ
„ „ eclipsed (moon)	اِنْخَسَفَ	„ „ amazed	اِنْدَهَلَ
„ be lowered	اِنْخَفَضَ	„ „ troubled	اِنْزَعَجَ
„ „ erased	اِنْدَثَرَ	„ „ bruised	اِنْسَحَقَ
„ „ obliterated (traces)	اِنْدَرَسَ	„ „ poured out	اِنْسَكَبَ
„ be repelled	اِنْدَفَعَ	„ slip away	اِنْسَلَّ
		„ be split	اِنْشَقَّ
		„ „ poured out	اِنْصَبَّ

To depart	إِنْصَرَفَ
„ proceed from	إِنْبَثَقَ
„ be cut (pen)	إِنْبَرَى
„ „ extended, mercy	إِنْبَسَطَ
„ be raised, sent	إِنْبَعَثَ
„ „ attracted	إِنْجَذَبَ
„ „ wounded	إِنْجَرَحَ
„ „ concealed	إِنْحَجَبَ
„ go down	إِنْحَدَرَ
„ deviate	إِنْحَرَفَ
„ be straitened	إِنْحَصَرَ
„ „ degraded	إِنْحَطَّ
„ „ broken	إِنْحَطَمَ
„ „ loosed	إِنْحَلَّ
„ stoop	إِنْحَنَى
„ be deceived	إِنْخَدَعَ
„ „ led	إِنْقَادَ
„ fall prostrate, to be spilt	إِنْكَبَّ
„ be broken, defeated	إِنْكَسَرَ
„ be eclipsed (sun)	إِنْكَسَفَ

To be disclosed	إِنْكَشَفَ
„ „ blotted out	إِنْمَحَى
„ „ pulled down	إِنْهَدَمَ
„ „ put to flight	إِنْهَزَمَ
„ rain heavily, shed tears	إِنْهَلَّ
„ be joined to	إِنْضَمَّ
„ „ printed	إِنْطَبَعَ
„ „ covered	إِنْطَبَقَ
„ „ thrown	إِنْطَرَحَ
„ depart	إِنْطَلَقَ
„ be bent, inclined	إِنْعَطَفَ
„ „ arched, coagulated	إِنْعَقَدَ
„ cleave to	إِنْعَكَفَ
„ be planted	إِنْغَرَسَ
„ „ plunged	إِنْغَمَسَ
„ „ opened	إِنْفَتَحَ
„ burst	إِنْفَجَرَ
„ be separated	إِنْفَصَلَ
„ „ cleft	إِنْفَلَقَ
„ „ distressed	إِنْقَبَضَ
„ „ extinguished	إِنْقَرَضَ

| To be finished | اِنْقَضَى | To be overturned | اِنْقَلَبَ |
| „ „ cut off, cease | اِنْقَطَعَ | | |

VII. اِفْتَعَلَ

To adduce an argument	اِحْتَجَّ	To begin	اِبْتَدَأَ
„ be on one's guard	اِحْتَرَسَ	„ originate	اِبْتَدَعَ
„ „ burnt	اِحْتَرَقَ	„ smile	اِبْتَسَمَ
„ venerate	اِحْتَرَمَ	„ be distant	اِبْتَعَدَ
„ gather wood	اِحْتَطَبَ	„ request	اِبْتَغَى
„ celebrate	اِحْتَفَلَ	„ swallow	اِبْتَلَعَ
„ despise	اِحْتَقَرَ	„ put to the test	اِبْتَلَى
„ endure	اِحْتَمَلَ	„ delight	اِبْتَهَجَ
„ contain	اِحْتَوَى	„ implore	اِبْتَهَلَ
„ use strategy	اِحْتَلَّ	„ follow	اِتَّبَعَ
„ hide oneself	اِحْتَبَأَ	„ ruminate	اِجْتَرَّ
„ experience	اِخْتَبَرَ	„ be gathered	اِجْتَمَعَ
„ invent	اِخْتَرَعَ	„ exert oneself	اِجْتَهَدَ
„ abridge	اِخْتَصَرَ	„ be kindled	اِسْتَعَرَ
„ be distinguished for	اِخْتَصَّ	„ draw water	اِسْتَقَى
		„ listen	اِسْتَمَعَ
„ take to oneself	اِتَّخَذَ	„ lean upon	اِسْتَنَدَ
„ be girded	اِتَّزَرَ	„ be strong	اِشْتَدَّ
		„ buy	اِشْتَرَى

To be kindled	اِشْتَعَلَ	To be ordained	اِرْتَسَم
„ „ occupied	اِشْتَغَلَ	„ „ pleased with	اِرْتَضَى
„ long for	اِشْتَهَى	„ tremble	اِرْتَعَدَ
„ long for	اِشْتَاقَ	„ rise, advance	اِرْتَقَى
„ be dyed	اِصْطَبَغَ	„ commit a crime	اِرْتَكَبَ
„ choose	اِصْطَفَى	„ suspect	اِرْتَابَ
„ make terms	اِصْطَلَحَ	„ despise, scorn	اِزْدَرَى
„ warm oneself	اِصْطَلَى	„ increase	اِزْدَادَ
„ lie down	اِضْطَجَعَ	„ cover oneself	اِسْتَتَرَ
„ be troubled	اِضْطَرَبَ	„ economise	اِقْتَصَدَ
„ compel	اِضْطَرَّ	„ limit oneself to	اِقْتَصَرَ
„ blaze	اِضْطَرَمَ	„ require	اِقْتَضَى
„ persecute	اِضْطَهَدَ	„ acquire	اِقْتَنَى
„ defraud	اِخْتَلَسَ	„ be grieved	اِكْتَأَبَ
„ be mixed	اِخْتَلَطَ	„ earn	اِكْتَسَبَ
„ invent, forge lies	اِخْتَلَقَ	„ be clothed	اِكْتَسَى
„ be leavened	اِخْتَمَرَ	„ „ satisfied	اِكْتَفَى
„ choose	اِخْتَارَ	„ surround	اِكْتَنَفَ
„ claim	اِدَّعَى	„ take refuge	اِلْتَجَأَ
„ be confused	اِرْتَبَكَ	„ undertake	اِلْتَزَمَ
„ tremble	اِرْتَجَفَ	„ look back	اِلْتَفَتَ
„ extemporize	اِرْتَجَلَ	„ meet together	اِلْتَقَى
„ apostatize	اِرْتَدَّ	„ seek for	اِلْتَمَسَ

To blaze, be inflamed	الْتَهَبَ	To draw near	اِقْتَرَبَ
„ be bent	الْتَوَى	„ commit crime	اِقْتَرَفَ
„ examine, try	اِمْتَحَنَ	„ obstain from	اِمْتَنَعَ
„ be mixed	اِمْتَزَجَ	„ be vigilant	اِنْتَبَهَ
„ „ filled	اِمْتَلَأَ	„ commit suicide	اِنْتَحَرَ
„ know, see	اِطَّلَعَ	„ choose	اِنْتَخَبَ
„ consider	اِعْتَبَرَ	„ be spread	اِنْتَشَرَ
„ excuse oneself	اِعْتَذَرَ	„ „ victorious	اِنْتَصَرَ
„ confess	اِعْتَرَفَ	„ await	اِنْتَظَرَ
„ separate oneself	اِعْتَزَلَ	„ be puffed up	اِنْتَفَخَ
„ take refuge	اِعْتَصَمَ	„ profit by	اِنْتَفَعَ
„ embrace	اِعْتَنَقَ	„ criticise	اِنْتَقَدَ
„ take care of	اِعْتَنَى	„ be transferred	اِنْتَقَلَ
„ be accustomed	اِعْتَادَ	„ choose	اِنْتَقَى
„ „ deceived	اِغْتَرَّ	„ have a relapse	اِنْتَكَسَ
„ wash oneself	اِغْتَسَلَ	„ rebuke, drive away	اِنْتَهَرَ
„ be enraged	اِغْتَاظَ	„ seize an opportunity	اِنْتَهَزَ
„ begin, conquer	اِفْتَتَحَ	„ come to an end	اِنْتَهَى
„ glory in	اِفْتَخَرَ	„ be shaken	اِهْتَزَّ
„ prey on	اِفْتَرَسَ	„ mind	اِهْتَمَّ
„ miss	اِفْتَقَدَ	„ be united	اِتَّحَدَ
„ think	اِفْتَكَرَ	„ „ wide	اِتَّسَعَ

To be joined	إِتَّصَلَ	To burn, blaze	إِتَّقَدَ
„ „ humble	إِتَّضَعَ	„ be pious, fear	إِتَّقَى
„ follow advice	إِتَّعَظَ	„ lean upon	إِتَّكَأَ
„ happen, agree	إِتَّفَقَ	„ trust in	إِتَّكَلَ

VIII. إِفْعَلَّ

To be white	إِبْيَضَّ	To be yellow	إِصْفَرَّ
„ „ red	إِحْمَرَّ	„ „ crooked	إِعْوَجَّ
„ „ green	إِخْضَرَّ	„ „ one-eyed	إِعْوَرَّ
„ „ blue	إِزْرَقَّ	„ „ dust-coloured	إِغْبَرَّ
„ „ brown	إِسْمَرَّ	„ „ dull	إِكْمَدَّ
„ „ black	إِسْوَدَّ		

IX. إِسْتَفْعَلَ

To approve	إِسْتَحْسَنَ	To employ a ser-	
„ send for one	إِسْتَحْضَرَ	vant	إِسْتَخْدَمَ
„ be worthy of	إِسْتَحَقَّ	„ draw out	إِسْتَخْرَجَ
„ find sweet	إِسْتَحْلَى	„ extract	إِسْتَخْلَصَ
„ be changed, be		„ rectify omission	إِسْتَدْرَكَ
impossible	إِسْتَحَالَ	„ seek proof, infer	إِسْتَدَلَّ
„ spare one's life,		„ be circular	إِسْتَدَارَ
be ashamed	إِسْتَحْيَا	„ seek mercy	إِسْتَرْحَمَ
„ seek information	إِسْتَخْبَرَ	„ recall	إِسْتَرَدَّ

To hire	اِسْتَأْجَرَ	To rest	اِسْتَقَرّ
„ ask permission	اِسْتَأْذَنَ	„ explore	اِسْتَقْرَى
„ seek safety	اِسْتَأْمَنَ	„ penetrate deeply,	
„ be polite, cultured	اِسْتَأْنَسَ	(affair)	اِسْتَقْصَى
„ recommence an action	اِسْتَأْنَفَ	„ be independent	اِسْتَقَلَّ
„ be worthy of	اِسْتَأْهَلَ	„ „ upright	اِسْتَقَامَ
„ „ arbitrary	اِسْتَبَدَّ	„ consider great	اِسْتَكْبَرَ
„ exchange	اِسْتَبْدَلَ	„ consider abundant	اِسْتَكْثَرَ
„ rejoice at good news	اِسْتَبْشَرَ	„ regard as a duty	اِسْتَلْزَمَ
„ consider ugly	اِسْتَبْشَعَ	„ draw attention to	اِسْتَلْفَتَ
„ consider remote	اِسْتَبْعَدَ	„ lie on one's back	اِسْتَلْقَى
„ seek the completion	اِسْتَتَمَّ	„ seek inspiration	اِسْتَلْهَمَ
„ except	اِسْتَثْنَى	„ seek help	اِسْتَمَدَّ
„ answer prayer	اِسْتَجَابَ	„ continue	اِسْتَمَرَّ
„ seek protection	اِسْتَجَارَ	„ ask a gift	اِسْتَمْنَحَ
„ profit	اِسْتَفَادَ	„ discover	اِسْتَنْبَطَ
„ loathe	اِسْتَقْبَحَ	„ deduce	اِسْتَنْتَجَ
„ meet, to be in front of	اِسْتَقْبَلَ	„ ask for water, be dropsical	اِسْتَسْقَى
		„ call to witness	اِسْتَشْهَدَ
		„ consult	اِسْتَشَارَ

To esteem of little account	إِسْتَصْغَر		„ seek aid	إِسْتَغَاثَ
„ find right	إِسْتَصْوَب		„ seek to understand	إِسْتَفْهَمَ
„ seek for information	إِسْتَطْلَعَ		„ seek help	إِسْتَنْجَدَ
„ enslave	إِسْتَعْبَدَ		„ ask fulfilment of a promise	إِسْتَنْجَزَ
„ hasten	إِسْتَعْجَلَ		„ disdain	إِسْتَنْكَفَ
„ make oneself ready	إِسْتَعَدَّ		„ incite	إِسْتَنْهَضَ
„ seek a favour	إِسْتَعْطَف		„ shine, be enlightened	إِسْتَنَارَ
„ consider great	إِسْتَعْظَمَ		„ mock	إِسْتَهْزَأَ
„ desire to know	إِسْتَعْلَمَ		„ begin speech	إِسْتَهَلَّ
„ use	إِسْتَعْمَلَ		„ deserve	إِسْتَوْجَبَ
„ borrow	إِسْتَعَارَ		„ deposit	إِسْتَوْدَعَ
„ seek help	إِسْتَعَان		„ seek payment	إِسْتَوْفَى
„ seek forgiveness	إِسْتَغْفَرَ		„ overpower	إِسْتَوْلَى
„ be rich, independent of	إِسْتَغْنَى		„ be awakened	إِسْتَيْقَظَ

X. إِفْعَوْعَلَ

To be hump-backed	إِحْدَوْدَبَ		To be about to do	إِخْلَوْلَقَ
„ „ „	إِحْقَوْقَفَ		„ „ covered with grass	إِعْشَوْشَبَ
„ „ sweet	إِحْلَوْلَى		„ „ be filled with tears, eyes	إِغْرَوْرَقَ
„ „ rough, rude	إِحْشَوْشَنَ			

QUADRILITERALS. فَعْلَلَ

To embellish	زَخْرَف	To make disciples	تَلْمَذَ
„ embroider	زَرْكَش	„ stammer	تَمْتَمَ
„ move	زَعْزَعَ	„ collect	جَمْهَرَ
„ shake	زَلْزَلَ	„ have the death-	
„ roar	زَمْجَرَ	rattle	حَشْرَجَ
„ clothe	سَرْبَلَ	„ appear (truth)	حَصْحَصَ
„ lower the head	طَأْطَأَ	„ neigh	حَمْحَمَ
„ fall in (the night)	عَسْعَسَ	„ open the eyes	
„ camp	عَسْكَرَ	widely	حَمْلَقَ
„ sift wheat	غَرْبَلَ	„ scribble	خَرْبَشَ
„ gargle	غَرْغَرَ	„ roll down	دَحْرَجَ
„ burst out laughing	قَهْقَهَ	„ buzz	دَنْدَنَ
„ shine	لَأْلَأَ	„ flutter	رَفْرَفَ
„ rinse	مَضْمَضَ	„ roll away	زَحْلَقَ
„ trouble	مَلْمَلَ	„ run quickly	هَرْوَلَ
„ wag the tail	بَصْبَصَ	„ sketch, plan	هَنْدَسَ
„ confound	بَلْبَلَ	„ suggest evil (devil)	وَسْوَسَ
„ interpret	تَرْجَمَ	„ wail	وَلْوَلَ

DERIVED FORMS OF THE QUADRILITERAL.

I. تَفَعْلَلَ

To roll along	تَدَحْرَجَ	To profess atheism	تَزَنْدَقَ
„ be shaken	تَزَعْزَعَ	„ put on trousers	تَسَرْوَلَ

To be rude, proud	تَعَجْرَفَ	To shine	تَلَأْلَأَ
„ „ conceited	تَغَطْرَسَ	„ follow a sect	تَمَذْهَبَ
„ philosophize	تَفَلْسَفَ	„ be restless in bed	تَمَلْمَلَ
„ go backwards	تَقَهْقَرَ		

II. اِفْعَنْلَلَ

To gather of press (crowds)	إِحْرَنْجَمَ	To have a protube-rant chest and a hollow back	اِقْعَنْسَسَ
„ lie on the back	إِسْلَنْقَى		

III. اِفْعَلَلَّ

To be intensely dark	إِدْلَهَمَّ	To vanish away	إِضْمَحَلَّ
„ stretch the neck to look	إِشْرَأَبَّ	„ enjoy tranquillity	إِطْمَأَنَّ
„ be high, proud	إِشْمَخَرَّ	„ shudder with honor	اِقْشَعَرَّ
		„ be intensely dark	اِكْفَهَرَّ

SUPPLEMENTS OF THE QUADRILITERAL.

To practise farriery	بَيْطَرَ	To stuff the crop	حَوْصَلَ
„ clothe one with a gown	جَلْبَبَ	„ hurl into an abyss	دَهْوَرَ
„ throw violenthy down	جَنْدَلَ	„ put a cap on any one	قَلْنَسَ

THE MORE COMMON FORMS OF TRILITERAL
MASDARS.

أَشْهَرُ أُوزانِ مَصَادِرِ ٱلثُّلَاثِيّ

18 فَعِيْلَة		1 فَعْل	
19 فُعَالَة		2 فُعْل	
20 فَاعِلَة		3 فِعْل	
21 فَعْلَة		4 فَعَل	
22 فُعْلَة		5 فُعُل	
23 فِعْلَة		6 فُعَل	
24 فَعَلَة		7 فَعِل	
25 فُعْلَى		8 فِعَل	
26 فَعْلَى		9 فُعُوْل	
27 فِعْلَى		10 فُعُوْلَة	
28 فُعْلَان		11 فِعَالَة	
29 فِعْلَان		12 فَعَالَة	
30 فَعَلَان		13 فَعَالِيَة	
31 تَفْعَال		14 فُعَال	
32 فَعْلُوْلَة		15 فَعَال	
33 مَفْعُوْل		16 فِعَال	
		17 فَعِيْل	

NOUNS OF ACTION OF TRILITERAL VERBS.

ٱلْمَصَادِرُ ٱلثَّلَاثِيَّة

‎1. فَعْل

Pushing, paying	دَفْع	Bringing	جَلْب
Sprinkling	رَشّ	Gathering	جَمْع
Thunder	رَعْد	Ignorance	جَهْل
Lifting	رَفْع	Digging	حَفْر
Throwing	رَمْي	Truth	حَقّ
Captivity	سَبْي	Loosing	حَلّ
Closing up	سَدّ	Praising	حَمْد
Shedding	سَفْك	Carrying	حَمْل
Enacting, sharpening	سَنّ	Writing	خَطّ
Longing	شَوْق	Study	دَرْس
Roasting	شَيّ	Knocking	طَرْق
Pardon	صَفْح	Taste	طَعْم
Beating	ضَرْب	Folding	طَيّ
Light	ضَوْء	Fickleness	طَيْش
Grinding	طَحْن	Justice	عَدْل
Eating	أَكْل	Living	عَيْش
Safety	آمْن	Washing	غَسْل
Cold	بَرْد	Grief	غَمّ
Lightning	بَرْق	Opening	فَتْح
Selling	بَيْع	Supposing, appointing	فَرْض

Superiority	فَضْل	Death	مَوْت
Understanding	فَهْم	Springing	نَبْع
Killing	قَتْل	Vow	نَذْر
Purpose	قَصْد	Assisting	نَصْر
Knocking	قَرْع	Sprinkling	نَضْح
Speech	قَوْل	Arranging, versifying	نَظْم
Cauterizing	كَيّ	Profiting	نَفْع
Glance	لَحْظ	Lamentation	نَوْح
Blame	لَوْم	Sleep	نَوْم
Praising	مَدْح	Obtaining	نَيْل
Stretching	مَدّ	Pulling down	هَدْم
Forbidding	مَنْع	Promise	وَعْد

فُعْل 2

Abasement, weakness	ذُلّ	Harm	ضُرّ
Ampleness	رُحْب	Weakness	ضُعْف
Cheapness	رُخْص	Oppression	ظُلْم
Abstemiousness	زُهْد	Excuse	عُذْر
Scoffing	سُخْر	Politeness, sociability	أُنْس
Disease	سُقْم	Stinginess	بُخْل
Drunkenness	سُكْر	Healing	بُرْء
Drinking	شُرْب	Slowness	بُطْء
Occupation	شُغْل	Vanity, falsehood	بُطْل
Thankfulness	شُكْر	Distance	بُعْد
Doing	صُنْع	Cowardice	جُبْن

Generosity	جُوْد	Holiness	قُدْس
Sorrow	حُزْن	Proximity	قُرْب
Beauty	حُسْن	Abhorrence	كُرْه
Judgment	حُكْم	Meanness	لُؤْم
Dream	حُلْم	Kindness, gentleness	لُطْف
Wickedness	خُبْث	Abiding	مُكْث
Experience	خُبْر	Reigning	مُلْك
Storing up	ذُخْر	Advice	نُصْح
Nakedness	عُرْي	Speaking	نُطْق
Difficulty	عُسْر	Dryness	يُبْس
Washing	غُسْل	Easiness	يُسْر
Spoiling	غُنْم	Luck	يُمْن
Vileness, ugliness	قُبْح		

3. فِعْل

Crime	إِثْم	Envy	حِقْد
Permission	إِذْن	Forbearance	حِلْم
Inheritance	إِرْث	Confusion	خِزْي
Righteousness	بِرّ	Fertility	خِصْب
Diligence, endeavour	جِدّ	Rememberance	ذِكْر
Skilfulness	حِذْق	Compassion	رِفْق
Covetousness	حِرْص	Being well watered	رِيّ
Depriving	حِرْم	Sorcery, seduction	سِحْر
Feeling	حِسّ	Drinking	شِرْب
Preservation	حِفْظ	Feeling, versifying	شِعْر

Truthfulness	صِدْق	Knowledge	عِلْم
Distress	ضِيْق	Adultery	فِسْق
Goodness	طِيْب	Saying	قِيْل
Passionate love	عِشْق		

4. فَعَل

Confusion, shame	خَجَل	Hoarseness	بَكَم
Dumbness	خَرَس	Leaving	بَرَح
Erring	خَطَأ	Leprosy	بَرَص
Diligence	دَأَب	Seeing	بَصَر
Slipping	زَلَق	Fatigue	تَعَب
Slipping	زَلَل	Fear, grief	جَزَع
Disgust	سَأَم	Patience	جَلَد
Anger	سَخَط	Caution	حَذَر
Generosity	سَخَا	Sorrow	حَزَن
Hisease	سَقَم	Envy	حَسَد
Dwelling	سَكَن	Swearing	حَلَف
Wakefulness, watching	سَهَر	Annoyance	ضَجَر
Grief	شَجَن	Request, seeking	طَلَب
Dignity	شَرَف	Coveting	طَمَع
Deafness	صَمَم	Victory	ظَفَر
Politeness	أَدَب	Sweating	عَرَق
Regret	أَسَف	Thirst	عَطَش
Corruption	أَسَن	Publicity	عَلَن
Hope	أَمَل	Doing	عَمَل

Blindness	عَمًى	Repentance	نَدَم
Anger	غَضَب	Moisture	نَدًى
Toy	فَرَح	Relationship	نَسَب
Failure	فَشَل	Looking	نَظَر
Despair	قَنَط	Fleeing	هَرَب
Generosity	كَرَم	Affection	هَوًى
Laziness	كَسَل	Fear	وَجَل
Hydrophobia	كَلَب	Swelling	وَرَم
Affection	كَلَف	Dirtiness	وَسَخ
Sickness	مَرَض	Deep sleep	وَسَن
Weariness	مَلَل		

5. فُعُل

Difficulty	عُسُر	Mercy	رُحْم
Holiness	قُدُس	Drunkenness	سُكُر
Meanness	لُؤُم	Excuse	عُذُر
Dreaming	حُلُم		

6. فُعَل

Consent	رُضًى	Request	بُغًى
Night-journey	سُرًى	Weeping	بُكًى
Guidance	هُدًى	Piety	تُقًى

7. فَعِل

Laughing	ضَحِك	Playing	لَعِب
Lying	كَذِب	Depriving	حَرِم

| Swearing | حَلَف | Stealing | سَرِق |
| Choking | خَنِق | | |

8. فِعَل

Heaviness	ثِقَل	Satisfaction	شِبَع
Satisfaction	رِضًى	Littleness	صِغَر
Annihilation	بِلًى	Greatness	عِظَم
Thickness	ثِخَن	Richness	غِنًى
Plumpness	سِمَن	Shortness	قِصَر

9. فُعُوْل

Compassion	حُنُوّ	Setting (sun, moon, or star)	أُفُول
Going forth	خُرُوج	Going forth	بُرُوز
Subjection, obedience	خُضُوع	Rising (sun)	بُزُوغ
Palpitation	خُفُوق	Reaching, maturity	بُلُوغ
Obscureness	خُمُول	Firmness	ثُبُوت
Entering	دُخُول	Sitting	جُلُوس
Approaching	دُنُوّ	Solidity	جُمُود
Returning	رُجُوع	Madness	جُنُون
Settling	رُسُوب	Happening	حُدُوث
Firmness	رُسُوخ	Arriving	حُصُول
Worship, prostration	سُجُود	Presence	حُضُور
Gladness	سُرُور	Staying, falling	حُلُول
Falling	سُقُوط		

Heat	حُمُوّ	Failing	قُصُور
Silence	سُكُوت	Sitting	قُعُود
Quietness	سُكُون	Hiding	كُمُون
Consolation	سُلُوّ	Descending	نُزُول
Exaltation	سُمُوّ	Growing, beginning	نُشُوء
Rising (sun)	شُرُوق	Execution	نُفُوذ
Proceeding	صُدُور	Aversion	نُفُور
Ascending	صُعُود	Growth	نُمُوّ
Rising	طُلُوع	Blowing (wind)	هُبُوب
Crossing	عُبُور	Falling	هُبُوط
Height	عُلُوّ	Attacking	هُجُوم
Setting (sun)	غُرُوب	Arriving	وُصُول
Deception	غُرُور	Coming	وُرُود
Languor, lukewarmness	فُتُور	Standing	وُقُوف
Coming	قُدُوم		

10. فُعُولَة

Manhood	كُهُولَة	Harshness	خُشُونَة
Manliness	مُرُوءَة	Tenderness	رُخُوصَة
Saltiness	مُلُوحَة	Dampness	رُطُوبَة
Softness	نُعُومَة	Heat	سَخُونَة
Ruggedness	وُعُوثَة	Ease	سُهُولَة
Ruggedness	وُعُورَة	Difficulty	صُعُوبَة
Dryness	يُبُوسَة	Sweetness	عُذُوبَة
Sourness	حُمُوضَة		

288

11. فِعَالَة

Swimming	سِبَاحَة	Protection	حِمَايَة
Office of a butler	سِقَايَة	Avoidance	حِيَادَة
Authority	سِيَادَة	Weaving	حِبَاكَة
Ruling, politics	سِيَاسَة	Lectureship	خِطَابَة
Travelling	سِيَاحَة	Caliphate	خِلَافَة
Accusation	شِكَايَة	Treachery	خِيَانَة
Dyeing	صِبَاغَة	Sewing	خِيَاطَة
Exchanging (money)	صِرَافَة	Knowledge	دِرَايَة
Handcraft	صِنَاعَة	Prefecture	إِمَارَة
Goldsmith's art	صِيَاغَة	Building	بِنَايَة
Hospitality	ضِيَافَة	Merchandise	تِجَارَة
Worship	عِبَادَة	Reciting	تِلَاوَة
Porterage	عِتَالَة	Tribute	جِبَايَة
Divination	عِرَافَة	Surgery	جِرَاحَة
Perfumery (trade)	عِطَارَة	Ploughing	حِرَاثَة
Building	عِمَارَة	Guarding	حِرَاسَة
Providence, care	عِنَايَة	Relating	حِكَايَة
Husbandry	فِلَاحَة	Indication, auctioneering	دِلَالَة
Reading	قِرَاءَة	Headship	رِئَاسَة
Leading	قِيَادَة	Suckling	رِضَاعَة
Writing	كِتَابَة	Agriculture	زِرَاعَة
Sufficience	كِفَايَة		

Navigation	مِلَاحَة	Protection	وِقَايَة
Carpentry	نِجَارَة	Stewardship	وِكَالَة
Guidance	هِدَايَة	Birth	وِلَادَة
Inheritance	وِرَاثَة	Governorship	وِلَايَة
Office of Vizier	وِزَارَة		

12. فَعَالَة

Safety	سَلَامَة	Honour, regard	كَرَامَة
Kindness	سَمَاحَة	Foulmouthedness	بَذَاءَة
Courage	شَجَاعَة	Skilfulness	بَرَاعَة
Misery	شَقَاوَة	Simplicity	بَسَاطَة
Testimony	شَهَادَة	Kindness,cheerfulness	بَشَاشَة
Chivalry	شَهَامَة	Stupidity	بَلَادَة
Friendliness	صَدَاقَة	Cowardice	جَبَانَة
Hardness	صَلَابَة	Boldness	جَسَارَة
Cheerfulness	طَلَاقَة	Ignorance	جَهَالَة
Purity	طَهَارَة	Youthfulness	حَدَاثَة
Comeliness	ظَرَافَة	Skilfulness	حَذَاقَة
Freshness	غَضَاضَة	Sweetness	حَلَاوَة
Stupidity	غَبَاوَة	Foolishness	حَمَاقَة
Vileness	قَبَاحَة	Depravity	خَبَاثَة
Holiness	قَدَاسَة	Losing	خَسَارَة
Contentedness	قَنَاعَة	Delicacy	دَمَاثَة
Denseness	كَثَافَة	Meaness, badness	رَدَاءَة

Happiness	سَعَادَة	Vigilance	نَبَاهَة
Easiness of style	سَلَاسَة	Repentance	نَدَامَة
Stability	مَتَانَة	Cleanliness	نَظَافَة
Inaccessibility	مَنَاعَة	Innocency	نَقَاوَة
Skilfulness	مَهَارَة	Meekness	وَدَاعَة

13. فَعَالِيَّة

Depravity	خَبَاثِيَّة	Openly	عَلَانِيَّة
Suitability	صَلَاحِيَّة	Skilfulness	فَرَاهِيَّة
Obedience	طَوَاعِيَة	Hating	كَرَاهِيَة
Madness	عَتَاهِيَة	Purity	نَزَاهِيَة

14. فُعَال

Weeping	بُكَاء	Cough	سُعَال
Singing to camels	حُدَاء	Consumption	سُلَال
Bellowing	خُوَار	Headache	صُدَاع
Choking, diphtheria	خُنَاق	Crying	صُرَاخ
Praying	دُعَاء	Shouting	صِيَاح
Giddiness	دُوَار	Sneezing	عُطَاس
Bleeding (nose)	رُعَاف	Hiccough, gasp	فُوَاق
Grumbling (camel)	رُغَاء	Great thirst	لُهَات
Hard breathing	زُحَار	Mewing	مُوَاء
Chatter (monkey)	زُقَاح	Crowing	نُعَاب
Rheum	زُكَام	Drowsiness	نُعَاس
Asking	سُؤَال	Lamentation	نُوَاح

Shouting	هُتَاف	Passionate love	هُيَام
Leaness	هُزَال		

15. فَعَال

Affliction	بَلَاء	Generosity	سَخَاء
Splendour	بَهَاء	Permission	سَمَاح
Firmness	ثَبَات	Misery	شَقَاء
Reward	جَزَاء	Straying	ضَلَال
Dryness	جَفَاف	Costliness	غَلَاء
Clearness, emigration	جَلَاء	Corruption	فَسَاد
Beauty	جَمَال	Vanishing	فَنَاء
Crossing, license	جَوَاز	Lapse, missing	فَوَات
Reaping	حَصَاد	Fatigue	كَلَال
Destruction	خَرَاب	Perfection	كَمَال
Losing	خَسَار	Success	نَجَاح
Secrecy	خَفَاء	Growing	نَمَاء
Abundance	رَخَاء	Fulfilment of promise	وَفَاء

16. فِعَال

Shouting	صِيَاح	Returning	إِيَاب
Light, brightness	ضِيَاء	Veiling	حِجَاب
Fleeing	فِرَار	Counting	حِسَاب
Rising, standing	قِيَام	Conclusion, end	خِتَام
Meeting, finding	لِقَاء	Nursing	رِضَاع
Shunning	نِفَار	Healing	شِفَاء
Refusing	إِبَاء	Fasting	صِيَام

17. فَعِيْل

Sighing	زَفِيب	Departure	رَحِيل
Snoring	شَخِير	Roaring	زَئِير
Braying, hiccough	شَهِيق	Neighing	صَهِيل
Trumpeting (elephant)	صَئِّي	Buzzing	طَنِين
Shouting	صَرِيخ	Clamour, roaring (sea)	عَجِيج
Gnashing	صَرِير	Hissing	فَحِيح
Creaking	صَرِيف	Praising	مَدِيح
Whistling	صَفِير	Barking	نَبِيح
Noise of boiling water	أَزِيز	Lamentation	نَحِيب
Groaning	أَنِين	Crowing	نَعِيب
Rustling (leaves)	حَفِيف	Braying	نَهِيق
Longing	حَنِين	Roaring	هَدِير
Murmur (water)	خَرِير	Sound of thunder	هَزِيم
Creeping	دَبِيب		

18. فَعِيْلَة

Estrangement	قَطِيعَة	Scorn, zeal	حَمِيَّة
Advice	نَصِيحَة	Youthfulness	شَبِيبَة
Supplication	وَسِيلَة	Accusation	شَكِيَّة
Slander	وَقِيعَة	Determination	عَزِيمَة
Prevention	حَرِيمَة	Plunder	غَنِيمَة
Rancour	حَقِيقَة	Judgment	قَضِيَّة

19. فُعَالَة

Request	بُغَايَة	Suddenness	فُجَاءَة
Completion	تُمَامَة	Tarrying	لُبَاثَة

20. فَاعِلَة

Disclosing	كَاشِفَة	Order	آمِرَة
Development	نَاشِئَة	Result	عَاقِبَة
Preserving, watch	وَاقِيَة	Siesta	قَائِلَة

21. فُعْلَة

Scoffing	سُخَرَة	Experience	خُبَرَة
Haste	سُرعَة	Preaching	خُطْبَة
Brownish	سُمرَة	Pace	خُطْوَة
Auburn	شُقرَة	Sight	رُؤيَة
Companionship	صُحبَة	Roughness	غُلظَة
Nakedness	عُريَة	Power	قُدرَة
Emigration	غُربَة	Freshness, consolation	قُرَّة
Desire, request	بُغيَة	Power	قُوَّة
Boldness	جُرأَة	Grammatical error	هُجنَة
Excellence	جُودَة		

22. فَعْلَة

Power	سَطوَة	Return	عَودَة
Distress, ill-luck	شَقوَة	Inattention	غَفلَة
Attack	صَولَة	Absence	غَيبَة

Zeal, jealousy	غَيرَة	Failure	خَيبَة
Surprise	فَجأَة	Invitation	دَعوَة
Hardness	قَسوَة	Mercy	رَأفَة
Sorrow	كَأبَة	Mercy	رَحمَة
Abundance	كَثرَة	Desire	رَغبَة
Curse	لَعنَة	Dread	رَهبَة
Rheum	نَزلَة	Slipping	زَلَّة
Ampleness	بَسطَة	Growth	نَشأَة
Repentance	تَوبَة	Revenge	نَقمَة
Perplexity	حَيرَة	Slip, error	هَفوَة
Fear	خَشيَة	Fear	هَيبَة
Solitude	خَلوَة	Old age	شَيبَة

23. فِعْلَة

Chastity	عِفَّة	Relationship	نِسبَة
Living	عِيشَة	Luxuriousness	نِعمَة
Might	غِرَّة	Intention	نِيَّة
Desire, blessedness	غِبطَة	Supremacy, empire	إِمرَة
Seduction	فِتنَة	Impetuosity	حِدَّة
Prudence	فِطنَة	Wisdom	حِكمَة
Littleness, rarity	قِلَّة	Experience	خِبرَة
Writing	كِتبَة	Service	خِدمَة
Praising	مِدحَة	Betrothal	خِطبَة
Bounty, (reproachful		Lightness	خِفَّة
for favours)	مِنَّة	Fear	خِيفَة

Dignity	رِفْعَة	Partnership, commu-	
Tenderness, thinness	رِقَّة	nion	شِرْكَة
Conduct	سِيرَة	Soundness	صِحَّة

24. فَعَلَة

Pity	شَفَقَة	Security	أَمَنَة
Haste	عَجَلَة	Affability	أَنَسَة
Victory	غَلَبَة	Contempt	أَنَفَة
Possessing, talent	مَلَكَة	Motion	حَرَكَة
Deliverance	نَجَاة	Life	حَيَاة

25. فُعْلَى

Nearness	زُلْفَى	Misfortune	بُؤْس
Dwelling	سُكْنَى	Vision	رُؤْيَا
Blessedness	طُوبَى	Returning	رُجْعَى
Encounter	لُقْيَا	Desire	رُغْبَى

26. فَعْلَى

Claim	دَعْوَى	Confidential whisper	نَجْوَى
Accusation	شَكْوَى		

27. فِعْلَى

Remembrance	ذِكْرَى

28. فُعْلَان

Reproof	عُتبَان	Reckoning	حُسْبَان
Forgiveness	غُفرَان	Sweetness	حُلوَان
Losing	فُقدَان	Carrying	حُملَان
Reading	قُرآن	Losing	خُسرَان
Approaching	قُربَان	Over-weighing	رُجحَان
Denying, ingratitude	كُفرَان	Consolation	سُلوَان
Decrease	نُقصَان	Thankfulness	شُكرَان
Vanity	بُطلَان	Overflowing, injustice	طُغيَان
Slander	بُهتَان		

29. فِعْلَان

Forgetting	نِسيَان	Knowing	عِرفَان
Forsaking	هِجرَان	Losing	فِقدَان
Finding	وِجدَان	Returning, arriving	قِدمَان
Coming	إِتيَان	Concealing	كِتمَان
Depriving, forbidding	حِرمَان		

30. فَعَلَان

Flowing	سَيَلَان	Shining	لَمَعَان
Rambling, flowing	طَوَفَان	Inclination	مَيَلَان
Flying	طَيَرَان	Raving	هَذَيَان
Boiling	غَلَيَان	Agitation, commotion	هَيَجَان
Boiling	فَورَان		
Overflowing	فَيَضَان	Longing	تَوَقَان

Wandering	تَيَهَان	Palpitation	خَفَقَان
Agitation	ثَوَرَان	Revolving	دَوَرَان
Running	جَرَيَان	Trembling	رَجَفَان
Wandering	جَوَلَان	Passing away	زَوَلَان
Avoidance	حَيَدَان		

31. تَفْعَال

Croaking	تَنْعَاب	Sprinkling	تَرشَاش
Paying ready money	تَنقَاد	Sipping, sucking	تَرشَاف
Sleep	تهجَاع	Asking	تَسْآل
Remembrance	تَذكَار	Pouring	تَسكَاب
Departing	تَرحَال		

32. فَعْلُولَة

Senility	شَيخُوخَة	Perishableness	بَيدُ ودَة
Spreading news	شَيعُوعَة	Separation, remote-	
Becoming	صَيرُورَة	ness	بَينُونَة
Siesta	قَيلُولَة	Avoidance	حَيدُ ودَة
Existence	كَينُونَة	Continuation	دَيمُومَة
Inclining	مَيلُولَة	Deviation	زَيغُوغَة
		Lordship	سَيدُ ودَة

33. مَفْعُول

Difficult	مَعسُور	Subject, placing	مَوضُوع
Understanding	مَعقُول	Promise	مَوعُود
Temptation	مَفتُون	Easiness	مَيسُور

Patience	مَجلُود	Oath	مَحلُوف
Exertion	مَجهُود	Return	مَرجُوع
Produce	مَحصُول	Restoring	مَردُود

ADJECTIVES RESEMBLING THE AGENT.

1. فَعْل

Easy	سَهْل	Deficient, low (price)	بَخْس
Clever, energetic	شَهْم	Righteous	بَرّ
Aged	شَيْخ	Smiling	بَشّ
Difficult	صَعْب	Firm, steady	ثَبْت
Hard	صَلْد	Chaste (language)	جَزْل
Thick, bulky	ضَخْم	Alive	حَيّ
Straight, narrow	ضَنْك	Deceiver	خَبّ
Sweet	عَذْب	Meek	دَمْث
Tender, sappy	غَضّ	Ragged	رَتّ
Rough	فَظّ	Broad	رَحْب
Thick (beard)	كَتّ	Soft, flexible	رَخْص
Pure	مَحْض	Ignoble	رَذْل
Soft, brittle	هَشّ	Tender	رَطْب
Rugged	وَعْر	Luxurious	رَغْد
		Compliant	سَمْح

2. فِعْل

| Thin | دِقّ | Rude | جِلْف |
| Filthy | رِجْس | Fertile | خِصْب |

Saltish	مِلْح	Pure	صِرْف
		Inexperienced	غِرّ

3. فُعْل

Hard	صُلْب	Pure, free	حُرّ
Heedless	غُفْل	Sweet	حُلْو
Bitter	مُرّ	Mean	دُوْن
Sour	مُزّ	Hot	سُخْن

4. فَعَل

Handsome	حَسَن	Hero	بَطَل
Filthy	نَجَس	Youth	حَدَث

5. فَعِل

Easy, (style)	سَلِس	Fragrant	أرِج
Unsociable	شَرِس	Liar	أفِك
Greedy	شَرِه	Ugly	بَشِع
Harsh tempered	شَكِس	Glutton	بَطِن
Merry	طَرِب	Joyful	بَهِج
Thirsty	ظَمِئ	Fatigued	تَعِب
Difficult	عَسِر	Unfortunate	تَعِس
Fragrant	عَطِر	Tasteless	تَفِه
Turbid	عَكِر	Rough	خَشِن
Blind	عَمِي	Dangerous	خَطِر
Drowned	غَرِق	Defiled	دَنِس

Eloquent	لَسِن	Angry	غَضِب
Gluttonous	لَهِم	Joyous	فَرِح
Rotten (eggs)	مَذِر	Timid	فَرِق
Filthy	نَجِس	Filthy	قَذِر
Glutton	نَهِم	Fragile	قَصِم
Timorous	وَجِل	Troubled	قَلِق
Pious	وَرِع	Despairing	قَنِط
Dirty	وَسِخ	Broken-hearted	كَئِب
Brazenfaced	وَقِح	Grieved	كَمِد
		Viscous	لَزِج

6. أَفْعَل

Dumb	أَخْرَس	Bobtailed	أَبْتَر
Green	أَخْضَر	Hoarse	أَبَحّ
Having one eye blue,		Piebald	أَبْرَش
the other black	أَخْيَف	Leper	أَبْرَص
Having eyes black and		Spotted	أَبْقَع
wide apart	أَدْعَج	White	أَبْيَض
Blackish	أَدْكَن	Bare (face, field)	أَجْرَد
Having a long chin	أَذْقَن	Shapely contour (neck)	أَجْيَد
Spotted	أَرْقَط	Humpbacked	أَحْدَب
Having bad eyes	أَرْمَد	Short-sighted	أَحْسَر
Blue	أَزْرَق	Red	أَحْمَر
Brownish, tawny	أَسْمَر	Fool	أَحْمَق
Black	أَسْوَد	Squint-eyed	أَحْوَل

Crooked	أَعْوَج	Having the tip of the	
One-eyed	أَعْوَر	nose cut off	أَشْرَم
Dust-coloured	أَغْبَر	Hairy	أَشْعَر
Blaze-faced	أَغَرّ	Auburn	أَشْقَر
Flat-nosed	أَفْطَس	Stiff-handed	أَشَلّ
Having the teeth apart	أَفْلَج	Hoary	أَشْمَط
Under lip chapped	أَفْلَح	Gray	أَشْهَب
Bald-headed	أَقْرَع	Red-tinged, (pupil)	أَشْهَل
Hook-nosed	أَقْنَى	Yellow	أَصْفَر
Having brown eyelids	أَكْحَل	Partially bald	أَصْلَع
Born blind	أَكْمَه	Deaf	أَصَمّ
Long-bearded	أَلْحَى	Deaf	أَطْرَش
Red-lipped	أَلْعَس	Lame	أَعْرَج
Blue-eyed, gray-eyed	أَمْلَح	Left-handed	أَعْسَر
Eyes wide apart	أَنْجَل	Night-blind	أَعْشَى
Clipped (bird's tail)	أَهْلَب	Tongue-tied	أَعْقَد
Hasty	أَهْوَج	Hare-lipped	أَعْلَم
Slender	أَهْيَف	Blear-eyed	أَعْمَش
Right-handed	أَيْمَن	Blind	أَعْمَى
		Long-necked	أَعْنَق

7. فَيْعِل

Evil	سَيِّء	Clear	بَيِّن
Narrow	ضَيِّق	Good	جَيِّد
Pleasant	طَيِّب	Religious	دَيِّن

Dying	مَيِّت	Intelligent	كَيِّس
		Soft	لَيِّن

8. فَعِيل

Merciful	رَحِيم	Polite, learned	أَدِيب
Evil, bad	رَدِيّ	Faithful	أَمِين
Companion	رَفِيق	Stingy	بَخِيل
Weak-minded	سَخِيف	Slow	بَطِيء
Swift	سَرِيع	Far	بَعِيد
Happy	سَعِيد	Stupid	بَلِيد
Foolish	سَفِيه	Thick	ثَخِين
Safe	سَلِيم	New	جَدِيد
Stout	سَمِين	Worthy	جَدِير
Strong	شَدِيد	Important, large	جَسِيم
Noble	شَرِيف	Great, glorious	جَلِيل
Ugly	شَنِيع	Sharp	حَدِيد
Sound	صَحِيح	Greedy	حَرِيص
Small	صَغِير	Sorrowful	حَزِين
Weak	ضَعِيف	Wise	حَكِيم
Long	طَوِيل	Vile	خَسِيس
Beautiful	ظَرِيف	Light, agile	خَفِيف
Old	عَتِيق	Fine, thin	دَقِيق
Wonderful	عَجِيب	Low	دَنِيء

Much, many	كَثِير	Broad	عَرِيض
Dense	كَثِيف	Dear, rare	عَزِيز
Generous	كَرِيم	Of high rank	عَلِيّ
Base	لَئِيْم	Deep	عَمِيق
Kind	لَطِيف	Common, universal	عَمِيم
Glorious	مَجِيد	Strange	غَرِيب
Good, handsome	مَلِيح	Thick, coarse	غَلِيظ
Lean	نَحِيف	Rich	غَنِيّ
Clean	نَظِيف	Poor	فَقِير
Valuable	نَفِيس	Old	قَدِيم
Honourable	وَجِيه	Near	قَرِيب
Humble	وَضِيع	Short	قَصِير
Orphan	يَتِيم	Strong	قَوِي
		Great	كَبِير

٩. فَاعِل

Firm	ثَابِت	Putrid, (water)	آجِن
Ignorant	جَاهِل	Stagnant	آسِن
Clever	حَاذِق	Cold	بَارِد
Hot	حَارّ	Righteous	بَارّ
Resolute	حَازِم	Brave	بَاسِل
Intensely black	حَالِك	Vain	بَاطِل
Sour	حَامِض	Oppressing	بَاغٍ

Barren	عَاقِر	Special	خَاصّ
Wise	عَاقِل	Traitor	خَائِن
Learned	عَالِم	Sinner	خَاطِئ
High	عَالٍ	Domesticated(animals)	دَاجِن
General, common	عَامّ	Continuous	دَائِم
Lukewarm	فَاتِر	Simpleton	سَاذِج
Wicked	فَاجِر	Thief	سَارِق
Hard	قَاسٍ	Sound	سَالِم
Cutting (sword)	قَاطِع	High	سَامٍ
Liar	كَاذِب	Sharp sword	صَارِم
Infidel	كَافِر	Clear	صَافٍ
Perfect	كَامِل	Carnivorous	ضَارٍ
Skilful	مَاهِر	Pure	طَاهِر
Imperfect	نَاقِص	Just	عَادِل
Complete	وَافٍ	Naked	عَارٍ

10. فَعْلَان

Satisfied, (food)	شَبْعَان	Hungry	جَوْعان
Lewd	شَهْوَان	Grieved	حَزْنَان
Thirsty	صَدْيَان	Perplexed	حَيْرَان
Thirsty	ظَمْآن	Ashamed	خَجْلَان
Perspiring	عَرْقَان	Abashed	خَزْيَان
Thirsty	عَطْشَان	Watered	رَيَّان
Impotent	عَيَّان	Drunken	سَكْران

Repentant	نَدْمَان	Choked	غَصَّان
Forgetful	نَسْيَان	Angry	غَضْبَان
Giddy (from wine)	نَشْوَان	Heedless	غَفْلَان
Sleepy	نَعْسَان	Joyous	فَرحَان
Fearful	هَيْبَان	Cripple	كَسْحَان
Slumbering	وَسْنَان	Grieved	لَهْفَان
Dejected	وَلْهَان	Full	مَلآن

11. فَعَال

Chaste (woman)	حَصان	Coward	جَبَان
Incurable	عَيَاء	Liberal	جَوَاد

12. فُعَال

Incurable	عُضَال	Brackish	أُجَاج
Incurable	عُقَام	Fatal	ذُعَاف and زُعَاف
Sweet (water)	فُرَات	Clear (water)	زُلَال
Magnanimous	هُمَام	Brave	شُجَاع
		Bulky	ضُخَام

MEASURES OF THE NOUNS OF EXCESS.

9 مِفْعِيْل	1 فَعَّال
10 فَاعِلَة	2 فَعَّالَة
11 فَعُّوْلَة	3 فِعِّيْل
12 فُعَل	4 فَعُوْل
13 فُعَّل	5 فَعِيْل
14 فُعُّوْل	6 فَاعُوْل
15 تِفْعَال	7 فُعَلَة
16 تِفْعَالَة	8 مِفْعَال

NOUNS OF EXCESS. صِيغُ الْمُبَالَغَة

1. فَعَّال

Learned	عَلَّام	Penitent	أَوَّاب
Perfidious	غَدَّار	Smiling	بَسَّام
Deceiver	غَرَّار	Weeper	بَكَّاء
Impostor	غَشَّاش	Forgiving (God)	تَوَّاب
Pardoner (God)	غَفَّار	Giant	جَبَّار
Bountiful	فَيَّاض	Traveller	جَوَّال
Murderer	قَتَّال	Traitor	خَوَّان
Subduer (God)	قَهَّار	Fosterer (God)	رَزَّاق
Liar	كَذَّاب	Thief	سَرَّاق
Benefactor	مَنَّان	Bloodthirsty	سَفَّاك
Timid	هَيَّاب	Drunkard	شَرَّاب
Giver	وَهَّاب	One who fasts	صَوَّام
		Covetous	طَمَّاع

‎2. فَعَّالَة‎

Learned	عَلَّامَة	Traveller	جَوَّالَة
Genealogist	نَسَّابَة	Traveller	رَحَّالَة
Timid	هَيَّابَة	Clamorous	صَخَّابَة

‎3. فِعِّيل‎

Veracious	صِدِّيق	Silent	سِكِّيت
Holy	قِدِّيس	Tippler	سِكِّير
Playful	لِعِّيب	Drunkard	شِرِّيب
		Wicked	شِرِّير

‎4. فَعُول‎

Chaste	طَهُور	Brave	جَسُور
Hasty	عَجُول	Ignorant	جَهُول
Forgiving	غَفُور	Merciful	رَحُوم
Zealous	غَيُور	Silent	سَكُوت
Fearful	هَيُوب	Thankful	شَكُور
Affectionate	وَدُود	Veracious	صَدُوق

‎5. فَعِيل‎

Sorrowful	كَئِيب	Merciful	رَحِيم
Thick (beard)	كَثِيث	Of close texture	صَفِيق
		Omniscient	عَلِيم

‎6. فَاعُول‎

Very timid	فَارُوق	Silent	سَاكُوت

7. فُعَلَة

Jolly	لُعَبَة	Wrestler	صُرَعَة
Censorious	لُوَمَة	Laugher	ضُحَكَة
Sleepy	نُوَمَة	Sweater	عُرَقَة
Mocker	هُزَّأَة	Timid	فُزَعَة

8. مِفْعَال

Liberal	مِعْطَاء	Spendthrift	مِتْلَاف
Daring	مِقْدَام	Delusive	مِخْلَاف
Loquacious	مِكْثَار	Docile	مِذْعَان
Lazy	مِكْسَال	Hospitable	مِضْيَاف
Bountiful	مِهْدَاء	Covetous	مِطْمَاع

9. مِفْعِيل

Using perfumes	مِعْطِير	Poor, destitute	مِسْكِين

10. فَاعِلَة

Reciter	رَاوِيَة	Treacherous	خَائِنَة
Distinguished	نَابِغَة	Crafty	دَاهِيَة

11. فَعُولَة

Grateful	مَنُونَة	Timid	فَرُوقَة
Timid	هَيُوبَة	Liar	كَذُوبَة
		Disgusted with	مَلُولَة

12. فُعْل

Holy	قُدْس	Heedless	غُفْل

‎١٣. فُعَّل‎

Changeable	قُلَّب Fickle	حُوَّل
	Deceitful	خُلَّب

‎١٤. فَعُّول‎

Everlasting	قَيُّوم Holy	قَدُّوس

‎١٥ and ١٦. تِفْعَال وتِفْعَالة‎

Humorist	تِلْعَابة Humorist	تِلْعَاب
	Glutton	تِلْقَام

NOUNS OF INSTRUMENT. ‎اِسْمُ ٱلْآلَة‎

‎١. مِفْعَل‎

Slaking trough	مِصْوَل Needlecase	مِثْبَر
Cooking-pot	مِطْبَخ File	مِبْرَد
Spindle	مِغْزَل Lancet	مِبْضَع
Bath	مِغْطَس Microscope	مِجْهَر
Handle	مِقْبَض Syringe	مِدَّقَن
Scissors	مِقَصّ Awl	مِدْرَز
Cutter	مِقْطَع Cannon	مِدْفَع
Frying-pan	مِقْلَى Telescope	مِرْقَب
Halter	مِقْوَد Fire-brand	مِسْعَر
Press, (hand or		Grindstone	مِسَنّ
hydraulic)	مِكْبَس Whetstone	مِشْحَذ
Tongs	مِلْقَط Fork	مِشَكّ

| Beak | مِنْسَر | Adze, chisel | مِنْحَت |
| Fork, kitchen | مِنْشَل | Spur | مِنْخَس |

2. مِفْعَال

Telescope	مِنْظَار	Needle-case	مِثْبَار
Bellows	مِنْفَاخ	Oar	مِجْذَاف
Bird's bill	مِنْقَار	Plough	مِحْرَاث
Chisel	مِنْقَاش	Syringe	مِحْقَان
Hand or hydraulic		Flute	مِزْمَار
press	مِكْبَاس	Probe	مِسْبَار
Measure	مِكْيَال	Lancet	مِشْرَاط
Saw	مِنْشَار	Lamp, torch	مِصْبَاح
Hoe	مِنْكَاش	Wooden lock	مِغْلَاق
Iron-shod staff, spur	مِهْمَاز	Key	مِفْتَاح
Balance	مِيزَان	Oar	مِقْذَاف
		Scissors	مِقْرَاض

3. مِفْعَلَة

Lathe	مِخْرَطَة	Needle-case	مِثْبَرَة
Looking-glass	مِرْآة	Censer	مِبْخَرَة
Sprinkler	مِرَشَّة	Pen-knife	مِبْرَأَة
Sand-sifter	مِرْمَلَة	Spittoon	مِتْفَلَة
Arrow	مِرْمَاة	Censer	مِجْمَرَة
Fan	مِرْوَحَة	Inkstand	مِحْبَرَة
Paper ruler	مِسْطَرَة	Pillow	مِخَدَّة

Broom	مِكْنَسَة	Filter	مِصْفَاة
Flat or box iron	مِكْوَاة	Squirt	مِضَخَّة
Press	مِلْزَمَة	Hand-mill	مِطْحَنَة
Spoon	مِلْعَقَة	Mallet	مِطْرَقَة
Duster	مِمْسَحَة	Umbrella	مِظَلَّة
Salt-cellar	مِمْلَحَة	Wine or olive press	مِعْصَرَة
Towel	مِنْشَفَة	Ladle	مِغْرَفَة
Girdle	مِنْطَقَة	Pen-case	مِقْلَمَة

WITH THE MEANING OF NOUN OF INSTRUMENT.

فِعَال

Shackle	عِقَال	A woman's covering	إِزَار
Swaddling clothes	قِمَاط	Shoe	حِذَاء
Head-veil	قِنَاع	Girth, girdle	حِزَام
Muffler	لِثَام	Blanket	دِثَار
Bridle, rein	لِجَام	Bandage	رِبَاط
Quilt	لِحَاف	Wine-skin	زِقَاق
Belt	نِطَاق	Curtain	سِتَار
Golden girdle	وِشَاح	Bandage	ضِمَاد

WITH THE MEANING OF NOUN OF INSTRUMENT.

فِعَالَة

Bandage	رِبَاطَة	Sword belt	حِمَالَة
Bandage	عِصَابَة	Support	دِعَامَة

312

Stick	هِرَاوَة	Support	عِضَادَة
Pillow	وِسَادَة	Suspender	عِلَاقَة
		Turban	عِمَامَة

THE IRREGULAR MEASURES. مُفْعَلَة and مُفْعَل

Sieve	مُنْخُل	Pestle	مُدُقّ
Soda or soap box	مُحَّرُضَة	Oil bottle	مُدْهُن
Antimony box	مُكَّحَلَة	Snuff-box	مُسْعُط

PRIMITIVE NOUNS OF INSTRUMENT.

Net	شَبَكَة	Needle	إِبْرَة
Drum	طَبْل	Double-headed axe	حِدَأَة
Pick-axe, hoe	فَأْس	Lance, spear	حَرْبَة
Trap	فَخّ	Bucket	دَلْو
Adze	قَدُوم	Wheel	دُوْلَاب
Lock	قُفْل	Ink-stand	دَوَاة
Pen	قَلَم	Lance	رُمْح
Tongs, pincers	كَلْبَتَان	Flint	زِنَاد
Pipe, screw	لَوْلَب	Lamp	سِرَاج
Catapult, ballista	مَنْجَنِيق	Knife	سِكِّين
Razor	مُوسَى	Arrow	سَهْم
Yoke	نِيْر	Sword	سَيْف

PROFESSIONS AND TRADES.

فَعَّال مُصَاغًا لِذَى حِرْفَة

Thrasher	دَرَّاس	Tiller	أَكَّار
Auctioneer	دَلَّال	Greengrocer	بَقَّال
Oil merchant	دَهَّان	Builder	بَنَّاء
Sower	زَرَّاع	Door-keeper	بَوَّاب
Oil-dealer	زَيَّات	Salesman	بَيَّاع
Jailer	سَجَّان	Surgeon	جَرَّاح
Water carrier	سَقَّاء	Butcher	جَزَّار
Butter dealer	سَمَّان	Shearer	جَزَّاز
Beggar	شَحَّاذ	Executioner	جَلَّاد
Dyer	صَبَّاغ	Camel-driver	جَمَّال
Money changer	صَرَّاف	Smith	حَدَّاد
Sportsman	صَيَّاد	Ploughman	حَرَّات
Cook	طَبَّاخ	Reaper	حَصَّاد
Printer	طَبَّاع	Wood-cutter	حَطَّاب
Drummer	طَبَّال	Barber	حَلَّاق
Miller	طَحَّان	Donkey-driver	حَمَّار
Porter	عَتَّال	Porter	حَمَّال
Grocer, perfumer	عَطَّار	Baker	خَبَّاز
Spinner	غَزَّال	Potter	خَزَّاف
Sheep owner	غَنَّام	Tailor	خَيَّاط
Miner	فَحَّام	Horseman	خَيَّال
Husbandman	فَلَّاح	Tanner	دَبَّاغ

Carpenter	نَجَّار	Butcher	قَصَّاب
Sculptor, stone-		Bleacher	قَصَّار
dresser	نَحَّات	Vine-dresser	كَرَّام
Copper-smith	نَحَّاس	Wheat measurer	كَيَّال
Carder	نَدَّاف	Butcher	لَحَّام
Engraver, stone-cutter	نَقَّاش	Sailor	مَلَّاح

MEASURES OF THE PLURAL OF PAUCITY.

أَوْزَانُ جَمْعِ ٱلْقِلَّةِ

1 أَفْعُل
2 أَفْعَال
3 أَفْعِلَة
4 فِعْلَة

MEASURES OF THE PLURAL OF MULTITUDE

أَوْزَانُ جَمْعِ ٱلْكَثْرَةِ

19 فُعَلَاء	10 فِعَال	1 فَعْل
20 أَفْعِلَاء	11 فِعَالَة	2 فُعْل
21 فُعْلَان	12 فُعُول	3 فَعَل
22 فِعْلَان	13 فُعُولَة	4 فُعَل
23 فَعَالَى	14 فَعْلَى	5 فِعَل
24 فُعَالَى	15 فِعْلَى	6 فُعُل
25 فَعَالِيّ	16 فَعِيل	7 فَعَلَة
26 فُعَالِيّ	17 فُعَّل	8 فُعَلَة
	18 فُعَّال	9 فِعَلَة

PLURAL OF PAUCITY. جَمْعُ ٱلْقِلَّة

1. أَفْعُل

English	Plural	Singular		English	Plural	Singular
Slave	أَعْبُد	عَبْد		Sea	أَبْحُر	بَحْر
Time, age	أَعْصُر	عَصْر		Eyelid	أَجْفُن	جَفْن
She-goat	أَعْنُز	عَنْز		Letters (al-	أَحْرُف	حَرْف
Eye	أَعْيُن	عَيْن		phabet		
Farthing	أَفْلُس	فَلْس		Breast-plate	أَدْرُع	دِرْع
Cup	أَكْوُس	كَأْس		Bucket	أَدْلٍ	دَلْو
Sheep, ram	أَكْبُش	كَبْش		Tears	أَدْمُع	دَمْع
Palm of the				House	أَدْوُر	دَار
hand	أَكُفّ	كَفّ		Cubit	أَذْرُع	ذِرَاع
Tongue	أَلْسُن	لِسَان		Head	أُرْوُس	رَأْس
Star	أَنْجُم	نَجْم		Spring-camp	أَرْبُع	رَتْع
Eagle	أَنْسُر	نَسْر		Foot	أَرْجُل	رِجْل
Soul	أَنْفُس	نَفْس		Line	أَسْطُر	سَطْر
Tiger	أَنْمُر	نَمِر		Lot, share	أَسْهُم	سَهْم
River	أَنْهُر	نَهْر		Mouth	أَشْهُر	شَهْر
Face, page	أَوْجُه	وَجْه		Rib	أَضْلُع	ضِلْع
Hand	أَيْدٍ	يَد		Fawn	أَظْبٍ	ظَبْي
				Back	أَظْهُر	ظَهْر

2. أَفْعَال

English	Plural	Singular		English	Plural	Singular
Ruins, traces	آثَار	أَثَر		Camel	آبَال	إِبِل
Appointed time	آجَال	أَجَل		Father	آبَاء	أَب

English	Plural	Singular	English	Plural	Singular
Eyelid	أَجْفَان	جَفْن	Sunday	آحَاد	أَحَد
Generation	أَجْيَال	جِيْل	Ear	آذَان	أُذُن
Jewish Doctor, Pontiff	أَخْبَار	حَبْر	Lion	آسَاد	أَسَد
Rope	أَحْبَال	حَبْل	Horizon	آفَاق	أُفُق
Young man	أَحْدَاث	حَدَث	Hill	آكَام	أَكَمَة
Party, troop	أَحْزَاب	حِزْب	Pain	آلَام	أَلَم
Grief	أَحْزَان	حُزْن	Favour	آلَآء	أَلًى
Sentence (in law	أَحْكَام	حُكْم	Hope	آمَل	أَمَل
Burden	أَحْمَال	حِمْل	Time	آذَآء	أَنًى
Lower jaw	أَحْنَاك	حَنَك	Well	آبَار	بِئْرُ
Condition, state	أَحْوَال	حَال	Righteous	أَبْرَار	بَرّ
Time	أَحْيَان	حِيْن	Hero	أَبْطَال	بَطَل
Alive	أَحْيَآء	حَيّ	Distance	أَبْعَاد	بُعْد
Adversary	أَخْصَام	خَصْم	First-born	أَبْكَار	بِكْر
Danger	أَخْطَار	خَطَر	Son	أَبْنَآء	إِبْن
Disease	أَدْوَآء	دَاء	Door	أَبْوَاب	بَاب
Rotation	أَدْوَار	دَوْر	Verse	أَبْيَات	بَيْت
Opinion	آرَآء	رَأْي	Equals in age	أَتْرَاب	تِرْب
Sustenance	أَرْزَاق	رِزْق	Fatigue	أَتْعَاب	تَعَب
Ripe dates	أَرْطَاب	رُطَب	Fruit	أَثْمَار	ثَمَر
Spirit	أَرْوَاح	رُوْح	Garment	أَثْوَاب	ثَوْب
			Grandfather	أَجْدَاد	جَدّ
			Bell	أَجْرَاس	جَرَس
			Body	أَجْسَاد	جَسَد

Malice	أَضْغَان	ضِغْن	Button	أَزْرَار	زِرّ
Edge	أَطْرَاف	طَرَف	Husband or wife	أَزْوَاج	زَوْج
Child	أَطْفَال	طِفْل	Cause	أَسْبَاب	سَبَب
Bird	أَطْيَار	طَيْر	Tribe	أَسْبَاط	سِبْط
Nail	أَظْفَار	ظُفْر	Screen	أَسْتَار	سِتْر
Number	أَعْدَاد	عَدَد	Current price	أَسْعَار	سِعْر
Enemy	أَعْدَآء	عَدُوّ	Book	أَسْفَار	سِفْر
Wedding	أَعْرَاس	عُرْس	Fish	أَسْمَاك	سَمَك
Grass	أَعْشَاب	عُشْب	Name	أَسْمَآء	إِسْم
Nests	أَعْشَاش	عُشّ	Tooth	أَسْنَان	سِنّ
Arm	أَعْضَاد	عَضُد	Whip	أَسْوَاط	سَوْط
Member,limb	أَعْضَآء	عُضْو	Market	أَسْوَاق	سُوق
Flag	أَعْلَام	عَلَم	Sword	أَسْيَاف	سَيْف
Work	أَعْمَال	عَمَل	Tree	أَشْجَار	شَجَر
Paternal uncle	أَعْمَام	عَمّ	Poetry	أَشْعَار	شِعْر
Neck	أَعْنَاق	عُنُق	Business,work	أَشْغَال	شُغْل
Year	أَعْوَام	عَام	Kind, sort	أَشْكَال	شَكْل
Branch	أَغْصَان	غُصْن	Longing	أَشْوَاق	شَوْق
Scabbard	أَغْمَاد	غِمْد	Thorn	أَشْوَاك	شَوْك
Joy	أَفْرَاح	فَرَح	Thing	أَشْيَآء	شَيْء
Individual	أَفْرَاد	فَرْد	Echo	أَصْدَآء	صَدَى
Mare	أَفْرَاس	فَرَس	Country	أَصْقَاع	صُقْع
Mouth	أَفْوَاه	فَمْ or فُوْه	Voice	أَصْوَات	صَوْت
Filth	أَقْذَار	قَذَر			

English	Plural	Singular	English	Plural	Singular
Angel	أَمْلاَك	مَلَك	Pole, axis, leader	أَقْطَاب	قُطْب
Wave	أَمْوَاج	مَوْج	Country	أَقْطَار	قُطْر
Possession, property	أَمْوَال	مَال	Lock	أَقْفَال	قُفْل
Water	أَمْوَاه	مَاء	Pen	أَقْلَام	قَلَم
Mile	أَمْيَال	مِيْل	Moon	أَقْمَار	قَمَر
Region	أَنْحَاء	نَحْو	Saying	أَقْوَال	قَوْل
Helper	أَنْصَار	نَصِير	People, crowd	أَقْوَام	قَوْم
River	أَنْهَار	نَهْر	Liver	أَكْبَاد	كَبِد
Light	أَنْوَار	نُور	Shoulder	أَكْتَاف	كَتِف
Tusk	أَنْيَاب	نَاب	Shroud	أَكْفَان	كَفَن
Tent-peg, stake	أَوْتَاد	وَتِد	Sleeve	أَكْمَام	كُمّ
Bow-string	أَوْتَار	وَتَر	Purse, bag	أَكْيَاس	كِيس
Pain	أَوْجَاع	وَجَع	Mind	أَلْبَاب	لُبّ
Leaf	أَوْرَاق	وَرَق	Side-glance	أَلْحَاظ	لَحْظ
Dirt	أَوْسَاخ	وَسَخ	Tone, melody	أَلْحَان	لَحْن
Time	أَوْقَات	وَقْت	Board	أَلْوَاح	لَوْح
Nest	أَوْكَار	وَكْر	Glory	أَمْجَاد	مَجْد
Child	أَوْلَاد	وَلَد	Territory	أَمْصَار	مِصْر
Day	أَيَّام	يَوْم	Salt	أَمْلاَح	مِلْح
			Property	أَمْلاَك	مِلْك

3. أَفْعِلَة

English	Plural	Singular	English	Plural	Singular
Leather bag	أَجْرِبَة	جِرَاب	Vessel	آنِيَة	إِنَاء
Wing	أَجْنِحَة	جَنَاح	Building	أَبْنِيَة	بِنَاء

Pillar	أَعْمِدَة	عَمُود	Foetus	أَجِنّه	جَنِين
Bridle	أَعِنّة	عِنَان	Apparatus	أَجهِزَة	جِهَاز
Food	أَغْذِيَة	غِذَاء	Answer	أَجوِبَة	جَواب
Crow	أَغْرِبَة	غُرَاب	Shoes	أَحْذِيَة	حِذَاء
Coverings	أَغْشِيَة	غِشَاء	Phantasm	أَخْيِلَة	خَيَال
Heart	أَفْئِدَة	فُؤَاد	Invocation	أَدعِيَة	دُعَاء
Mattress	أَفْرِشَة	فِرَاش	Proof	أَدِلَّة	دَلِيل
Shirt	أَقْمِصَة	قَمِيص	Brain	أَدمِغَة	دِمَاغ
Measurement	أَقيِسَة	قِيَاس	Medicine	أَدوِيَة	دَوَاء
Garment	أَكسِيَة	كِسَاء	Handmill	أَرحِيَة	رَحىً
Dress	أَلبِسَة	لِبَاس	Loaf	أَرغِفَة	رَغِيف
Counterpane	أَلحِفَة	لِحَاف	Porch	أَروِقَة	رِوَاق
Goods	أَمتِعَة	مَتَاع	Reins	أَزِمّة	زِمَام
Example	أَمثِلَة	مِثَال	Time	أَزمِنَة	زَمَان
Place	أَمكِنَة	مَكَان	Question	أَسئِلَة	سُؤَال
Woven	أَنسِجَة	نَسِيج	Mirage	أَسرِبَة	سَرَاب
Portion	أَنصِبَة	نَصِيب	Bed	أَسِرّة	سَرِير
Air	أَهوِيَة	هَوَاء	Armour, arms	أَسلِحَة	سِلَاح
Den of wild			Camel's hump	أَسْنِمَة	سَنَام
beasts	أَوجِرَة	وَجَار	Spear head	أَسِنّة	سِنَان
Valley	أَودِيَة	وَاد	Beverage	أَشرِبَة	شَرَاب
Jugular vein	أَوردَة	وَرَد	Sun's rays	أَشِعّة	شُعَاع
Vessel	أَوعِيَة	وِعَاء	Spleen	أَطحِلَة	طِحَال
			Food	أَطعِمَة	طَعَام

فِعْلَة .4

Lad	غُلَام	غِلْمَة	Brother	إِخْوَة	أَخْ
Youth	فَتًى	فِتْيَة	Neighbour	جِيْرَة	جَار
Boy	وَلَد	وِلْدَة	Boy	صِبْيَة	صَبِيّ

PLURALS OF MULTITUDE. جُمُوع ٱلْكَثْرَة

فَعْل .1

Friend	صَاحِب	صَحْب	Party of Riders	رَكْب	رَاكِب
Guest	نَازِل	نَزْل	Party of travel-		
Envoy	وَافِد	وَفْد	lers	سَفْر	مُسَافِر
			Party of drin-		
			kers	شَرْب	شَارِب

فُعْل .2

Blue	أَزْرَق	زُرْق	Piebald	بُرْش	أَبْرَش
Brown	أَسْمَر	سُمْر	Leper	بُرْص	أَبْرَص
Black	أَسْوَد	سُوْد	White	بِيْض	أَبْيَض
Auburn	أَشْقَر	شُقْر	Bare, smooth-		
Withered hand	أَشَلّ	شُلّ	faced	جُرْد	أَجْرَد
Fine-nosed	أَشَمّ	شُمّ	Red	حُمْر	أَحْمَر
Red-tinged			Squint-eyed	حُوْل	أَحْوَل
(eye)	أَشْهَل	شُهْل	Dumb	خُرْس	أَخْرَس
Hoary	أَشْيَب	شِيْب	Green	خُضْر	أَخْضَر
Partially bald	أَصْلَع	صُلْع	Spotted	رُقْط	أَرْقَط

One-eyed	غُوْر	أَعْوَر	Deaf	صُمّ	أَصَمّ
Spotted-face			Lame	عُرْج	أَعْرَج
(horse)	غُرّ	أَغَرّ	Tongue-tied	عُقْل	أَعْقَل
Bald-headed	قُرْع	أَقْرَع	Blind	عُمْي	أَعْمَي
Hasty	هُوْج	أَهْوَج	Crooked	عُوْج	أَعْوَج

3. فَعَل

| Column | عَمَد | عَمُود | Ring, ferrule | حَلَق | حَلْقَة |
| Goat | مَعَز | مَعْزَى | Servant | خَدَم | خَادِم |

4. فُعَل

Underclothing	حُلَل	حُلَّة	Knot (in wood)	أُبَن	أُبْنَة
Scorpion's			Family	أُسَر	أُسْرَة
sting	حُمَّى	حُمَة	Nation	أُمَم	أُمَّة
Lecture	خُطَب	خُطْبَة	Desire	بُغًى	بُغْيَة
Step	خُطًى	خُطْوَة	Low-lying land	بُقَع	بُقْعَة
Pearl	دُرَر	دُرَّة	Channel, canal	تُرَع	تُرْعَة
Shower	دُفَع	دُفْعَة	Suspicion	تُهَم	تُهَمَة
Summit	ذُرًى	ذُرْوَة	Wide-sleeved		
Sight	رُوًى	رُوْيَة	cloak	جُبَب	جُبَّة
Vision	رُوًى	رُوْيَا	Corpse	جُثَث	جُثَّة
Hill	رُبًى	رُبْوَة	Sentence	جُمَل	جُمْلَة
Patch	رُقَع	رُقْعَة	Argument	حُجَج	حُجَّة
Knee	رُكَب	رُكْبَة	Room	حُجَر	حُجْرَة
Law	سُنَن	سُنَّة	Ditch	حُفَر	حُفْرَة
Twig	شُعَب	شُعْبَة	Clyster	حُقَن	حُقْنَة

Window	كُوًى	كُوَّة	Picture	صُوَر	صُورَة
Morsel	لُقَم	لُقْمَة	Edge of a sword	ظُبًى	ظُبَة
Small quantity, bright spot	لُمَع	لُمْعَة	Apparatus	عُدَد	عُدَّة
			Button-hole	عُرًى	عُرْوَة
Duration	مُدَد	مُدَّة	Knot	عُقَد	عُقْدَة
Eye	مُقَل	مُقْلَة	Wages	عُمَل	عُمْلَة
Wish	مُنًى	مُنْيَة	Room	غُرَف	غُرْفَة
Heart-blood	مُهَج	مُهْجَة	Opportunity	فُرَص	فُرْصَة
Copy (book)	نُسَخ	نُسْخَة	Dome, pavilion	قُبَب	قُبَّة
Nape of the neck	نُقَر	نُقْرَة	Kiss	قُبَل	قُبْلَة
Drop	نُقَط	نُقْطَة	Village	قُرًى	قَرْيَة
Fine-point	نُكَت	نُكَتَة	Power, faculty	قُوًى	قُوَّة
Number	نُمَر	نُمْرَة	Anxiety	كُرَب	كُرْبَة
Turn, paroxysm	نُوَب	نَوْبَة	Ball, bomb, marble	كُلَل	كُلَّة
Opportunity	نُهَز	نُهْزَة			

٥. فِعَل

Strategy	حِيَل	حِيْلَة	Needle	إِبَر	إِبْرَة
Service	خِدَم	خِدْمَة	Pool	بِرَك	بِرْكَة
Rag	خِرَق	خِرْقَة	Few, piece	بِضَع	بِضْعَة
Steady rain	دِيَم	دِيْمَة	Church	بِيَع	بِيْعَة
Responsibility	ذِمَم	ذِمَّة	Poll-tax	جِزًى	جِزْيَة
Departure	رِحَل	رِحْلَة	Craft, trade	حِرَف	حِرْفَة
Parcel	رِزَم	رِزْمَة	Portion	حِصَص	حِصَّة
Decayed bones	رِمَم	رِمَّة	Wisdom	حِكَم	حِكْمَة

Paragraph	فِقَر	فِقْرَة	Suspicion	رِيَب	رِيْبَة
Fragment	فِلَق	فِلْقَة	Feather	رِيَش	رِيْشَة
Water-skin	قِرَب	قِربَة	Article of mer-		
Tale	قِصَص	قِصَّة	chandise	سِلَع	سِلْعَة
Piece	قِطَع	قِطْعَة	Walk, conduct	سِيَر	سِيرَة
Peak	قِمَم	قِمَّة	Sect	شِيَع	شِيعَة
Fragment	كِسَر	كِسْرَة	Disposition	شِيَم	شِيمَة
Mosquito-			Paradigm		
curtain	كِلَل	كِلَّة	(Gram.)	صِيَغ	صِيغَة
Beard	لِحَى	لِحْيَة	Villages	ضِيَع	ضَيْعَة
Trial	مِحَن	مِحْنَة	Example	عِبَر	عِبْرَة
Sect	مِلَل	مِلَّة	Cause, plea,		
Gift, grace	مِنَن	مِنَّة	illness	عِلَل	عِلَّة
Relation	نِسَب	نِسْبَة	Disturbance	فِتَن	فِتْنَة
Grace, favour	نِعَم	نِعْمَة	Party, division	فِرَق	فِرْقَة
Energy, zeal	هِمَم	هِمَّة	Intelligence	فِطَن	فِطْنَة

6. فُعْل

Veil	حُجُب	حِجَاب	She-ass	أُتُن	أَتَان
Girdle	حُزُم	حِزَام	Large veil	أُزُر	إِزَار
Horse	حُصُن	حِصَان	Foundation	أُسُس	أَسَاس
Donkey	حُمُر	حِمَار	Frame	أُطُر	إِطَار
Gulf	خُلُج	خَلِيج	Large carpet	بُسُط	بِسَاط
Muffler	خُمُر	خِمَار	Inclosure	جُدُر	جِدَار

Mattress	فُرُش	فِرَاش	Blanket	دُثُر	دِثَار
Darkness	قُتُم	قَتَام	Bond, tie	رُبُط	رِبَاط
Back of the head	قُذُل	قَذَال	Apostle	رُسُل	رَسُول
Rod	قُضُب	قَضِيب	Way	سُبُل	سَبِيل
Train	قُطُر	قِطَار	Cloud	سُحُب	سَحَاب
Book	كُتُب	كِتَاب	Lamp	سُرُج	سِرَاج
Bridle	لُجُم	لِجَام	Bedstead	سُرُر	سَرِير
Counterpane	لُحُف	لِحَاف	Fire	سُعُر	سَعِير
Town	مُدُن	مَدِينَة	Sail	شُرُع	شِرَاع
Bed	مُهُد	مِهَاد	Star, flame	شُهُب	شِهَاب
Handle (knife)	نُصُب	نِصَاب	Patient	صُبُر	صَبُور
Night-time	هُزُع	هَزِيع	Book	صُحُف	صَحِيفَة
Band, rope	وُثُق	وِثَاق	Road	طُرُق	طَرِيق
			Shackle	عُقُل	عِقَال
			Pillar	عُمُد	عَمُود

٧. فَعَلَة

Keeper	حَفَظَة	حَافِظ	Guilty	أَثَمَة	آثِم
Weaver	حَاكَة	حَائِك	Eater	أَكَلَة	آكِل
Servant	خَدَمة	خَادِم	Righteous	بَرَرَة	بَارّ
Treasurer	خَزَنَة	خَازِن	Seller	بَاعَة (بَيَعَة)	بَائِع
Sinner	خَطَأَة	خَاطِئ	Ignorant	جَهَلَة	جَاهِل
Traitor	خَوَنَة	خَائِن	Envious	حَسَدَة	حَاسِد
Low, base	سَفَلَة	سَافِل	Grandson	حَفَدَة	حَفِيد

Scribe	كَاتِب	كَتَبَة	Lord, chief	سَائِد	سَادَة
Liar	كَاذِب	كَذَبَة	Manager	سَائِس	سَاسَة
Unbeliever	كَافِر	كَفَرَة	Goldsmith	صَائِغ	صَاغَة
Perfect	كَامِل	كَمَلَة	Seeker, student	طَالِب	طَلَبَة
Priest	كَاهِن	كَهَنَة	Worshipper	عَابِد	عَبَدَة
Rebellious	مَارِد	مَرَدة	Workman	عَامِل	عَمَلَة
Crafty	مَاكِر	مَكَرة	Labourer	فَاعِل	فَعَلَة
Skilful	مَاهِر	مَهَرة	Murderer	قَاتِل	قَتَلَة
Narrator	نَاقِل	نَقَلَة	Reader	قَارِئ	قَرَأَة

8. فُعَلَة

Narrator	رَاوٍ	رُوَاة	Falcon	بَازٍ (بَازِي)	بُزَاة
Adulterer	زَانٍ	زُنَاة	Oppressor	بَاغٍ (بَاغِي)	بُغَاة
Messenger	سَاعٍ	سُعَاة	Builder	بَانٍ	بُنَاة
Cup-bearer	سَاقٍ	سُقَاة	Tax-gatherer	جَابٍ	جُبَاة
Cruel	طَاغٍ	طُغَاة	Criminal	جَانٍ	جُنَاة
Haughty	عَاتٍ	عُتَاة	Camel-driver	حَادٍ	حُدَاة
Naked	عَارٍ	عُرَاة	Bare-footed	حَافٍ	حُفَاة
Rebel	عَاصٍ	عُصَاة	Protector	حَامٍ	حُمَاة
Raider	غَازٍ	غُزَاة	Sinner	خَاطٍ	خُطَاة
Cruel, hard	قَاسٍ	قُسَاة	Caller, suppliant	دَاعٍ	دُعَاة
Judge	قَاضٍ	قُضَاة	Shepherd	رَاعٍ	رُعَاة
Iron-clad, brave	كَمِيّ	كُمَاة	Archer	رَامٍ	رُمَاة

Walker, infantry	مُشاة	ماشٍ	
Guide	هُداة	هادٍ	
Calumniator	وُشاة	واشٍ	
Governor	وُلاة	والٍ	

٩. فِعَلَة

Shield	تِرَسَة	تُرْس	Elephant	فِيَلَة	فِيْل
Well	جِبَبَة	جُبّ	Monkey	قِرَدَة	قِرْد
Bear	دِبَبَة	دُبّ	Sleeve	كِمَمَة	كُمّ
Husband	زِوَجَة	زَوْج	Cat	هِرَرَة	هِرّ

١٠. فِعَال

Hill	إِكام	أَكَمَة	Camel	جِمال	جَمَل
Sea	بِحَار	بَحْر	Rope	حِبال	حَبْل
Torrent-bed	بِطاح	بَطْحَاء	Stone	حِجَار	حَجَر
Mule	بِغال	بَغْل	Lance, bayonet	حِراب	حَرْبَة
Low-lying land	بِقاع	بُقْعَة	Sheep	خِراف	خَرُوف
Town	بِلاد	بَلَد	Good quality	خِصال	خَصْلَة
Hill	تِلال	تَلّ	Tent	خِيام	خَيْمَة
Mountain	جِبال	جَبَل	Rudder	دِفاف	دُفَّة
Forehead	جِباه	جَبْهَة	Blood	دِمَاء	دَمّ
Kid	جِدَاء	جَدْي	Wolf	ذِئاب	ذِئْب
Wound	جِراح	جُرح	Man	رِجال	رَجُل
Jar	جِرار	جَرَّة	Thin	رِقاق	رَفِيق
Pup	جِرَاء	جَرْو	Spear, lance	رِماح	رُمْح
Deep dish	جِفان	جَفْنَة	Sand	رِمال	رَمْل

Ascent	عِقَاب	عَقَبَة	Wind	رِيَاح	رِيح
Child, family	عِيَال	عَيِّل	Swift	سِرَاع	سَرِيع
Angry	غِضَاب	غَضْبَان	Basket	سلَال	سَلّ
Trap	فِخَاخ	فَخّ	Stout	سِمَان	سَمِين
Short	قِصَار	قَصِير	Arrow	سِهَام	سَهْم
Fortress	قِلَاع	قَلْعَة	Mountain-		
Heel, ankle	كِعَاب	كَعْب	path	شِعَاب	شِعْب
Dog	كِلَاب	كَلْب	Net	شِبَاك	شَبَكَة
Base	لِئَام	لَئِيم	Difficult	صِعَاب	صَعْب
Side-glance	لِحَاظ	لَحْظ	Temper	طِبَاع	طَبْع
Water	مِيَاه	مَاء	Long	طِوَال	طَوِيل
Ewe	نِعَاج	نَعْجَة	Fawn	ظِبَـآء	ظَبْي
Sandal	نِعَال	نَعْل	Slave, servant	عِبَاد	عَبْد
She-camel	نِيَاق	نَاقَة	Thirsty	عِطَاش	عَطْشَان
Sleeping	نِيَام	نَائِم	Bone	عِظَام	عَظْم
Abyss	وِهَاد	وَهْدَة	Great	عِظَام	عَظِيم

11. فِعَالَة

Calyx of a			Camel	جِمَالَة	جَمَل
flower	كِمَامَة	كِم	Stone	حِجَارة	حَجَر
			Companion	صِحَابة	صَاحِب

12. فُعُول

Sea	بُحُور	بَحْر	Origin	أُصُول	أَصْل
Full-moon	بُدُور	بَدْر	Affair	أُمُور	أَمْر

328

English	Plural	Singular
Hand-writing	خُطُوط	خَطّ
Wine	خُمُور	خَمْر
String, thread	خُيُوط	خَيْط
Lesson	دُرُوس	دَرْس
Debt	دُيُون	دَيْن
Male	ذُكُور	ذَكَر
Head	رُؤُوس	رَأْس
Spring-camp	رُبُوع	رَبْع
Thunder	رُعُود	رَعْد
Seed	زُرُوع	زَرْع
Flower	زُهُور	زَهْر
Prison	سُجُون	سِجْن
Saddle	سُرُوج	سَرْج
Roof	سُطُوح	سَطْح
Line, row	سُطُور	سَطْر
Roof	سُقُوف	سَقْف
Poison	سُمُوم	سُمّ
Affair	شُؤُون	شَأْن
Explanation	شُرُوح	شَرْح
Hair	شُعُور	شَعَر
Doubt	شُكُوك	شَكّ
Sun	شُمُوس	شَمْس
Witness	شُهُود	شَاهِد
Month	شُهُور	شَهْر
Plate, dish	صُحُون	صَحْن

English	Plural	Singular
Tower	بُرُوج	بُرْج
Lightning	بُرُوق	بَرْق
Seed	بُزُور	بِزْر
Belly	بُطُون	بَطْن
House	بُيُوت	بَيْت
Border-land	تُخُوم	تَخْم
Hill	تُلُول	تَلّ
Breast	(ثُدُوّ) ثُدِيّ	ثَدْي
Snow	ثُلُوج	ثَلْج
Bridge	جُسُور	جِسْر
Eyelid	جُفُون	جَفْن
Skin	جُلُود	جِلْد
Side	جُنُوب	جَنْب
Army	جُنُود	جُنْد
Pocket	جُيُوب	جَيْب
Grain	حُبُوب	حَبّ
Limit, boundary	حُدُود	حَدّ
War	حُرُوب	حَرْب
Particle	حُرُوف	حَرْف
Fortress	حُصُون	حِصْن
Field	حُقُول	حَقْل
Cheek	خُدُود	خَدّ
Adversary	خُصُوم	خَصْم

Chest	صُدُور	صَدْر	Difference	فُرُوق	فَرْق
Rank	صُفُوف	صَفّ	Season, chapter, part	فُصُول	فَصْل
Cymbal	صُنُوج	صَنْج	Farthing	فُلُوس	فَلْس
Kind, sort	صُنُوف	صِنْف	Art, handicraft	فُنُون	فَنّ
Molar-tooth	ضُرُوس	ضِرْس	Monkey	قُرُود	قِرْد
Rib	ضُلُوع	ضِلْع	Priest	قُسُوس	قِسّ
Drum	طُبُول	طَبْل	Rind	قُشُور	قِشْر
Rite, cere-			Castle	قُصُور	قَصْر
mony	طُقُوس	طَقْس	Back, nape of		
Bird	طُيُور	طَيْر	neck	قِفِيّ	قَفَا
Vessel, enve-			Heart	قُلُوب	قَلْب
lope, adverb	ظُرُوف	ظَرْف	Sail of ship	قُلُوع	قَلْع
Back	ظُهُور	ظَهْر	Bow	قِسِيّ	قَوْس
Calf	عُجُول	عِجْل	Cup	كُؤُوس	كَأْس
Root, vein	عُرُوق	عِرْق	Vineyard	كُرُوم	كَرْم
Time, epoch	عُصُور	عَصْر	Palm of hand	كُفُوف	كَفّ
Stick	(عُصُوّ) عِصِيّ	عَصَا	Flesh	لُحُوم	لَحْم
Mind	عُقُول	عَقْل	Meadow	مُرُوج	مَرْج
Vice, defect	عُيُوب	عَيْب	Star	نُجُوم	نَجْم
Eye	عُيُون	عَيْن	Vow	نُذُور	نَذْر
Branch	غُصُون	غُصْن	Soul	نُفُوس	نَفْس
Cloud	غُيُوم	غَيْم	Tiger	نُمُور	نَمِر
Examination	فُحُوص	فَحْص	Anxiety	هُمُوم	هَمّ
Twig	فُرُوع	فَرْع			

13. فُعُولَة

Hawk	صُقُورة	صَقْر	Husband	بُعُولَة	بَعْل
Paternal			Burden	حُمُولَة	حِمْل
Uncle	عُمُومَة	عَمّ	Maternal		
Tiger	نُمُورَة	نَمِر	Uncle	خُؤُولَة	خَال
			Male	ذُكُورة	ذَكَر

14. فَعْلَى

Weak	ضَعْفَى	ضَعِيف	Hireling	أَجْرَى	أَجِير
Murderer	قَتْلَى	قَتِيل	Captive	أَسْرَى	أَسِير
Wounded	قَرْحَى	قَرِيح	Wounded	جَرْحَى	جَرِيح
Stung	لَدْغَى	لَدِيغ	Stupid	حَمْقَى	أَحْمَق
Sick	مَرْضَى	مَرِيض	Dispersed	حَمْقَى	شَتِيت
Dead	مَوْتَى	مَيْت	Prostrated in		
Perishing	هَلْكَى	هَالِك	wrestling¹	صَرْعَى	صَرِيع
			Weak	ضَعْفَى	ضَعِيف

15. فِعْلَى

Pole-cat	ظِرْبَى	ظَرِبان	Partridge	حِجْلَى	حَجَل

16. فَعِيل

Servant	عَبِيد	عَبْد	Cow	بَقِير	بَقَر
			Donkey	حَمِير	حِمَار

‏فُعَّل‎ .17

White-haired	‏شُيَّب‎	‏شَائِب‎	Stingy	‏بُخَّل‎	‏بَاخِل‎
Reprover	‏عُذَّل‎	‏عَاذِل‎	Brave	‏بُسَّل‎	‏بَاسِل‎
Unadorned	‏عُطَّل‎	‏عَاطِل‎	Reclining on		
Barren	‏عُقَّر‎	‏عَاقِر‎	the chest	‏جُثَّم‎	‏جَاثِم‎
Raider	‏غُزَّى‎	‏غَازٍ‎	Envious	‏حُسَّد‎	‏حَاسِد‎
Absent	‏غُيَّب‎	‏غَائِب‎	Kneeling	‏رُكَّع‎	‏رَاكِع‎
Liar	‏كُذَّب‎	‏كَاذِب‎	Worshipper	‏سُجَّد‎	‏سَاجِد‎
Adviser	‏نُصَّح‎	‏نَاصِح‎	Law-giver	‏شُرَّع‎	‏شَارِع‎
Sleeping	‏نُوَّم‎	‏نَائِم‎	Eye-witness	‏شُهَّد‎	‏شَاهِد‎

‏فُعَّال‎ .18

Mischievous	‏شُطَّار‎	‏شَاطِر‎	Ignorant	‏جُهَّال‎	‏جَاهِل‎
Artizan	‏صُنَّاع‎	‏صَانِع‎	Clever	‏حُذَّاق‎	‏حَاذِق‎
Worshipper	‏عُبَّاد‎	‏عَابِد‎	Guardian	‏حُرَّاس‎	‏حَارِس‎
Reprover	‏عُذَّال‎	‏عَاذِل‎	Envious	‏حُسَّاد‎	‏حَاسِد‎
Workman	‏عُمَّال‎	‏عَامِل‎	Keeper	‏حُفَّاظ‎	‏حَافِظ‎
Sick-visitor	‏عُوَّاد‎	‏عَائِد‎	Servant	‏خُدَّام‎	‏خَادِم‎
Wicked	‏فُجَّار‎	‏فَاجِر‎	Rider	‏رُكَّاب‎	‏رَاكِب‎
Reader	‏قُرَّآء‎	‏قَارِئٌ‎	Ascetic	‏زُهَّاد‎	‏زَاهِد‎
Highwayman	‏قُطَّاع‎	‏قَاطِع‎	Visitor, pilgrim	‏زُوَّار‎	‏زَائِر‎
Leader	‏قُوَّاد‎	‏قَائِد‎	Thief	‏سُرَّاق‎	‏سَارِق‎
Scribe	‏كُتَّاب‎	‏كَاتِب‎	Traveller	‏سُيَّاح‎	‏سَائِح‎
Infidel	‏كُفَّار‎	‏كَافِر‎	Commentator	‏شُرَّاح‎	‏شَارِح‎

Members of Parliament	نَائِب	نُوَّاب
Heir	وَارِث	وُرَّاث

Priest	كَاهِن	كُهَّان
Hermit	نَاسِك	نُسَّاك
Adviser	نَاصِح	نُصَّاح
Watchman	نَاظِر	نُظَّار

19. فُعَلَآء

Caliph, successor	خَلِيفَة	خُلَفَآء
Fit, suited for	خَلِيق	خُلَقَآء
Intruder	دَخِيل	دُخَلَاء
Chief	رَئِيس	رُؤَسَآء
Merciful	رَحِيم	رُحَمَآء
ompanion	رَفِيق	رُفَقَآء
Watcher	رَقِيب	رُقَبَآء
Chief	زَعِيم	زُعَمَآء
Happy	سَعِيد	سُعَدَآء
Ambassador	سَفِير	سُفَرَآء
Foolish	سَفِيه	سُفَهَآء
Sickly	سَقِيم	سُقَمَآء
Noble	شَرِيف	شُرَفَآء
Partner	شَرِيك	شُرَكَآء
Poet	شَاعِر	شُعَرَآء
Weak	ضَعِيف	ضُعَفَآء
Elegant	ظَرِيف	ظُرَفَآء
Companion	عَشِير	عُشَرَآء

Guilty	أَثِيم	أُثَمَآء
Polite, learned	أَدِيب	أُدَبَآء
Prince	أَمِير	أُمَرَآء
Faithful	أَمِين	أُمَنَآء
Stingy	بَخِيل	بُخَلَاء
Intelligent	بَصِير	بُصَرَآء
Stupid	بَلِيد	بُلَدَآء
Eloquent	بَلِيغ	بُلَغَآء
Unlucky	تَعِيس	تُعَسَآء
Coward	جَبَان	جُبَنَآء
Worthy, fit	جَدِير	جُدَرَآء
Companion	جَلِيس	جُلَسَآء
Ignorant	جَاهِل	جُهَلَا
Sorrowful	حَزِين	حُزَنَآء
Wise	حَكِيم	حُكَمَآء
Wicked	خَبِيث	خُبَثَآء
Orator	خَطِيب	خُطَبَآء

Anointed	مَسِيح مُسَحَآء	Mighty	عَظِيم عُظَمَآء
Steady	مَكِين مُكَنَآء	Intelligent	عَاقِل عُقَلَآء
Intelligent	نَجِيب نُجَبَآء	Commissioner	عَمِيل عُمَلَآء
Jester, boon		Stranger	غَرِيب غُرَبَآء
companion	نَدِيم نُدَمَآء	Eloquent	
Guest	نَزِيل نُزَلَآء	speaker	فَصِيح فُصَحَآء
Adviser	نَصِيح نُصَحَآء	Excellent	فَاضِل فُضَلَآء
Defender	نَصِير نُصَرَآء	Poor	فَقِير فُقَرَآء
Equal	نَظِير نُظَرَآء	Ancient	قَدِيم قُدَمَآء
Honourable	وَجِيه وُجَهَآء	Comrade	قَرِين قُرَنَآء
Meek	وَدِيع وُدَعَآء	Great	كَبِير كُبَرَآء
Minister	وَزِير وُزَرَآء	Generous	كَرِيم كُرَمَآء
Mediator	وَسِيط وُسَطَآء	Surety	كَفِيل كُفَلَآء
Humble	وَضِيع وُضَعَآء	Base	لَئِيم لُؤَمَآء
		Kind, delicate	لَطِيف لُطَفَآء

20. أَفْعِلَآء

Intimate		Innocent	بَرِيّ أَبْرِيَآء
friend	خَلِيل أَخِلَّآء	Pious	تَقِيّ أَتْقِيَآء
Adopted son	دَعِيّ أَدْعِيَآء	Glorious	جَلِيل أَجِلَّآء
Guide	دَلِيل أَدِلَّآء	Beloved	حَبِيب أَحِبَّآء
Mean	دَنِيّ أَدْنِيَآء	Sharp	حَدِيد أَحِدَّآء
Sagacious	ذَكِيّ أَذْكِيَآء	Peculiar	
Submissive	ذَلِيل أَذِلَّآء	friend	خَاص أَخِصَّآء

Foolish	أَغْبِيَآء	غَبِيّ	Evil	أَرْدِيَآء	رَدِيّ
Rich	أَغْنِيَآء	غَنِيّ	Slave	أَرِقَّآء	رَقِيق
Relative	أَقْرِبَآء	قَرِيب	Generous	أَسْخِيَآء	سَخِيّ
Powerful	أَقْوِيَآء	قَوِيّ	Stingy	أَشِحَّآء	شَحِيح
Intelligent	أَلِبَّآء	لَبِيب	Strong	أَشِدَّآء	شَدِيد
Prophet	أَنْبِيَآء	نَبِيّ	Miserable	أَشْقِيَآء	شَقِيّ
Relative by			Sound	أَصِحَّآء	صَحِيح
marriage	أَنْسِبَآء	نَسِيب	Friend	أَصْدِقَآء	صَدِيق
Pure	أَنْقِيَآء	نَقِي	Sincere		
Friend	أَوِدَّآء	وَدِيد	friend	أَصْفِيَآء	صَفِيّ
Testator,			Physician	أَطِبَّآء	طَبِيب
executor	أَوْصِيَآء	وَصِي	Precious,		
Benefactor	أَوْلِيَآء	وَلِيّ	friend	أَعِزَّآء	عَزِيز
			Sick	أَعِلَّآء	عَلِيل

21. فُعْلَان

Fore-arm,			Camels	بُعْرَان	بَعِير
cubit	ذِرعَان	ذِرَاع	Town, country	بُلدَان	بَلَد
Male	ذُكْرَان	ذَكَر	Wall, inclo-		
Shepherd	رُعيَان	رَاعٍ	sure	جُدرَان	جِدَار
Loaf	رُغْفان	رَغِيف	Lamb	حُملَان	حَمَل
Rider	رُكبَان	رَاكِب	Gulf	خُلجَان	خَلِيج
Monk	رُهبَان	رَاهِب	Intimate		
Youth	شُبَّان	شَاب	friend	خُلَّان	خَلِيل

Clergyman	قُسَّان	قِسِيس	Boy	صُبيَان	صَبِيّ
Stick	قُضبَان	قَضِيب	Cross	صُلبَان	صَلِيب
Flock	قُطعَان	قَطِيع	Back	ظُهرَان	ظَهْر
Beehive	قُفرَان	قَفِير	Blind	عُميَان	أَعمَى
Shirt	قُمصَان	قَمِيص	Pool	غُدرَان	غَدِير
Hill	كُثبَان	كَثِيب	Horseman	فُرسَان	فَارِس
			Weaned	فُصلَان	فَصِيل

22. فِعْلَان

Leg	سِيقَان	سَاق	Brother (friend)	إِخوَان	أَخ
Sparrow-hawk	صِردَان	صُرَد	Crown	تِيجَان	تَاج
Eagle	عِقبَان	عُقاب	Ox, bull	ثِيرَان	ثَوْر
Wood, rod	عِيدَان	عُوْد	Rat	جِرذَان	جُرَذ
Crow	غِربَان	غُرَاب	Neighbour	جِيرَان	جَار
Gazelle	غِزلَان	غَزَال	Whale	حِيتَان	حُوت
Lad	غِلمَان	غُلاَم	Wall	حِيطَان	حَائِط
Mouse	فِثرَان	فَأُر	Sheep	خِرفَان	خَرُوف
Youth	فِتيَان	فَتَى	Worm	دِيدَان	دُوْد
Fire	نِيرَان	نَار	Fly, flies	ذِبَّان	ذُبَاب

23. فَعَالَى

Pregnant	حَبَالَى	حُبْلَى	Widow, widower	أَيَامَى	أَيِّم
Sorrowful	حَزانَى	حَزِين			

Virgin	عَذْرَاء	عَذَارَى	Law-suit	دَعْوَى	دَعَاوَى
Penitent	نَدْمَان	نَدَامَى	Satisfied	شَبْعَان	شَبَاعَى
Orphan	يَتِيم	يَتَامَى	Pure	طَاهِر	طَهَارَى

24. فُعَالَى

Unique, one by one	فَرْد	فُرَادَى	Intoxicated	سَكْرَان	سُكَارَى
Lazy	كَسْلَان	كُسَالَى			

25. فَعَالِي

Chair	كُرْسِيّ	كَرَاسٍ	Land	أَرْض	أَرَاضٍ
Night	لَيْل	لَيَالٍ	People, family	أَهْل	أَهَالٍ
Interior angle of the eye	مُوق	مَـاقٍ	Desert	صَحْرَاء	صَحَارٍ
			Bottle	قِنِّينَة	قَنَانٍ

26. فَعَالِيّ

Upper Room	عِلِّيَّة	عَلَالِيّ	Desert	بَرِّيَّة	بَرَارِيّ
Chair	كُرْسِيّ	كَرَاسِيّ	Chameleon	حِرْبَاء	حَرَابِيّ
Fleet camels	مَهْرِيَّة	مَهَارِيّ	Concubine	سَرِّيَّة	سَرَارِيّ
			Desert	صَحْرَاء	صَحَارِيّ

PLURAL OF PLURALS. أَوْزَانُ مُنْتَهَى ٱلْجُمُوعِ

6 فَوَاعِل	1 فَعَالِل
7 فَوَاعِيل	2 فَعَالِيل
8 مَفَاعِل	3 أَفَاعِل
9 مَفَاعِيل	4 أَفَاعِيل
10 تَفَاعِيل	5 فَعَائِل

PLURAL OF PLURALS. مُنْتَهَى ٱلْجُمُوعِ

1. فَعَالِل

Black			Hare	أَرَانِب	أَرْنَب
locust	جَنَادِب	جُنْدُب	Head veil	بَخَانِق	بُخْنُق
Stocking	جَوَارِب	جَوْرَب	Isthmus	بَرَازِخ	بَرْزَخ
Substance,			Bud	بَرَاعِم	بُرْعُم
jewel, pearl	جَوَاهِر	جَوهَر	Veil	بَرَاقِع	بُرْقُع
Fish scales	حَرَاشِف	حُرْشُف	Dragoman,		
Colocynth	حَنَاظِل	حَنْظَل	interpreter	تَرَاجِم	تُرْجُمَان
Large Knife	خَنَاجِر	خَنْجَر	Fox	ثَعَالِب	ثَعْلَب
Silver coin	دَرَاهِم	دِرْهَم	Breast of		
Copy-book,			man	ثَنَادِىَ	تَنْدُؤَة
register	دَفَاتِر	دَفْتَر	Wild calf	جَآذِر	جُؤْذُر
White silk			Army	جَحَافِل	جَحْفَل
cloth	دَمَاقِس	دِمَقْس	Brook, list	جَدَاوِل	جَدْوَل
Bracelet	دَمَالِج	دُمْلُج	Skull	جَمَاجِم	جُمْجُمَة

22

English	Plural	Singular	English	Plural	Singular
Parasang, league	فَرَاسِخ	فَرْسَخ	Embellishment	زَخَارِف	زُخْرُف
Caravansary	فَنَادِق	فُنْدُق	Fins	زَعَانِف	زُعْنُفَة
Biretta	قَلَانِس	قَلَنْسُوَة	Tortoise	سَلَاحِف	سُلَحْفاة
Consul	قَنَاصِل	قُنْصُل	Banner	سَنَاجِق	سَنْجَق
Bridge	قَنَاطِر	قَنْطَرة	Party of men	شَرَاذِم	شَرْذَمَة
Hedgehog	قَنَافِذ	قُنْفُذ	Frog	ضَفَادِع	ضِفْدَع
Poultice, salve	مَرَاهِم	مَرْهَم	Bitter thing, colocynth	عَلَاقِم	عَلْقَم
Tumult	مَعَامِع	مَعْمَعَة	Nightingale	عَنَادِل	عَنْدَلِيب
Hoopoe	هَدَاهِد	هُدْهُد	Elements	عَنَاصِر	عُنْصُر
Evil thought	وَسَاوِس	وَسْوَاس	Spider	عَنَاكِب	عَنْكَبُوت
			Darkness	غَياهِب	غَيْهَب

٢. فَعَالِيل

English	Plural	Singular	English	Plural	Singular
Circular oven	تَنَانِير	تَنُّور	Jug	أَبَارِيق	إِبْرِيق
The constellation			Hackney	بَرَاذِين	بِرْذَوْن
			Bribe	بَرَاطِيل	بَرْطِيل
			Flea	بَرَاغِيث	بُرْغُوث
Dragon	تَنَانِين	تِنِّين	Volcano	بَرَاكِين	بُرْكَان
Snake	ثَعَابِين	ثُعْبَان	Barrel	بَرَامِيل	بَرْمِيل
Root	جَرَاثِيم	جُرْثُومَة	Proof	بَرَاهِين	بُرْهَان
Outer garment	جَلَابِيب	جِلْبَاب	Garden	بَسَاتِين	بُسْتَان
			Disciple	تَلَامِيذ	تِلْمِيذ

Crowd	جَمَاهِير	جُمْهُور
Elephant's trunk	خَرَاطِيم	خُرْطُوم
Soft twig	خَرَاعِيب	خُرْعُوب
Anklet	خَلَاخِيل	خَلْخَال
Pig	خَنَازِير	خِنْزِير
Gold coin	دَنَانِير	دِينَار
Knife	سَكَاكِين	سِكِّين
Sultan	سَلَاطِين	سُلْطَان
Window	شَبَابِيك	شُبَّاك
Devil	شَيَاطِين	شَيْطَان
Box	صَنَادِيق	صُنْدُوق
Well, cistern	صَهَارِيج	صِهْرِيج
Turkish cap	طَرَابِيش	طَرْبوش
Peacock	طَوَاوِيس	طَاوُوس

Bird	عَصَافِير	عُصْفُور
Demon	عَفَارِيت	عِفْرِيت
Drug	عقاقير	عَقَّار
Bunch of grapes	عَنَاقِيد	عُنْقُود
Sieve	غَرَابِيل	غِرْبَال
Cartilage	غَضَارِيف	غُضْرُوف
Paradise	فَرَادِيس	فِرْدَوْس
Paper	قَرَاطِيس	قِرْطَاس
Felt gloves	قَفَافِيز	قُفَّاز
Lamp	قَنَادِيل	قِنْدِيل
Hundred-weight	قَنَاطِير	قَنْطَار
Guitar	قَيَاثِير	قِيْثَار
Pamphlet	كَرَارِيس	كُرَّاسَة
Hole, fissure	نَخَارِيب	نُخْرُوب

٣. أَفَاعِل

Thumb	أَبَاهِم	إِبْهَام
Finger	أَصَابِع	إِصْبَع
Finger tip	أَنَامِل	أُنْمُلَة
Stranger	أَبَاعِد	أَبْعَد
Foreigner	أَجَانِب	أَجْنَبِيّ

Enigma	أَحَاجِ	أُحْجِيَّة
Middle of the sole	أَخَامِص	أَخْمَاص
Poor widow	أَرَامِل	أَرْمَلَة
Name	(أَسَامِي) أَسَامِ	اِسْم

Scorpion	أَفَاعٍ	أَفْعَى	Bracelet	أَسَاوِر	سِوَار
Relative	أَقَارِب	أَقْرَب	Smallest	أَصَاغِر	أَصْغَر
Greatest	أَكَابِر	أَكْبَر	Nails	أَظَافِر	أَظْفُر
Most generous	أَكَارِم	أَكْرَم	Foreigner	أَعَاجِم	أَعْجَم
Goat	أَمَاعِز	أُمْعُوزَة	Song	أَغَانٍ	أُغْنِيَّة

4. أَفَاعِيل

Path, method	أَسَالِيب	أُسْلُوب	Palace, arched hall	أَوَاوِين	إِيوَان
Nails	أَظَافِير	أَظَافِر	Vanity	أَبَاطِيل	أَبَاطِل
Song	أَغَانِيّ	أُغْنِيَّة	Enigma	أَحَاجِيّ	أُحْجِيَّة
District	أَقَالِيم	إِقْلِيم	Story	أَحَادِيث	أُحْدُوثَة
Saying	أَقَاوِيل	أَقْوَال	See-saw	أَرَاجِيح	أُرْجُوحَة
Falsehood	أَكَاذِيب	أُكْذُوبَة	Poem	أَرَاجِيز	أُرْجُوزَة
Crown	أَكَالِيل	إِكْلِيل	Week	أَسَابِيع	أُسْبُوع
Poem, declamation	أَنَاشِيد	أُنْشُودَة	Handwriting	أَسَاطِير	أُسْطُورَة

5. فَعَائِل

Cards	بَطَائِق	بِطَاقَة	Throne	أَرَائِك	أَرِيكَة
Lining of clothes	بَطَائِن	بِطَانَة	Deer	أَيَائِل	إِيَّل
Amulet	تَمَائِم	تَمِيمَة	Creature	بَرَايَا (بَرَائِي)	بَرِيَّة
News-paper	جَرَائِد	جَرِيدَة	Good news, Gospel	بَشَائِر	بِشَارَة

English	Plural	Singular	English	Plural	Singular
Curtain	سَتَائِر	سِتَارَة	Crime	جَرَائِر	جَرِيرَة
Cloud	سَحَائِب	سَحَابة	Crime	جَرَائِم	جَرِيمَة
Secret, heart	سَرَائِر	سَرِيرَة	Small garden	جَنَائِن	جُنَيْنَة
Body of troops	سَرَايَا (سَرَائِي)	سَرِيَّة	Trap, net	حَبَائِل	حِبَالَة
Insult	شَتَائِم	شَتِيمَة	Fruit garden	حَدَائِق	حَدِيقَة
Nature	طَبَائِع	طَبِيعَة	Sheepfold	حَظَائِر	حَظِيرَة
Miracle	عَجَائِب	عَجِيبَة	Ditch	حَفَائِر	حَفِيرَة
Old Woman	عَجَائِز	عَجُوز	Provision-bag	حَقَائِب	حَقِيبَة
Resolution	عَزَائِم	عَزِيمَة	Reality	حَقَائِق	حَقِيقَة
Gift	عَطَايَا (عَطَائِي)	عَطِيَّة	Treasury	خَزَائِن	خِزَانَة
Important affair	عَظَائِم	عَظِيمَة	Loss	خَسَائِر	خِسَارَة
Turban	عَمَائِم	عِمَامَة	Sin	خَطَايَا (خَطَائِي)	خَطِيَّة
Wonderful event	غَرَائِب	غَرِيبَة	Bee-hive	خَلَايَا (خَلَائِي)	خَلِيَّة
Instinct	غَرَائِز	غَرِيزَة	Minute	دَقَائِق	دَقِيقَة
Booty	غَنَائِم	غَنِيمَة	Victim	ذَبَائِح	ذَبِيحَة
Prey	فَرَائِس	فَرِيسَة	Savings	ذَخَائِر	ذَخِيرَة
Muscle	فَرَائِص	فَرِيصَة	Damage	رَزَايَا (رَزَائِي)	رَزِيَّة
Precept	فَرَائِض	فَرِيضَة	Subjects	رَعَايَا (رَعَائِي)	رَعِيَّة
Virtue, merit	فَضَائِل	فَضِيلَة			

English	Plural	Singular
Defect, vice	نَقَائِص	نَقِيصَة
Present	هَدَايَا (هَدَائِي)	هَدِيَّة
Deposit	وَدَائِع	وَدِيعَة
Pillow	وَسَائِد	وِسَادَة
Means	وَسَائِط	وَاسِطَة
Means	وَسَائِل	وَسِيلَة
Commandment	وَصَايَا (وَصَائِي)	وَصِيَّة
Event, fight	وَقَائِع	وَقِيعَة

English	Plural	Singular
Memory	قَرَائِح	قَرِيحَة
Necklace	قَلَائِد	قَلَادَة
Squadron	كَتَائِب	كَتِيبَة
Church	كَنَائِس	كَنِيسَة
Quiver	كَنَائِن	كِنَانَة
Nicety of language	لَطَائِف	لَطِيفَة
Roll	لَفَائِف	لُفَافَة
Death	مَنَايَا (مَنَائِي)	مَنِيَّة
Result	نَتَائِج	نَتِيجَة
Advice	نَصَائِح	نَصِيحَة

٦. فَوَاعِل

English	Plural	Singular
Maid	جَوَارٍ	جَارِيَة
Mosque	جَوَامِع	جَامِع
Side	جَوَانِب	جَانِب
Prize	جَوَائِز	جَائِزَة
Eye-brow	حَوَاجِب	حَاجِب
Accident	حَوَادِث	حَادِثَة
Senses	حَوَاسّ	حَاسَّة
Marginal notes	حَوَاشٍ	حَاشِيَة
Hoof	حَوَافِر	حَافِر
Want	حَوَائِج	حَاجَة

English	Plural	Singular
Vessel	أَوَانٍ	آنِيَة
Hastiness	بَوَادِر	بَادِرَة
Man-of-war	بَوَارِج	بَارِجَة
Jar	بَوَاطٍ	بَاطِيَة
Cause	بَوَاعِث	بَاعِث
Spice	تَوَابِل	تَابِل
Fixed (star)	ثَوَابِت	ثَابِت
Penetrating (mind)	ثَوَاقِب	ثَاقِب
Second	ثَوَانٍ	ثَانِيَة
Bird of prey	جَوَارِح	جَارِحَة

English	Plural	Singular
Ring	خَوَاتِم	خَاتَم
Property	خَوَاصّ	خَاصَّة
Beast	دَوَابّ	دَابَّة
Misfortune	دَوَاهٍ	دَاهِيَة
Circle	دَوَائِر	دَائِرَة
Lock of hair	ذَوَائِب	ذُؤَابَة
Hill	رَوَابٍ	رَابِيَة
Swift-running running	سَوَابِح	سَابِحَة
Precedence	سَوَابِق	سَابِقَة
Streamlet	سَوَاقٍ	سَاقِيَة
Moustaches	شَوَارِب	شَارِب
Street	شَوَارِع	شَارِع
Sea-shore	شَوَاطِئ	شَاطِئ
Proof	شَوَاهِد	شَاهِد
Thunderbolt	صَوَاعِق	صَاعِقَة
Neighing	صَوَاهِل	صَاهِل
Outskirt	ضَوَاحٍ	ضَاحِيَة
Seal, stamp	طَوَابِع	طَابِع
Divorced	طَوَالِق	طَالِق
Portion, rite	طَوَائِف	طَائِفَة
Obstacle	عَوَارِض	عَارِضَة
Storm	عَوَاصِف	عَاصِفَة
Capital (town)	عَوَاصِم	عَاصِمَة
Kind feeling	عَوَاطِف	عَاطِفَة
Result	عَوَاقِب	عَاقِبَة
World	عَوَالِم	عَالَم
Grammatical regent	عَوَامِل	عَامِل
Common people	عَوَامّ	عَامَّة
Habit, custom	عَوَائِد	عَادَة
Shoulder	عَوَاتِق	عَاتِق
Secret	غَوَامِض	غَامِضَة
Fruit	فَوَاكِه	فَاكِهَة
Profit	فَوَائِد	فَائِدَة
Front-part, foremost feathers	قَوَادِم	قَادِمَة
Boat	قَوَارِب	قَارِب
Rule, foundation	قَوَاعِد	قَاعِدَة
Caravan	قَوَافِل	قَافِلَة

English	Plural	Singular	English	Plural	Singular
Rhyme	قَوَافٍ	قَافِيَة	Distinguished	نَوَابِغ	نَابِغَة
Mould	قَوَالِب	قَالَب	Region	نَوَاحٍ	نَاحِيَة
Glittering	لَوَامِع	لَامِع	Curiosity	نَوَادِر	نَادِرَة
Cattle	مَوَاشٍ	مَاشِيَة	Fore-lock	نَوَاصٍ	نَاصِيَة
Table, food	مَوَائِد	مَائِدَة	Loophole	نَوَافِذ	نَافِذَة
Harbour	مَوَانٍ	مِينَا	Misfortune	نَوَائِب	نَائِبَة

7. فَوَاعِيل

English	Plural	Singular	English	Plural	Singular
Strait	بَوَاغِيز	بُوغَاز	Mill	طَوَاحِين	طَاحُون
Drain	بَوَالِيع	بَالُوعَة	Lantern	فَوَانِيس	فَانُوس
Spy	جَوَاسِيس	جَاسُوس	Bottle	قَوَارِير	قَارُورَة
Sack	جَوَالِيق	جُوَالِق	Dictionary, ocean	قَوَامِيس	قَامُوس
Buffalo	جَوَامِيس	جَامُوس	Rule	قَوَانِين	قَانُون
Wheel	دَوَالِيب	دَوْلَاب	Law	نَوَامِيس	نَامُوس
Court, collection of poetry	دَوَاوِين	دِيوَان			

8. مَفَاعِل

English	Plural	Singular	English	Plural	Singular
Funeral	مَآتِم	مَأْتَم	Veil	مَآزِر	مِئْزَرَة
Noteworthy fact	مَآثِر	مَأْثَرَة	Food	مَآكِل	مَأْكَل
Aim, desire	مَآرِب	مَأْرَب	Dwelling	مَآوٍ	مَأْوَى
			Discussion	مَبَاحِث	مَبْحَث

Anchor	مَرَاسٍ	مِرْسَاة	Censer	مَبَاخِر	مِبْخَرَة
Pastorage	مَرَاعٍ	مَرْعًى	Origin, prin-		
Bed	مَرَاقِد	مَرْقَد	ciple	مَبَادِئ	مَبْدَأ
Mosque	مَسَاجِد	مَسْجِد	File	مَبَارِد	مِبْرَد
Paper-ruler	مَسَاطِر	مِسْطَرَة	Beneficence	مَبَارّ	مَبَرَّة
Dwelling	مَسَاكِن	مَسْكَن	Water-course	مَجَارٍ	مَجْرَى
Evil deed	مَسَاوٍ	مَسَاءَة	Council	مَجَامِع	مَجْمَع
Difficulty	مَشَاقّ	مَشَقَّة	Ink-pot	مَحَابِر	مِحْبَرَة
Bed	مَضَاجِع	مَضْجَع	Orbit of		
Damage	مَضَارّ	مَضَرَّة	the eye	مَحَاجِر	مَحْجِر
Kitchen	مَطَابِخ	مَطْبَخ	Meeting		
Printing-			place	مَحَافِل	مَحْفِل
press	مَطَابِع	مَطْبَعَة	Store	مَخَازِن	مَخْزَن
Mine	مَعَادِن	مَعْدِن	Claw	مَخَالِب	مِخْلَب
Exhibition	مَعَارِض	مَعْرِض	School	مَدَارِس	مَدْرَسَة
Battle	مَعَارِك	مَعْرَكَة	Burying-		
Manger	مَعَالِف	مَعْلِف	place	مَدَافِن	مَدْفِن
Manufacture	مَعَامِل	مَعْمَل	Rite, sect	مَذَاهِب	مَذْهَب
Meaning	مَعَانٍ	مَعْنًى	Mirror	مَرَآءٍ	مِرْآة
Resort	مَعَاهِد	مَعْهَد	High rank	مَرَاتِب	مَرْتَبَة
Defect	مَعَايِب	مَعَاب	Dirge, elegy	مَرَاثٍ	مَرْثَاة
Plantation	مَغَارِس	مَغْرِس	Mercy	مَرَاحِم	مَرْحَمَة
Spindle	مَغَازِل	مِغْزَل	Anchorage	مَرَاسٍ	مَرْسًى

English	Plural	Singular	English	Plural	Singular
Goad	مَنَاخِس	مِنْخَس	Cave	مَغَاوِر	مَغَارَة
Sieve	مَنَاخِل	مُنْخُل	Desert	مَفَاوِز	مَفَازَة
Lodging	مَنَازِل	مَنْزِل	Cemetery	مَقَابِر	مَقْبَرَة
View	مَنَاظِر	مَنْظَر	Design, purpose	مَقَاصِد	مَقْصِد
Virtue	مَنَاقِب	مَنْقَبَة			
Shoulder	مَنَاكِب	مَنكِب	Frying-pan	مَقَالٍ	مِقْلَى
Watering-place	مَنَاهِل	مَنْهَل	Elementary school	مَكَاتِب	مَكْتَب
Windward	مَهَابّ	مَهَبّ	Library	مَكَاتِب	مَكْتَبَة
Refuge	مَهَارِب	مَهْرَب	Gain	مَكَاسِب	مَكْسَب
Place of peril	مَهَالِك	مَهلِك	Broom	مَكَانِس	مِكْنَسَة
Time of meeting	مَوَاسِم	مَوسِم	Stratagem	مَكَايِد	مَكِيدَة
Place	مَوَاضِع	مَوضِع	Delight	مَلَاذّ	مَلَذَّة
Gift	مَوَاهِب	مَوهِبَة	Theatre	مَلَاعِب	مَلْعَب
			Spoon	مَلَاعَق	مِلْعَقَة
			Nostril	مَنَاخِر	مَنْخِر

9. مَفَاعِيل

English	Plural	Singular	English	Plural	Singular
Famous	مَشَاهِير	مشْهُور	1½ Dirhem	مَثَاقِيل	مِثْقَال
Torch	مَصَابِيح	مِصْبَاح	Wounded	مَجَارِيح	مَجْرُوح
Folding door	مَصَارِيع	مِصْرَاع	Mad	مَجَانِين	مَجْنُون
Key	مَفَاتِيح	مِفْتَاح	Psalm	مَزَامِير	مَزْمُور
Upper room	مَقَاصِير	مَقْصُورَة	Destitute	مَسَاكِين	مِسْكِين
			Nail	مَسَامِير	مِسْمَار

English	Plural	Singular	English	Plural	Singular
Bird's bill	مَنَاقِير	مِنْقَار	Key	مَقَالِيد	مِقْلَاد
Spur	مَهَامِيز	مِهْمَاز	Cursed	مَلَاعِين	مَلْعُون
Compact	مَوَاثِيق	مِيثَاق	Nose	مَنَاخِير	مِنْخَار
House utensil	مَوَاعِين	مَاعُون	Veil	مَنَادِيل	مِنْدِيل
Subject	مَوَاضِيع	مَوْضُوع	Saw	مَنَاشِير	مِنْشَار
Born, off-spring	مَوَالِيد	مَوْلُود	Letters patent	مَنَاشِير	مَنْشُور
			Balloon	مَنَاطِيد	مِنْطَاد
			Bellows	مَنَافِيخ	مِنْفَاخ

10. تَفَاعِيل

English	Plural	Singular	English	Plural	Singular
Commentary	تَفَاسِير	تَفْسِير	History	تَوَارِيخ	تَأْرِيخ
Tradition	تَقَالِيد	تَقْلِيد	Edition	تَآلِيف	تَأْلِيف
Image, statue	تَمَاثِيل	تِمْثَال	Misfortune	تَبَارِيح	تَبْرِيح
Crocodile	تَمَاسِيح	تِمْسَاح	Composition	تَرَاكِيب	تَرْكِيب
			Canticle	تَسَابِيح	تَسْبِحَة
			Amulet	تَعَاوِيذ	تَعْوِيذَة

A ة IS ADDED TO SOME MEASURES:

English	Plural	Singular	English	Plural	Singular
Sagacious man	جَهَابِذَة	جَهْبَذ	Satan	أَبَالِسَة	إِبْلِيس
Disciple	تَلَامِذة	تِلْمِيذ	Bishop	أَسَاقِفة	أُسْقُف
Broker	سَمَاسِرة	سِمْسَار	Veterinary surgeon	بَيَاطِرة	بَيْطَار
Chemist	صَيَادِلة	صَيْدَلِيّ	Patriarch	بَطَارِقة	بِطْرِيق

English	Arabic	Arabic		English	Arabic	Arabic
Satrap	مَوَازِبة	مَرْزُبَان		Money-changer	صَيَارِفة	صَيْرَفِيّ
Bishop	مَطَارِنة	مَطْرَان		Caesar	قَيَاصِرة	قَيْصَر
Angel	مَلَائِكة	مَلَاك		Cardinal	كَرَادِلة	كَرْدِينَال

TRILITERAL VERBS ARRANGED
ACCORDING TO THEIR MEDIAL RADICAL IN THE PRETERITE AND AORIST, WITH THEIR NOUNS OF ACTION IN COMMON USE.

1 فَعَلَ يَفْعِلُ
2 فَعَلَ يَفْعُلُ
3 فَعَلَ يَفْعَلُ
4 فَعِلَ يَفْعَلُ
5 فَعُلَ يَفْعُلُ
6 فعِلَ يفعِلُ

فَعَلَ يَفْعِلُ

English	Arabic	Arabic		English	Arabic	Arabic
To be fulfilled	تَمامًا	تَمَّ		To take shelter	إِوَاءً	أَوَى
„ wander	تَيَهانًا	تَاهَ		„ cut (a pen)	بَرْيًا	بَرَى
„ form, mix with water	جَبْلًا	جَبَلَ		„ seek	بَغْيًا	بَغَى
„ exert oneself	جِدًّا	جَدَّ		„ weep	بُكاءً	بَكَى
„ draw	جَذْبًا	جَذَبَ		„ pass the night	مَبِيتًا	بَاتَ
„ run	جَرْيًا	جَرَى		„ sell	بَيْعًا	بَاعَ
				„ be distant	بَيْنُونةً	بَانَ

To sit	جُلُوسًا	جَلَس	To bury	دَفْنًا	دَفَن
„ gather fruit	جَنْيًا	جَنَى	„ eulogise	رِثَاءً	رَثَى
„ impose	حَتْمًا	حَتَم	„ return	رُجُوعًا	رَجَع
„ omit	حَذْفًا	حَذَف	„ relate	رِوَايَةً	رَوَى
„ deprive	حِرْمَانًا	حَرَم	„ increase	زِيَادَةً	زَاد
„ pack up	حَزْمًا	حَزَم	„ err	زَيَغَانًا	زَاغ
„ dig	حَفْرًا	حَفَر	„ take captive	سَبْيًا	سَبَى
„ swear	حَلِفًا	حَلَف	„ steal	سَرِقَةً	سَرَق
„ shave	حِلَاقَةً	حَلَق	„ circulate (blood)	سَرَيَانًا	سَرَى
„ carry	حَمْلاً	حَمَل	„ shed blood	سَفْكًا	سَفَك
„ protect	حِمَايَة	حَمَى	„ give to drink	سَقْيًا	سَقَى
„ surround	حُيُوقًا	حَاف	„ travel	سِيَاحَةً	سَاح
„ weave	حِيَاكَةً	حَاك	„ march	سَيْرًا	سَار
„ be in season	حَيْنُونَةً	حَان	„ flow	سَيَلَانًا	سَال
„ kneel	خُرُورًا	خَرَّ	„ revile	شَتْمًا	شَتَم
„ vanish be eclipsed	خَسْفًا	خَسَف	„ buy	شِرَاءً	شَرَى
„ subdue	خَفْضًا	خَفَض	„ be transparent	شُفُوفًا	شَفَّ
„ mix	خَلْطًا	خَلَط	„ roast	شَيًّا	شَوَى
„ fail	خَيْبَةً	خَاب	„ become grey	شَيْبًا	شَاب
„ sew	خِيَاطَةً	خَاط			
„ know	دِرَايَةً	دَرَى			

To rebel	عِصْيَانًا	عَصَى	To become old	شَيْخُوْخَةً	شَاخَ
„ incline towards, join to	عَطْفًا	عَطَفَ	„ be sound, right	صِحَّةً	صَحَّ
„ tie	عَقْدًا	عَقَدَ	„ dismiss, spend	صَرْفًا	صَرَفَ
„ persevere	عَكْفًا	عَكَفَ	„ cry out, crow	صِيَاحًا	صَاحَ
„ feed cattle	عَلْفًا	عَلَفَ	„ become	صَيْرُوْرَةً	صَارَ
„ be faulty	عَيْبًا	عَابَ	„ make a noise	ضَجِيْجًا	ضَجَّ
„ live	مَعِيْشَةً	عَاشَ	„ beat	ضَرْبًا	ضَرَبَ
„ plant	غَرْسًا	غَرَسَ	„ be lost	ضَيَاعًا	ضَاعَ
„ spin	غَزْلًا	غَزَلَ	„ „ narrow	ضِيْقًا	ضَاقَ
„ wash	غَسْلًا	غَسَلَ	„ leap	طُفُوْرًا	طَفَرَ
„ forgive	غُفْرَانًا	غَفَرَ	„ fold	طَيًّا	طَوَى
„ conquer	غَلَبَةً	غَلَبَ	„ be agreeable	طِيْبًا	طَابَ
„ boil	غَلَيَانًا	غَلَى	„ fly	طَيَرَانًا	طَارَ
„ be absent	غَيْبًا	غَابَ	„ happen	عَرْضًا	عَرَضَ
„ seduce	فِتْنَةً	فَتَنَ	„ know	مَعْرِفَةً	عَرَفَ
„ flee	فِرَارًا	فَرَّ	„ resolve	عَزْمًا	عَزَمَ
enact, suppose	فَرْضًا	فَرَضَ	„ prevent	عِصْمَةً	عَصَمَ
„ bleed	فَصْدًا	فَصَدَ			
„ separate	فَصْلًا	فَصَلَ			
„ overflow	فَيَضَانًا	فَاضَ			

To incline	مَالَ	مَيَلَانًا
„ abandon	نَبَذَ	نَبْذًا
„ throb	نَبَضَ	نَبْضًا
„ take away	نَزَعَ	نَزْعًا
„ descend	نَزَلَ	نُزُوْلًا
„ attribute	نَسَبَ	نِسْبَةً
„ winnow, scatter	نَسَفَ	نَسْفًا
„ speak	نَطَقَ	نُطْقًا
„ prohibit, attain	نَهَى	نَهْيًا
„ intend	نَوَى	نِيَّةٌ
„ shout	هَتَفَ	هُتَافًا
„ put to flight	هَزَمَ	هَزِيْمَةً
„ break, bruise	هَشَمَ	هَشْمًا
„ digest	هَضَمَ	هَضْمًا
„ perish	هَلَكَ	هَلَاكًا
„ be agitated (sea)	هَاجَ	هِيَاجًا
„ love passionately	هَامَ	هُيَامًا

To grasp	قَبَضَ	قَبْضًا
„ throw, vomit	قَذَفَ	قَذْفًا
„ join	قَرَنَ	قَرْنًا
„ gnaw	قَرَضَ	قَرْضًا
„ purpose	قَصَدَ	قَصْدًا
„ decide, die, fulfil	قَضَى	قَضَاءً
„ jump	قَفَزَ	قَفْزًا
„ fry	قَلَى	قَلْيًا
„ measure	قَاسَ	قِيَاسًا
„ lie	كَذَبَ	كَذِبًا
„ gain	كَسَبَ	كَسْبًا
„ break	كَسَرَ	كَسْرًا
„ uncover	كَشَفَ	كَشْفًا
„ suffice	كَفَى	كِفَايَةً
„ be weary	كَلَّ	كَلًّا
„ slap	لَطَمَ	لَطْمًا
„ touch	لَمَسَ	لَمْسًا
„ be fitting	لَاقَ	لِيَاقَةً
„ „ tender, kind	لَانَ	لِيْنًا
„ possess	مَلَكَ	مُلْكًا

English	Arabic (verbal noun)	Arabic (verb)
To bury alive	وَأْدًا	وَأَدَ
„ leap	وُثُوْبًا	وَثَبَ
„ trust	ثِقَةً	وَثَقَ
„ be necessary	وُجُوْبًا	وَجَبَ
„ find	وِجْدَانًا	وَجَدَ
„ come	وُرُوْدًا	وَرَدَ
„ weigh	وَزْنًا	وَزَنَ
„ load	وَسْقًا	وَسَقَ
„ brand	سِمَةً	وَسَمَ
„ calumniate	وِشَايَةً	وَشَى
„ describe	صِفَةً	وَصَفَ

English	Arabic (verbal noun)	Arabic (verb)
To arrive, join	صِلَةً	وَصَلَ
„ promise	عِدَةً	وَعَدَ
„ exhort	عِظَةً	وَعَظَ
„ come	وُفُوْدًا	وَفَدَ
„ fulfil a compact	وَفْيًا	وَفَى
„ burn	وُقُوْدًا	وَقَدَ
„ stand	وُقُوْفًا	وَقَفَ
„ quard	وِقَايَةً	وَقَى
„ shed tears	وَكْفًا	وَكَفَ
„ entrust	وَكْلًا	وَكَلَ
„ beget	وِلَادَةً	وَلَدَ
„ be weak	وَهْيًا	وَهَى

فَعَلَ يَفْعُلُ

English	Arabic (verbal noun)	Arabic (verb)
To take	أَخْذًا	أَخَذَ
„ eat	أَكْلًا	أَكَلَ
„ command	أَمْرًا	أَمَرَ
„ direct one's steps	أَمًّا	أَمَّ
„ return	إِيَابًا	آبَ
„ publish	بَثًّا	بَثَّ
„ give freely	بَذْلًا	بَذَلَ
„ appear	بُرُوْزًا	ابَرَزَ

English	Arabic (verbal noun)	Arabic (verb)
To spread out	بَسْطًا	بَسَطَ
„ assault	بَطْشًا	بَطَشَ
„ be vain	بُطْلًا	بَطَلَ
„ attain	بُلُوْغًا	بَلَغَ
„ wet	بَلًّا	بَلَّ
„ recite, read	تِلَاوَةً	تَلَا
„ repent	تَوْبَةً	تَابَ
„ stand firm	ثُبُوْتًا	ثَبَتَ
„ pierce	ثَقْبًا	ثَقَبَ

To envy	حَسْدًا	حَسَدَ	To rise, (dust, war), be roused	ثَوَرَانًا	ثَارَ
„ assemble	حَشْرًا	حَشَرَ	„ set a fracture	جَبْرًا	جَبَرَ
„ reap	حَصْدًا	حَصَدَ	„ drag	جَرًّا	جَرَّ
„ be present	حُضُورًا	حَضَرَ	„ shear	جَزًّا	جَزَّ
„ put, fall in price	حَطًّا	حَطَّ	„ touch, feel	جَسًّا	جَسَّ
„ rub	حَكًّا	حَكَّ	„ polish, emigrate	جَلَاءً	جَلَا
„ dream	حُلْمًا	حَلَمَ	„ be liberal, excellent	جُوْدًا	جَادَ
„ be changed	حَوْلًا	حَالَ	„ oppress	جَوْرًا	جَارَ
„ betray	خِذْلَانًا	خَذَلَ	„ pass, be lawful	جَوَازًا	جَازَ
„ pierce, traverse	خَرْقًا	خَرَقَ	„ hunger	جُوعًا	جَاعَ
„ trace, write	خَطًّا	خَطَّ	„ wander	جَوَلَانًا	جَالَ
„ step	خَطْوًا	خَطَا	„ urge	حَثًّا	حَثَّ
„ create	خَلْقًا	خَلَقَ	„ veil	حَجْبًا	حَجَبَ
„ tan	دَبْغًا	دَبَغَ	„ make a pilgrimage	حَجًّا	حَجَّ
„ enter	دُخُولًا	دَخَلَ	„ hinder, sequester	حَجْزًا	حَجَزَ
„ study	دَرْسًا	دَرَسَ	„ happen	حُدُوثًا	حَدَثَ
„ call	دُعَاءً	دَعَا	„ guard	حِرَاسَةً	حَرَسَ
„ knock, pound	دَقًّا	دَقَّ			
„ guide	دَلَالَةً	دَلَّ			
„ approach	دُنُوًّا	دَنَا			
„ revolve	دَوَرَانًا	دَارَ			
„ dilute	دَوْفًا	دَافَ			
„ continue	دَوَامًا	دَامَ			

To be quiet	سُكُوْتًا	سَكَتَ	To melt	ذَوَبَانًا	ذَابَ
„ dwell	سُكْنَى	سَكَن	„ quake	رَجَفَانًا	رَجَف
„ boil	سَلْقًا	سَلَقَ	„ stone	رَجْمًا	رَجَمَ
„ behave, go along	سُلُوْكًا	سَلَكَ	„ hope	رَجَاءً	رَجَا
„ enact, sharpen	سَنًّا	سَنَّ	„ restore	رَدًّا	رَدَّ
„ grieve, be evil	سُوءًا	سَاء	„ disapprove	رَذْلًا	رَذَلَ
„ be chief	سِيَادَةً	سَادَ	„ prescribe, sketch	رَسْمًا	رَسَمَ
„ drive	سَوْقًا	سَاقَ	„ sprinkle	رَشًّا	رَشَّ
„ revile	شَتْمًا	شَتَمَ	„ refuse	رِفْضًا	رفَضَ
„ perceive	شُعُوْرًا	شَعَرَ	„ dance	رقْصًا	رقَص
„ split	شَقًّا	شَقَّ	„ run	رَكْضًا	ركَض
„ doubt	شَكًّا	شَكَّ	„ desire strongly	مَرَامًا	رَامَ
„ complain	شِكَايَةً	شَكَا	„ interdict	زَجْرًا	زَجَرَ
„ smell	شَمًّا	شَمَّ	„ pass away	زَوَالًا	زَالَ
„ pour	صَبًّا	صَبَّ	„ precede, outstrip	سَبْقًا	سَبَقَ
„ dye, baptize	صَبْغًا	صَبَـح	„ veil	سَتْرًا	سَتَرَ
„ start	صُدُوْرًا	صَدَرَ	„ prostrate oneself	سُجُوْدًا	سَجَدَ
„ tell the truth	صِدْقًا	صَدَقَ	„ please, rejoice	سُرُوْرًا	سَرَّ
„ polish	صَقْلًا	صَقَل	„ assail	سَطْوَةً	سَطَا
„ be silent	صَمْتًا	صَمَتَ	„ pour	سَكْبًا	سَكَبَ
„ fast	صِيَامًا	صَامَ			

To return	عَوْدًا	عَادَ	To preserve	صِيَانَةً	صَانَ	
„ feed	عِيَالَةً	عَالَ	„ injure	ضَرًّا	ضَرَّ	
„ float	عَوْمًا	عَامَ	„ dress a			
„ act trea-			wound	ضَمْدًا	ضَمَدَ	
cherously	غَدْرًا	غَدَرَ	„ drive away	طَرْدًا	طَرَدَ	
„ disappear,			„ knock, come			
set (sun)	غُرُوبًا	غَرَبَ	by night	طَرْقًا	طَرَقَ	
„ deceive	غُرُورًا	غَرَّ	„ ask	طَلَبًا	طَلَبَ	
„ be languid,			„ appear,			
lukewarm	فُتُورًا	فَتَرَ	rise	طُلُوعًا	طَلَعَ	
„ spread	فَرْشًا	فَرَشَ	„ walk			
„ be empty	فَرَاغًا	فَرَغَ	around	طَوَفَانًا	طَافَ	
„ „ corrupt	فَسَادًا	فَسَدَ	„ suppose,			
„ loose	فَكًّا	فَكَّ	suspect	ظَنًّا	ظَنَّ	
„ miss, elapse	فَوْتًا	فَاتَ	„ worship	عِبَادَةً	عَبَدَ	
„ diffuse			„ cross	عُبُورًا	عَبَرَ	
(perfume)	فَوَحَانًا	فَاحَ	„ be proud	عُتُوًّا	عَتَا	
„ boil over	فَوَرَانًا	فَارَ	„ stumble	عُثُورًا	عَثَرَ	
„ win	فَوْزًا	فَازَ	„ count	عَدًّا	عَدَّ	
„ surpass	فَوْقًا	فَاقَ	„ run	عَدْوًا	عَدَا	
„ kill	قَتْلًا	قَتَلَ	„ help	عَضْدًا	عَضَدَ	
„ reside	قُطُونًا	قَطَنَ	„ sneeze	عُطَاسًا	عَطَسَ	
„ sit	قُعُودًا	قَعَدَ	„ pardon	عَفْوًا	عَفَا	
„ lead	قِيَادَةً	قَادَ	„ inhabit,			
„ say	قَوْلًا	قَالَ	live long	عُمْرًا	عَمَرَ	

To grant	مَنًّا	مَنَّ	To rise	قِيَامًا	قَامَ
„ die	مَوْتًا	مَات	„ write	كِتَابَةً	كَتَبَ
„ grow	نَبَاتًا	نَبَتَ	„ conceal	كِتْمَانًا	كَتَمَ
„ sift	نَخْلًا	نَخَلَ	„ toil	كَدًّا	كَدَّ
„ bewail, call	نَدْبًا	نَدَبَ	„ clothe	كَسْوًا	كَسَا
„ spread, saw	نَشْرًا	نَشَرَ	„ stay, refrain from	كَفًّا	كَفَّ
„ assist, give victory	نَصْرًا	نَصَرَ	„ lurk	كُمُونًا	كَمَنَ
„ look	نَظَرًا	نَظَرَ	„ be	كِيَانًا	كَانَ
„ blow	نَفْخًا	نَفَخَ	„ roll, wrap	لَفًّا	لَفَّ
„ penetrate	نُفُوذًا	نَفَذَ	„ gather	لَمًّا	لَمَّ
„ bore	نَقْبًا	نَقَبَ	„ amuse	لَهْوًا	لَهَا
„ chisel	نَقْشًا	نَقَشَ	„ spit	مَجًّا	مَجَّ
„ decrease	نُقْصَانًا	نقص	„ efface	مَحْوًا	مَحَا
„ fill the place of	نِيَابَةً	نَابَ	„ cleave the water(ship)	مَخْرًا	مَخَرَ
„ lament	نَوْحًا	نَاحَ	„ spread	مَدًّا	مَدَّ
„ abandon	هَجْرًا	هَجَرَ	„ pass	مَرًّا	مَرَّ
„ flee	هَرَبًا	هَرَبَ	„ mix	مَزْجًا	مَزَجَ
„ rain fast	هَطْلًا	هَطَلَ	„ chew	مَضْغًا	مَضَغَ
„ affright	هَوْلًا	هَالَ	„ rain	مَطَرًا	مَطَرَ
„ be easy, base	هَوْنًا	هَانَ	„ delay	مَطْلًا	مَطَلَ
			„ abhor	مَقْتًا	مَقَتَ
			„ circumvent	مَكْرًا	مَكَرَ

فَعِلَ يَفْعَلُ

To be hot	حَمِيَ حُمُوًّا	To permit	أَذِنَ إِذْنًا
„ „ enraged	حَنِقَ حَنَقًا	„ be sleepless	أَرِقَ أَرَقًا
„ live	حَيِيَ حَيَاةً	„ approach	أَزِفَ أَزَفًا
„ be ashamed	خَجِلَ خَجَلًا	„ regret	أَسِفَ أَسَفًا
„ lose	خَسِرَ خُسْرَانًا	„ be ac- customed	أَلِفَ أَلْفًا
„ be afraid	خَشِيَ خَشْيَةً	„ be secure	أَمِنَ أَمْنًا
„ snatch	خَطِفَ خَطْفًا	„ „ innocent	بَرِئَ بَرَاءةً
„ fear	خَافَ خَوْفًا	„ depart	بَرِحَ بَرَحًا
„ be amazed	ذَهِلَ ذُهُولًا	„ be ugly	بَشِعَ بَشَاعَةً
„ suck	رَضِعَ رَضَاعَةً	„ remain	بَقِيَ بَقَاءً
„ desire	رَغِبَ رَغْبَةً	„ be worn out	بَلِيَ بِلاءً
„ ascend gra- dually	رَقِيَ رُقِيًّا	„ follow	تَبِعَ تِبَاعًا
„ be safe	سَلِمَ سَلَامًا	„ trade	تَجِرَ تِجَارَةً
„ hear	سَمِعَ سَمْعًا	„ be tired	تَعِبَ تَعَبًا
„ keep awake at night	سَهِرَ سَهَرًا	„ „ spoilt, perish	تَلِفَ تَلَفًا
„ be satisfied	شَبِعَ شِبَعًا	„ get drunk	ثَمِلَ ثَمَلًا
„ witness	شَهِدَ شَهَادَةً	„ be grieved	حَزِنَ حُزْنًا
„ ascend	صَعِدَ صُعُودًا	„ keep, learn by heart	حَفِظَ حِفْظًا
„ be annoyed	ضَجِرَ ضَجَرًا	„ praise	حَمِدَ حَمْدًا
„ laugh	ضَحِكَ ضَحِكًا		

To be restless, anscious	قَلَقًا	قَلِقَ	To gain, conquer	ظَفَرًا	ظَفِرَ
„ despair	قُنُوطًا	قَنِطَ	„ be thirsty	ظَمَأً	ظَمِئَ
„ be content with	قَنَاعَةً	قَنِعَ	„ wonder	عَجْبًا	عَجِبَ
„ be strong	قُوَّةً	قَوِيَ	„ lack	عُدْمًا	عَدِمَ
„ become old	كِبَرًا	كَبِرَ	„ sweat	عَرَقًا	عَرِقَ
„ dislike	كَرَاهِيَةً	كَرِهَ	„ bite	عَضًّا	عَضَّ
„ be lazy	كَسَلًا	كَسِلَ	„ perish	عَطَبًا	عَطِبَ
„ be complete, perfect	كَمَالًا	كَمِلَ	„ thirst	عَطَشًا	عَطِشَ
„ abide	لُبْثًا	لَبِثَ	„ know	عِلْمًا	عَلِمَ
„ insist upon	لَجَاجَةً	لَجَّ	„ work	عَمَلًا	عَمِلَ
„ lick	لَحْسًا	لَحِسَ	„ be drowned	غَرَقًا	غَرِقَ
„ overtake	لَحَاقًا	لَحِقَ	„ pay a fine or tax	غَرَامَةً	غَرِمَ
„ be necessary	لُزُومًا	لَزِمَ	„ cover	غِشَايَةً	غَشِيَ
„ stick	لُصُوقًا	لَصِقَ	„ be angry	غَضَبًا	غَضِبَ
„ play	لَعِبًا	لَعِبَ	„ slip, err	غَلَطًا	غَلِطَ
„ meet, find	لُقْيَانًا	لَقِيَ	„ take booty	غُنْمًا	غَنِمَ
„ gulp	لَهْمًا	لَهِمَ	„ rejoice	فَرَحًا	فَرِحَ
„ be sick	مَرَضًا	مَرِضَ	„ finish, be empty	فَرَاغًا	فَرِغَ
			„ pass away	فَنَاءً	فَنِيَ
			„ understand	فَهْمًا	فَهِمَ

To touch	مَسًّا	مَسَّ
„ be wearied of	مَلَلًا	مَلَّ
„ repent	نَدَمًا	نَدِمَ
„ forget	نِسْيَانًا	نَسِيَ
„ stick in	نُشُوبًا	نَشِبَ
„ be dry	نَشَفًا	نَشِفَ
„ obtain	نَيْلًا	نَالَ
„ sleep	نَوْمًا	نَامَ
„ be decrepit	هَرَمًا	هَرِمَ
„ perish	هَلَاكًا	هَلِكَ
To desire, love هَوًى		هَوِيَ
„ reverence, fear	مَهَابَةً	هَابَ
„ sink into mire	وَحَلًا	وَحِلَ
„ contain	سَعَةً	وَسِعَ
„ tread	وَطْأً	وَطِئَ
„ despair	يَأْسًا	يَئِسَ
„ be dry	يُبْسًا	يَبِسَ
„ „ awake	يَقْظَةً	يَقِظَ

فَعَلَ يَفْعَلُ

To search	بَحْثًا	بَحَثَ
„ begin	بَدَاءَةً	بَدَأَ
„ send, raise the dead	بَعْثًا	بَعَثَ
„ deny	جُحُودًا	جَحَدَ
„ wound	جَرْحًا	جَرَحَ
„ put begin	جَعْلًا	جَعَلَ
„ gather	جَمْعًا	جَمَعَ
„ speak openly	جَهْرًا	جَهَرَ
„ deceive	خِدَاعًا	خَدَعَ
To be humble	خُشُوعًا	خَشَعَ
„ submit	خُضُوعًا	خَضَعَ
„ strip, pull off	خَلْعًا	خَلَعَ
„ refute, annul	دَحْضًا	دَحَضَ
„ push, repel	دَفْعًا	دَفَعَ
„ slaughter	ذَبْحًا	ذَبَحَ
„ store	ذُخْرًا	ذَخَرَ
„ go	ذَهَابًا	ذَهَبَ
„ see	رُؤْيَةً	رَأَى
„ outweigh	رُجْحَانًا	رَجَحَ

To examine	فَحْصًا	فَحَصَ	To depart	رَحِيْلًا	رَحَلَ
„ strike fire, slander	قَدْحًا	قَدَحَ	„ leak,		
„ read	قِرَاءةً	قَرَأ	„ sweat	رَشْحًا	رَشَحَ
„ knock	قَرْعًا	قَرَعَ	„ lift up	رَفْعًا	رَفَعَ
„ cut	قَطْعًا	قَطَعَ	„ kneel	رُكُوْعًا	رَكَعَ
„ subdue, conquer	قَهْرًا	قَهَرَ	„ creep	زَحْفًا	زَحَف
„ check a horse	كَبْحًا	كَبَحَ	„ sow	زَرْعًا	زَرَعَ
			„ swim	سِبَاحَةً	سَبَحَ
„ err grammatically	لَحْنًا	لَحَن	„ pasture	سُرُوْحًا	سَرَحَ
„ burn	لَذْعًا	لَذَعَ	„ radiate, spread	سُطُوْعًا	سَطَعَ
„ sting	لَسْعًا	لَسَعَ	„ permit	سَمَاحًا	سَمَحَ
„ curse	لَعْنًا	لَعَن	„ mediate	شِفَاعَةً	شَفَعَ
„ glance	لَمْحًا	لَمَحَ	„ throw down	صَرْعًا	صَرَعَ
„ shine	لَمَعَانًا	لَمَعَ	„ pardon	صَفْحًا	صَفَحَ
„ praise	مَدْحًا	مَدَحَ	„ make	صُنْعًا	صَنَعَ
„ anoint, wipe	مَسْحًا	مَسَحَ	„ melt	صَهْرًا	صَهَرَ
„ disfigure	مَسْخًا	مَسَخَ	„ grind	طَحْنًا	طَحَن
„ fill	مَلأً	مَلأ	„ cast	طَرْحًا	طَرَحَ
„ grant	مَنْحًا	مَنَحَ	„ pierce	طَعْنًا	طَعَن
„ forbid	مَنْعًا	مَنَعَ	„ overflow	طُفُوْحًا	طَفَحَ
			„ appear	ظُهُوْرًا	ظَهَرَ
			„ open	فَتْحًا	فَتَحَ

To pillage	نَهْبًا	نَهَبَ
,, flow	نَهْرًا	نَهَرَ
,, rise	نُهُوْضًا	نَهَضَ
,, hurry, flow fast	هَرَعًا	هَرَعَ
,, place	وَضْعًا	وَضَعَ
,, lap	وُلُوْغًا	وَلَغَ
,, grant	هِبَةً	وَهَبَ

To be distant	نَأْيًا	نَأَى
,, succeed	نَجَاحًا	نَجَحَ
,, hew	نِحَاتَةً	نَحَتَ
,, slay	نَحْرًا	نَحَرَ
,, grow up	نَشْأَةً	نَشَأَ
,, advise	نُصْحًا	نَصَحَ
,, sprinkle	نَضْحًا	نَضَحَ
,, croak	نَعِيْقًا	نَعَقَ
,, marry	نِكَاحًا	نَكَحَ

فَعَلَ يَفْعُلُ

To be elegant	بَهْجَةً	بَهُجَ
,, ,, heavy	ثِقَلًا	ثَقُلَ
,, ,, cowardly	جُبْنًا	جَبُنَ
,, ,, courageous	جُرْأَةً	جَرُؤَ
,, harden, freeze	جُمُوْدًا	جَمُدَ
,, be young, fresh	حَدَاثَةً	حَدُثَ
,, be resolute	حَزَامَةً	حَزُمَ
,, ,, of noble birth	حَسَبًا	حَسُبَ
,, be beautiful	حُسْنًا	حَسُنَ

To be well educated, refined	أَدَبًا	أَدُبَ
,, be strong, brave	بَأْسًا	بَؤُسَ
,, be avaricious	بُخْلًا	بَخُلَ
,, excel in knowledge	بَرَاعَةً	بَرُعَ
,, be simple	بَسَاطَةً	بَسُطَ
,, see	بَصَرًا	بَصُرَ
,, be slow	بُطْأً	بَطُؤَ
,, ,, gallant	بَطَالَةً	بَطُلَ
,, ,, distant	بُعْدًا	بَعُدَ
,, ,, stupid	بَلَادَةً	بَلُدَ

To be small	صَغَّرًا	صَغُرَ	To be impregnable	حَصَانَةً	حَصُنَ
,, hard	صَلَابَةً	صَلُبَ	,, be forbearing	حِلْمًا	حَلُمَ
,, suit, be good	صَلَاحِيَةً	صَلُحَ	,, be corrupt	خُبْثًا	خَبُثَ
,, be weak	ضُعْفًا	ضَعُفَ	,, dote	خَرَافَةً	خَرُفَ
,, ,, pure, chaste	طَهَارَةً	طَهُرَ	,, be rough	خُشُونَةً	خَشُنَ
,, be just	عَدْلًا	عَدُلَ	,, ,, gentle	دَمَاثَةً	دَمُثَ
,, ,, sweet	عُذُوبَةً	عَذُبَ	,, fade	ذُبُولًا	ذَبُلَ
,, ,, difficult	عُسْرًا	عَسُرَ	,, be wide	رُحْبًا	رَحُبَ
,, ,, great	عَظَمَةً	عَظُمَ	,, ,, sedate	رَصَانَةً	رَصُنَ
,, treat harshly	عَنْفًا	عَنُفَ	,, ,, moist, damp	رُطُوبَةً	رَطُبَ
,, be strange	غَرَابَةً	غَرُبَ	,, be ugly	سَمَاجَةً	سَمُجَ
,, ,, thick, rough	غِلْظَةً	غَلُظَ	,, ,, agreeable, generous	سَمَاحَةً	سَمُحَ
,, be great	فَخَامَةً	فَخُمَ	,, be easy	سُهُولَةً	سَهُلَ
,, ,, skilful	فَرَاهَةً	فَرُهَ	,, ,, courageous	شَجَاعَةً	شَجُعَ
,, ,, wide	فَسَاحَةً	فَسُحَ	,, be noble	شَرَفًا	شَرُفَ
,, ,, eloquent	فَصَاحَةً	فَصُحَ	,, ,, quick witted	شَهَامَةً	شَهُمَ
,, be excellent	فَضْلًا	فَضُلَ	,, be difficult	صُعُوبَةً	صَعُبَ
,, be ugly	قُبْحًا	قَبُحَ			
,, ,, holy	قَدَاسَةً	قَدُسَ			

To be renowed نَبَاهَةً نَبُهَ

„ „ of noble birth نَجَابَةً نَجُبَ

„ be clean نَظَافَةً نَظُفَ

„ „ smooth نُعُومَةً نَعُمَ

„ „ brief وَجَازَةً وَجُزَ

„ „ respected وَجَاهَةً وَجُهَ

„ be meek وَدَاعَةً وَدُعَ

„ „ pious وَرَاعَةً وَرُعَ

„ „ wide وُسْعًا وَسُعَ

„ „ handsome وَسَامَةً وَسُمَ

„ be humble ضَعَةً وَضُعَ

„ „ plentiful وَفَارَةً وَفُرَ

„ become an orphan يُتْمًا يَتُمَ

„ be easy يُسْرًا يَسُرَ

To be old, prior قِدَمًا قَدُمَ

„ be near قُرْبًا قَرُبَ

„ „ short قِصَرًا قَصُرَ

„ „ tall كُبْرًا كَبُرَ

„ „ plentiful كَثْرَةً كَثُرَ

„ „ generous كَرَمًا كَرُمَ

„ „ perfect كَمَالًا كَمُلَ

„ arrive at maturity كُهُولَةً كَهُلَ

„ be mean لُؤْمًا لَؤُمَ

„ „ gracious لَطَافَةً لَطُفَ

„ „ strong مَتَانَةً مَتُنَ

„ „ barren مَحَالَةً مَحُلَ

„ „ manly مُرُوَّةً مَرُوَ

„ „ salty مُلُوحَةً مَلُحَ

„ „ pretty مَلَاحَةً مَلُحَ

„ „ inaccessible مَنَاعَةً مَنُعَ

فَعِلَ يَفْعِلُ

To swell وَرَمًا وَرِمَ

„ come after وِلَايَةً وَلِيَ

„ despair يَأْسًا يَئِسَ

„ wither يُبْسًا يَبِسَ

To count حُسْبَانًا حَسِبَ

„ live in comfort نِعْمَةً نَعِمَ

„ trust ثِقَةً وَثِقَ

„ inherit وِرَاثَةً وَرِثَ

THE END.